50 Hikes in New Jersey

50 *Hikes*

In New Jersey

Walks, Hikes & Backpacking Trips
from the Kittatinnies to Cape May

Fourth Edition

Daniel Chazin

NEW YORK–NEW JERSEY
TRAIL CONFERENCE

THE COUNTRYMAN PRESS
Woodstock, Vermont

AN INVITATION TO THE READER

Over time trails can be rerouted and signs and landmarks altered. If you find that changes have occurred on the routes described in this book, please let us know so that corrections may be made in future editions. The author and publisher also welcome other comments and suggestions. Address all correspondence to:

Editor, 50 Hikes Series
The Countryman Press
P.O. Box 748
Woodstock, VT 05091

Maps by Erin Greb Cartography,
© The Countryman Press
Book design by Glenn Suokko
Text composition by Eugenie S. Delaney
Frontispiece photo by Daniel Chazin
Interior photographs by the author unless otherwise specified

Published by The Countryman Press,
P.O. Box 748, Woodstock, VT 05091
Distributed by W. W. Norton & Company, Inc.,
500 Fifth Avenue, New York, NY 10110

Printed in the United States of America

10 9 8 7 6 5 4 3 2 1

Acknowledgments

I would like to begin by acknowledging the contributions of my good friends Stella Green, Bruce Scofield, and H. Neil Zimmerman, the authors of the first two editions of the book. They selected the hikes to include in the book and scouted out all of the hike routes. Although many of the hike descriptions have been changed for this edition, the basic structure of the book and most of the historical and background material have been retained from the previous editions. We owe Neil, Stella, and Bruce a real debt of gratitude for making this book possible.

In 2012, Neil, Stella and Bruce graciously donated their rights to this book to the New York–New Jersey Trail Conference (NY–NJTC). For this edition, I have undertaken to revise and update the book on behalf of the NY–NJTC. This afforded me the opportunity, over the past year, to follow some of these beautiful hikes for the first time and to re-hike others.

I wish to thank Estelle Anderson, Gene Giordano, Bob Jonas, John Moran, Linda Rohleder, Brian Sniatkowski, Douglas Vorolieff, and Daniela Wagstaff for reviewing the descriptions of various hikes and making helpful suggestions. My friends Dan Crane, Ben Hutt and Garrett Kroner accompanied me on trips to check out some of the hikes in this book, for which I am grateful. I also wish to acknowledge the contributions of Dan Balogh, Claus Holzapfel, Richard Pillar, and Daniela Wagstaff—each of whom contributed one or more photos for this book.

Although the maps for each hike were prepared by The Countryman Press, the GPS tracks for each map were supplied by Jeremy Apgar, the NY–NJTC's talented cartographer.

– Daniel Chazin

50 Hikes in New Jersey at a Glance

HIKE	COUNTY	DISTANCE (miles)	DIFFICULTY
1. South of High Point	Sussex	6.3	M/S
2. Rattlesnake Swamp to Catfish Pond	Warren	5	M
3. Mount Tammany	Warren	3.5	M/S
4. Appalachian Trail Backpack	Warren/Sussex	28.2	S
5. Schuber Trail, End to End	Bergen	7.2	S
6. Ramapo Lake, Ramapo Mountain State Forest	Passaic/Bergen	5.1	M
7. Ringwood Manor Circular	Passaic	3	E
8. Skylands Manor	Passaic	5.4	M
9. Lake Sonoma and Overlook Rock	Passaic	4	M
10. Wyanokie Circular	Passaic	7.2	M/S
11. Carris Hill	Passaic	4	M/S
12. Torne Mountain–Osio Rock	Passaic	2.3 or 3.7	E/M
13. Terrace Pond	Passaic	4.5	M
14. Bearfort Ridge	Passaic	7	M/S
15. Pequannock Watershed	Passaic	8 or 9.5	M/S
16. Wawayanda State Park	Sussex/Passaic	7.5	E/M
17. Appalachian Trail Stairway to Heaven	Sussex	5	M/S
18. Pyramid Mountain	Morris	3	E/M
19. Mount Hope Historical Park	Morris	2.7	E
20. Mahlon Dickerson Reservation	Morris	4.7	E/M
21. Jenny Jump State Forest	Warren	5	M
22. Point Mountain	Hunterdon	3.5	M
23. Schooley's Mountain County Park	Morris	2.8	E/M
24. Black River Trails	Morris	6.6	M/S
25. Merrill Creek Reservoir	Warren	7.5	E

RISE (feet)	TIME (hours)	VIEWS	KIDS	CAMP	X-C SKI	FALLS	SHUTTLE	
								DIFFICULTY E Easy M Moderate S Strenuous **RISE** M Minimal **SHUTTLE** O Optional
500	4	★		★				Open ridges with views
500	3	★		★				Rugged and remote trail, good views
1,200	3	★						Steep climb and descent, views, heavily used
2,750	17	★		★		★	★	3-day backpack or walk as day hikes (use 2 cars)
800	5	★		★		★	★	Ridge walk with streams, lakes, views & history
700	3.5	★			★			Views, lake, stone ruins of mansion
250	2	★	★					History, Manor House
1,000	4	★			★			Manor house, gardens, views
700	3	★	★		★			Scenic lake and panoramic views
1,500	6.5	★			★			Two peaks and two mines, rock scrambling
800	4	★			★			Steep, rocky sections, good views
425–650	2.5 or 3.5	★			★			Stunning, 360-degree views
350	3.5	★						Rock scrambling, glacial lake
1,200	5.5	★						Great views, rock ledges
400	6	★				★	O	Historic features, views, deep woods
530	4	★		★				Rhododendron stands, lakes, historic furnace
1,000	3	★						Fabulous views
390	2.5	★	★					Unusual boulders, views
350	2	★						Historic mines
400	3	★	★	★	★			Unusual pine swamp, views, cross-country skiing
950	3.5	★						Glacial boulders, good views, lake
535	2.5	★		★				River, farm fields, rocky ridge, views
500	1.5	★				★		River gorge, waterfall, views
800	4					★	★	Grist mill, wild river gorge, meadows
400	4	★	★		★			Walk around scenic reservoir, historic ruins

50 Hikes in New Jersey at a Glance

HIKE	COUNTY	DISTANCE (miles)	DIFFICULTY
26. Jockey Hollow	Morris	5.6	E/M
27. Scherman-Hoffman Wildlife Sanctuary	Morris	1.5	E
28. Palisades	Bergen	5.75	E
29. Rockleigh Woods Sanctuary and Lamont Reserve	Bergen	2.4	E/M
30. High Mountain	Passaic	4	M
31. South Mountain Reservation	Essex	8.7	M
32. Watchung Reservation	Union	6.5	M
33. Washington Valley Park	Somerset	5.7	M
34. Sourland Mountain Preserve	Somerset	4.7	E/M
35. Washington Crossing to Scudder's Falls	Mercer	6	E
36. D & R Canal, Bull's Island to Prallsville	Hunterdon	3 or 6	E/M
37. D & R Canal, Kingston to Rocky Hill	Somerset	4	E/M
38. D & R Canal, Weston to East Millstone	Somerset	4.2	E
39. Cheesequake State Park	Middlesex	3.3	E/M
40. Hartshorne Woods Park	Monmouth	2.7	E/M
41. Allaire State Park	Monmouth	3.7	E
42. Cattus Island	Ocean	3.2	E
43. Island Beach State Park	Ocean	3.7	E
44. Wells Mills County Park	Ocean	4.5	M
45. Bass River State Forest	Burlington/Ocean	4.2	E
46. Brendan T. Byrne (Lebanon) State Forest	Burlington	8.1	M/S
47. Carranza Memorial to Apple Pie Hill	Burlington	8.2 or 5.2	M/S
48. Mullica River Wilderness	Burlington	7.5 or 8.5	M/S
49. Parvin State Park	Salem	4.6	E/M
50. Belleplain State Forest, East Creek Trail	Cape May	7	M

RISE (feet)	TIME (hours)	VIEWS	KIDS	CAMP	X-C SKI	FALLS	SHUTTLE	
670	3	★		★				Revolutionary War historic site
300	1							Interesting trees and boulders; scenic river walk
600	3.5	★	★		★			River walk, history
400	1.5	★	★					Pleasant hike on western slope of Palisades
400	5.5	★	★					Panoramic view of New York City skyline
750	6	★			★	★		Views, waterfall, historic features, unusual rocks
500	4	★						Suburban park, historic village and cemetery
550	3	★			★			Walk along reservoir, historic Chimney Rock
500	3		★					Interesting fields, huge boulders
100	3		★		★		O	Historic features, towpath
M	2 or 3.5		★		★		O	Pedestrian suspension bridge, historic mill
M	2		★		★			Historic features, water, easy walking
M	2		★		★			Tranquil, peaceful section of D&R Canal
200	2	★	★	★				Freshwater and cedar swamps, varied woods
300	1.5							Holly and oak forests, mountain laurel thickets
120	2.5	★	★					Historic Allaire Village
M	2	★	★					Views of marsh and bay
M	2.5	★	★					Ocean and bay views
500	3							Hills in the Pinelands
M	2		★		★			Sand roads, cedar bog
M	5	★		★				Explores cedar swamps and cranberry bogs
166	4–5	★		★			O	Classic Pinelands hiking with a view
200	5							Deep in the Pinelands
M	5		★					History, lake
M	4.5	★	★	★				Lake, fishing, beautiful woodlands

DIFFICULTY
E Easy
M Moderate
S Strenuous

RISE
M Minimal

SHUTTLE
O Optional

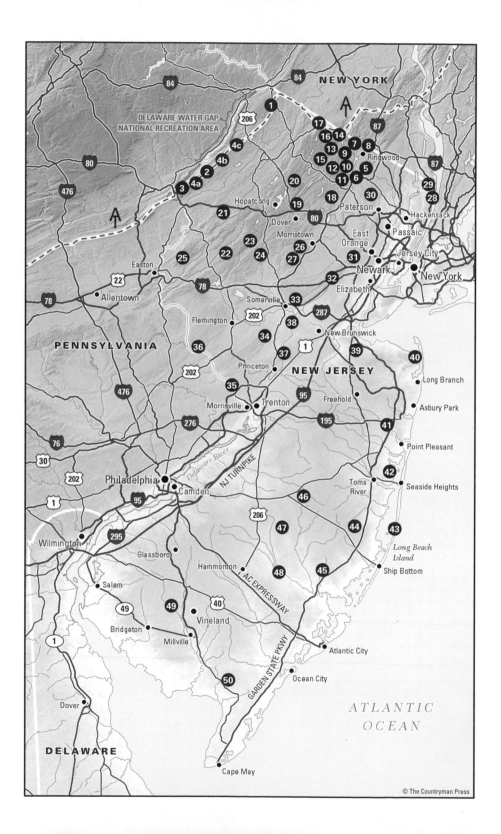

Contents

COASTAL PLAIN

Introduction

New Jersey boasts an abundance of fine hiking trails. The famous Appalachian Trail crosses the northern part of the state, as does most of the 150-mile Highlands Trail; the 60-mile Delaware & Raritan Canal State Park extends from New Brunswick to Raven Rock, north of Trenton; the 50-mile Batona Trail traverses the New Jersey Pinelands; and the Long Path commences its journey northward on the Palisades at the George Washington Bridge. Some trails are located on old roads and footpaths that existed prior to the acquisition of the land for public use, and some date back to the Depression and the federally funded Civilian Conservation Corps, whose members built park and recreation facilities still used today. Many trails, including the Appalachian Trail, are maintained by volunteers, whose dedication is evidenced by the fresh paint marks, water bars, and trails cleared of blowdowns and other hazards.

Hiking in the Garden State is varied, from the flat sandy trails in the southern part of the state to the hilly and rocky highlands in the north. There are swamps, beach areas, woods, and grasslands. Nine-tenths of New Jersey borders water; of its 480 miles of boundary, all but 48 are along either the seacoast or a riverbed. Except for the northwest section, the typical New Jersey landscape is a low, flat plain filled with meandering streams; four-fifths of the state is no more than 400 feet above sea level, and most of it is less than 100. The high point, in the northwest corner, is 1,803 feet above sea level.

THE GEOLOGY AND TOPOGRAPHY OF NEW JERSEY

Geologists divide New Jersey into four primary provinces. In the northwest, running roughly southwest to northeast, is the Appalachian Ridge and Valley Province, containing the highest elevations in the state. Here, in what was once a major mountain range (since leveled by erosion), is a series of parallel valleys and ridges composed of faulted and folded Paleozoic (Cambrian to mid-Devonian) sandstones and conglomerates between 375 and 540 million years old. The mountains we see today are former marine basins of sandstone, shale, and limestone, tipped by the compression of moving continental plates, which have eroded at varying rates, creating a series of parallel ridges and shallow valleys. Hawk sightings along the main ridges are frequent during the fall migration. The Delaware Water Gap National Recreation Area, Worthington and Stokes State Forests, and High Point State Park together preserve nearly all the mountainous portions of this province. The Appalachian Trail follows the crest of the main ridge, the Kittatinny Mountains, for more than 40 miles on its way from Georgia to Maine. The hiking in this province can be challenging because of steep inclines and extremely rocky footing.

Southeast of the Ridge and Valley Province and paralleling it lies the New Jersey Highlands Province. This mountainous area is composed primarily of Precambrian gneisses, granites, and schists, which formed between 750 million and 1.3 billion years ago. These rocks were formed from high pressures and temperatures deep within the Earth. From a distance, the Highlands appear to be a mass of elevated land at a constant elevation. But the Highlands have a very rugged topography with erratic and disconnected ridges and deep valleys between them. The elevations of the flat-topped summits characteristic of this province lie only a few hundred feet lower than those of the Kittatinny Mountains. The range extends north into New York State as the Hudson Highlands and south into Pennsylvania as the Reading Prong. Hikers will find not only more trails in this province than in any other in the state but also numerous lakes and reservoirs. The province includes Ramapo Mountain State Forest, Ramapo Valley County Reservation, Norvin Green State Forest, Ringwood State Park, Wawayanda State Park, and the vast holdings of the city of Newark, which supply drinking water to New Jersey's largest city. A number of other state and county parks and forests preserve segments of the natural features of the area.

Comprising most of northeastern and central New Jersey, the Piedmont Lowlands Province is a low-lying plain composed mainly of Mesozoic (Triassic and Jurassic) sandstones and shales that are 190 to 240 million years old. It is separated from the Highlands by a fault line that runs from Mahwah, in the north, to Milford, on the Delaware River. The Ramapo Fault in the northern part of the state shows this distinction dramatically, the boundary being apparent to the discerning eye on both road and contour maps. The more erosion-resistant Highlands rise above the Piedmont by as much as 800 feet in this region. Within the Piedmont Province, evidence of former rifting is found in a series of old lava flows that have withstood erosion

better than the shales and sandstones and now stand as mountain ridges. Following the deposition of shales and sandstones, rifting of the North American plate occurred in several places. Rifts are where a series of openings form between the Earth's surface and the hot mantle miles below the surface. Basalt and related rock is formed from such mantle extrusions. One such rift, to the east of present-day New Jersey, continued to expand and became the Atlantic Ocean. The rift that is now in New Jersey failed to open, leaving behind a number of igneous flows and intrusions. Just across the Hudson River from New York stand the Palisades, the eastern edges of a sill of igneous rock that in places rises more than 500 feet above the river. Farther west are the Watchung Hills, roughly parallel ridges made up of the resistant edges of westward-sloping, basaltic lava flows, which rise about 250 feet above the surrounding plans. Cushetunk Mountain and others near it are somewhat similar features called *dikes*. Composed of diabase, related to basalt, they are found in the southwestern portion of the province, where it extends into central New Jersey.

Extensive development has marred much of the natural beauty of the Piedmont Lowlands Province, though a few parks offer an opportunity to explore what was once the forest frontier of the New York region. The Palisades Interstate Park preserves much of the northern portion of the rock ramparts overlooking the Hudson. Several reservations along the crest of the first Watchung Ridge and the Round Valley Recreation Area on Cushetunk Mountain preserve some of the remaining high woodlands. In this province are also found several tracts of land that, though low and flat, offer some interesting hiking possibilities. The federally owned Great Swamp Wildlife Refuge and neighboring county parks have miles of trails, some on boardwalk, that penetrate the wetlands of a former glacial lake of immense proportions. From Raven Rock on the Delaware River to New Brunswick on the Raritan, the towpath of the old Delaware & Raritan Canal (now a state park) offers the hiker 66 miles of wooded walkway along a quiet but very alive body of water. During its heyday, the canal was the scene of intense activity. In fact, for a while, the Delaware & Raritan Canal did more business than the much better known Erie Canal in New York State.

Encompassing nearly all of New Jersey south of an imaginary line drawn between New Brunswick and Trenton is the Coastal Plain, the largest geomorphic province in the state. This entire area is composed of ocean and stream deposits of sands, silts, and clays laid down during the late Mesozoic to the early Cenozoic (late Cretaceous to Miocene) eras, 50 to 80 million years ago. The lowest elevations in the state are here, ranging from only a few hundred feet above sea level inland to water level on the seashore. From the gently rolling topography of the Pinelands to the sandy beaches along New Jersey's 127-mile coast, this province offers the hiker an environment very different from that found in the rest of the state. The Pinelands (also known as the Pine Barrens), a sparse pine and scrub oak forest of about 1 million acres, has been saved in large measure from the pressures of development. The heart of the Pinelands is preserved in several state forests, the largest of which is Wharton, headquartered at the old bog iron–mining town of Batsto. The Batona Trail (named for the BAck TO NAture Club of Philadelphia) penetrates the forest for some 50 miles from Lake Absegami to Ong's Hat. This marked footpath passes deep cedar swamps, parallels rivers of cedar water, and climbs Apple Pie Hill, at 205 feet the highest summit in the Pinelands. Throughout the Pinelands are sand roads—some more than 200 years old—that make for excellent walking through this wilderness of pines.

Several areas along the Jersey coast have been preserved in their original state, in tremendous contrast to the overdevelopment that has occurred elsewhere. Here, dunes, marshes, and moving sands pushed by the ocean currents present interesting walking opportunities. The New Jersey coast lies along the Atlantic Flyway, the route taken by migrating birds as they wing their way toward warmer climates. To avoid crowds, we recommend that the coast be hiked during the off-season.

LONG-DISTANCE TRAILS

Three long-distance trails pass through New Jersey. The Appalachian Trail (AT), a National Scenic Trail, enters from Pennsylvania at the Delaware Water Gap on its 2,185-mile journey from Georgia to Maine. From the Delaware Water Gap, it heads northeast along the ridge of the Kittatinny Mountains for 45 miles, then turns east and parallels the New Jersey–New York state boundary for another 25 miles until it turns north and heads into New York State. Blazed with white rectangles, the AT is administered by the Appalachian Trail Conservancy, headquartered in Harpers Ferry, West Virginia. Responsibility for the section of the AT in New Jersey has been delegated to the New York–New Jersey Trail Conference, and it is maintained by volunteers.

The Long Path (LP), blazed in parakeet aqua, begins its northward journey at the George Washington Bridge. For years, its northern terminus was at the town of Windham in the Catskills, but it has now been extended north to the Mohawk Valley. It is maintained by volunteers of the New York–New Jersey Trail Conference, and there is a plan to extend the trail into the Adirondacks.

The first 10 miles of the LP are in New Jersey. The Shawangunk Ridge Trail (SRT) was established as a trail alternative to the LP road walk through Orange County. Only 3.1 miles are located in New Jersey–the remaining miles are in New York.

The 150-mile Highlands Trail (HT) links the Delaware and Hudson Rivers, traversing many county, state, and federal parks. It is the result of cooperation among the New York–New Jersey Trail Conference, the New Jersey Conservation Foundation, and the National Park Service. There is a plan to extend the HT across the Hudson River and into Connecticut.

THE NATURE OF HIKING

Being out in the woods entails a certain element of risk. All hikers should be prepared with emergency gear and be able to look after themselves. Taking minimum precautions will ensure that your trip is pleasant. Enjoy your hobby.

The times assigned for the hikes in this book are based on an average pace, allowing for breaks and to explore interesting features along the way. Some hikers will be able to complete the hikes faster than the assigned time; some will take longer. Every hiker develops a pace at which he or she feels most comfortable. The slow amble with frequent stops that many beginning hikers adopt soon gives way to a more rhythmic stride. Begin with short walks on a regular basis and, as skills and muscle power build, move on to more challenging hikes. In addition to the physical elation of exercising in the outdoors, hobbies such as birdwatching, tree and flower identification, wildlife observation, photography, and local history can be made a part of almost any hike.

To enjoy the outdoors requires a certain amount of planning. Study the route and allow sufficient time to complete the trip before darkness falls. Some prefer hiking alone, but it is safer and generally more enjoyable to hike with a small group. A group of four people is recommended; if someone is injured, two of the hikers can go for help while one stays with the injured party. Large groups tend to destroy the feeling of isolation that one experiences in the wilderness and can spoil the hike for others who encounter the large groups along the way. If you decide to hike alone, tell someone dependable where you are hiking and when you expect to return, and do not deviate from the established plan.

As a hiker, your body is your resource. It needs enough food to keep energy levels high; above all, it needs water, and it should not be pushed to the point of exhaustion. Hiking is pleasurable if adequate preparations are taken. Keep your body at a comfortable temperature–neither so warm that excessive perspiration occurs, nor so cold or wet that hypothermia becomes a problem. Getting wet, either from rain or sweat, should be avoided. Hypothermia can creep up unawares. The outdoor temperature does not have to be very low. You can become hypothermic in 50-degree weather if there is rain or wind and you are unprepared. Watch your companions for signs of poor reflex actions–excessive stumbling, the need for frequent rest stops, or a careless attitude toward clothing and equipment. Once uncontrollable shivering has started, it may only be a matter of minutes before the body temperature has cooled beyond the point of recovery. Immediate warmth for the afflicted person is the only solution.

Suitable clothing and equipment are essential as safeguards against emergencies. It is assumed–and highly recommended–that new hikers will start their hiking careers during the warmer months, so the pieces of equipment discussed here are only the basics. Winter hiking is superb, with fewer people in the woods, no bugs, and a completely different feeling from summertime hiking, but remember: Rocks may be icy, wet leaves and lichen make rocks slippery, and clothing and equipment must be adjusted to fit the conditions.

Clothing

While clothing is largely a matter of personal choice, there are some important rules that should be followed. Cotton clothing should be avoided, especially in cold weather. When cotton becomes wet, it is heavy, dries slowly, and does not retain warmth. Instead wear nylon or polypropylene, especially next to your body. Wearing layers of clothing is recommended; this way, one can remove a layer or two if one gets too warm and put them back on at rest stops to avoid getting chilled. For emergency use, we recommend you carry a wool shirt or sweater, wool or polypropylene hat and gloves, a small flashlight, a simple first-aid kit, a pocket knife, toilet paper, and—in summer—bug repellent. In winter, it is a good idea to bring Stabilicers, MicroSpikes, or similar lightweight devices that provide traction on icy portions of the trail. If you would be helpless without your eyeglasses, carry an extra pair.

Boots

It is essential that one wear well-fitting, rubber-soled footwear on all hikes. Some hikers prefer lightweight sneakers, and these are minimally adequate for most hikes described in this book. However, lightweight hiking boots provide ankle support—something that sneakers do not provide. Many hikers choose to wear hiking boots on all but the easiest hikes, and they are strongly recommended for backpacking and for the more rugged hikes. If you need new boots, to ensure a good fit, take with you to the store the socks you plan to wear on the trail (see below). There should be ample room in the boots so your toes are not cramped, and there should not be much forward movement of your feet in them. Most good outfitters employ salespeople experienced enough to advise on boot choice. If possible, walk around in your home or office for several days before determining whether the pair you purchased will be suitable for hiking. Your first hike in new boots should be a short one, and should a "hot spot" form on your foot, stop immediately and apply moleskin or molefoam to reduce the likelihood of a blister forming.

Socks

To help prevent blisters, wear two pairs of socks with hiking boots: an inner pair of lightweight polypropylene or wool and an outer of thicker wool.

Rain/wind protection

Ideally, your rain jacket should have a hood. The hood will prevent cold wind from penetrating between your collar and neck. Remember, though, that hiking will generate perspiration, and some rain jackets will retain wetness inside the garment even if it is not raining. A waterproof, breathable fabric such as Gore-Tex is highly recommended.

Pack

A lightweight day pack is indispensable for carrying those pieces of equipment that you will need to take with you on the trail. Most day packs are basically small backpacks that ride high on the back. Some of the newer fanny packs, as well as a hybrid called a lumbar pack, will hold nearly as much as a small backpack and may be more comfortable.

You will want to take with you these items:

Water

The time has long since passed when you could be refreshed at that beautiful stream by drinking the pure, cold water. *Giardia lamblia* and other intestinal parasites and bacteria have destroyed that pleasure. Always carry water with you. The amount you need to take will vary depending on the length of the hike, the temperature and humidity, and your personal needs. Some people require more water than others. One quart may suffice for a moderate hike in cool temperatures, but you might need two or three quarts if you take the same hike on a hot summer day. Monitor your urine, and if it is dark, increase your water intake, particularly in colder weather when thirst is not as apparent as it is in the heat.

Lunch

Even if lunch is not planned on the trail, take an emergency ration—fruit, trail mix, a chocolate bar, or "gorp" (good old raisins and peanuts—with M&Ms, if you wish).

Maps

The maps in this guide, along with the text, are all you really need for these hikes. As you become experienced, though, you may want to explore areas in more depth. Each hike refers you to other maps, as keyed at the end of this introduction. For hiking in New Jersey, it is not usually necessary to carry a compass, particularly if you are on a described hike; however, if you stray from the trail, having a map and compass—and knowing how to use them—can return you to the path or to civilization. Today, the Global Positioning System (GPS) is an additional navigational tool. When used in conjunction with mapping software, a GPS unit can produce a map of the hike just walked.

You will need a good New Jersey road map to find your way to the trailheads. Each hike tells you how to reach the trailhead itself, but getting to the nearby town from where the directions begin is often up to you. New Jersey, like most states, publishes an official highway map, and it is free. Write to the New Jersey Division of Travel and Tourism, P.O. Box 820, Trenton, NJ 08625; call 609-292-2470 or 1-800-VISITNJ (1-800-847-4865) or go to www.state.nj.us/travel. Even if you have a GPS receiver in your car, it is a good idea to bring along a map, as GPS receivers sometimes fail to work properly.

Geocaching

This is a high-tech treasure hunt. In 2000, a new dimension was added to the adventure of being outdoors. A game called geocaching, which uses Global Positioning System (GPS) technology, was designed and developed in the Seattle area and now delights more than 6 million participants. Caches are mostly hidden containers, sometimes plastic, sometimes metal, that contain a log book and trinkets, with its coordinates posted on a log page accessed on the Web at www.geocaching.com. Players choose code names for themselves, enter a zip code, and find the names and coordinates for caches in their vicinity. Then it's up to the skill of the player to use a portable GPS unit to find the treasure. The pleasure is in the hunt, though. When the cache is found, the cacher signs the log using his *nom de plume*, replaces what he removes from the cache with an item of equal value, and then logs his find on the cache page, which keeps track of the number of "finds." It is estimated that caches exist in every state and in more than 200 countries, and there are many variations on the main theme.

Letterboxing is a similar pastime (www.letterboxing.com), but instead of a GPS using satellites to obtain coordinates, this game uses instructions and puzzles to help hikers locate the treasure, and you need a rubber stamp and pad to validate the find. Other sites such as www.navicache.com are also available.

FACTS FOR HIKERS
Trail markers
The trails in the Garden State are mostly color coded with paint blazes on trees. Sometimes metal or plastic tags affixed to trees with nails substitute for paint. Three blazes in a triangle indicate the beginning or the end of a trail, and major turns are indicated by two blazes, with the turn direction indicated by the upper blaze.

Ideally, trail blazes are spaced so that you can easily see the next as you move along the trail. At times, blazes become obscured by new growth or blowdowns, or, if a trail is not maintained properly, they may become faded. The hikes described in this book are mostly on marked trails, but we cannot vouch for the quality of the marking, which varies from trail to trail.

Ticks and Chiggers
During the hot summer, in grassy areas with damp soils, hikers may come into contact with chiggers. Chiggers are a species of mite and are parasitic on humans only in the juvenile stage of their life cycle. They are extremely small and are identifiable by only the itchy red spots that appear after the mite has attached itself to the skin. Welts may appear for several days after exposure as the mites move around the body. Immersion of the affected areas with alcohol is recommended as a treatment.

Ticks are a problem in New Jersey and other nearby states. Lyme disease is not to be trifled with. The deer tick *(Ixodes scapularis)* that carries Lyme disease is very small (the size of a period in this text). Do not confuse it with the common wood tick, which is the size of a match head, or—when engorged with blood—the size of a pea. Deer ticks are more abundant in shore areas where deer are common. A bite from an infected deer tick will often result in a rash (sometimes, but not always, in the shape of a bull's-eye), which should be immediately treated by a doctor. Learn to look for and remove ticks after hiking in an infested area. Long-sleeved shirts and pants with the legs tucked into socks are a must in these areas. Spray your feet and legs with a tick repellent containing DEET. A flier on Lyme disease is available from the New Jersey State Department of Health, P.O. Box 360, Trenton, NJ 08625; call 609-292-7837. Or check the Web site of the New York–New Jersey Trail Conference at www.nynjtc.org.

Wildlife
The black bear is the largest animal in New Jersey, and is native to the Garden State. In recent years, the bear population has increased, particularly in areas close to Pennsylvania, and near areas in New Jersey where new homes have invaded the territory once exclusively the domain of these animals.

Food smells attract bears, and in many cases they learn that where there are campsites there will be food. When camping, it is advisable to use a commercial bear-proof box (available from outfitters) to store all foods, as well as such items as soap, deodorant, and toothpaste. Never store anything edible in the tent or shelter, and prepare meals at least 100 feet away from your tent. Do not take the clothing worn while cooking into the tent, because food odors and food spatters cling to fabric.

The next best protection from bears is to hang food from a tree branch in odor-proof bundles, making sure that the packages hang at least 10 feet above the ground, and well away from the tree's trunk. Bears are smart animals and have been known to retrieve these caches, so it is advisable to use a tree branch far away from your tent. There is a trend among parks to supply metal bear-proof lockers to campers, and you should use these if they are available.

If a bear should come into camp, banging pots will sometimes scare the animal away. Remember, though, that a human is smaller than a bear—males usually weigh between 135 and 350 pounds.

Information and advice on black bears is available on the New Jersey Division of Fish and Wildlife Web site at www.njfishandwild life.com. Click on the Black Bear link in the Education pane.

Because rodents have sharp teeth and are good climbers, they can cause much damage to packs and tents if they detect food smells, so similar precautions should be taken to store food items away from camp.

Mountain bikes

When this book was first published in 1987, there were no bicycles on New Jersey trails. But modern technology has produced a rugged bicycle that can withstand trail use, and today's mountain bikes can traverse terrain once reserved for the hiker alone. The popularity of these new bicycles has been growing, and by the early 1990s many New Jersey trails had experienced sharp increases in use. User conflicts soon arose, and continue to be a problem in many places. Mountain bike riders assumed that the trails made and maintained by hikers were there for them to share. Hikers resented the encroachment and trail destruction mountain bikes can cause—though mountain-biking proponents often deny these problems—and fought to have them banned or limited in parks and forests, because mountain bikes create many erosion problems and intrude on the natural setting many hikers seek. Equestrians resented the speed at which some bikers travel along trails, scaring their horses. These problems are still with us, and policies are constantly being shaped and reshaped. If mountain biking is of concern to you, you may wish to contact the park or forest where you will be hiking for information on policies and complaints, or to express your opinion.

Parking fees

Many state parks and forests charge moderate fees for parking, normally between Memorial Day weekend and Labor Day weekend. Weekday rates are lower than weekend rates, and Tuesdays are free. A New Jersey State Park Pass is available, which provides free entry to all parks for one year. State residents older than 62 can obtain a free parking pass, good at any time. Passes can be purchased at any park or forest office.

Hunting

New Jersey has a short deer hunting season, usually in December. Avoid hiking in hunting areas during firearms season. Check with the local park office, the New Jersey Department of Environmental Protection, or the New York–New Jersey Trail Conference for specific dates. As of this writing, there is no hunting in New Jersey on Sundays.

TRAIL ETIQUETTE

There is a certain etiquette to hiking. Two of the most important phrases to remember are the familiar "take only photographs, leave only footprints" and "carry out what you carry in." If every user of our woods followed these guidelines, litter would not be a problem. Many concerned hikers carry empty garbage bags in their packs and pick up litter they find along the trails and carry it out.

Some trails border or cross private property. NO TRESPASSING signs should be honored and care taken to respect the rights of private landowners. A few thoughtless walkers can damage good relations built up over the years with trail neighbors.

On the trail, give way to the person walking uphill. If there are trail registers, carefully fill out the first register on your hike, and sign out at the last.

On overnights at existing shelters, remember that lean-tos should be available for all who need to use them. On those wet and windy nights, cheerfully make room for latecomers. Pack away all evidence that you have been there, and leave the shelter exactly as you would wish to find it on arrival.

Before beginning your backpacking hike, check whether fires are permitted in the area. Where fires are permitted, no live trees should be cut for firewood, and the fire should be contained in the fireplace provided at many shelters. It is courteous to gather enough dead wood so that the next occupant can at least get another fire started. Wood is in short supply in frequently camped areas. Whether you build them for atmosphere or for smudge (keeping mosquitoes away), keep fires small and safe. A small, lightweight backpacking stove is preferable for cooking. These are inexpensive, cook food quickly, and, unlike fires, keep pots from blackening.

There are certain areas in the United States—on the beaches of the Colorado River in the Grand Canyon, for instance—where human body waste has become such a problem that now it is required that all human excrement be carried out. With the increasing number of people using New Jersey trails, it is not unthinkable that in the future we might all be required to carry out our personal waste. To avoid this inconvenience, use the outhouse where one is provided, and otherwise be a "copy cat"—act as a feline does. Choose a spot far away from any water and the trail, remove the layer of leaves and twigs, dig a hole at least 3 inches deep in the soil with either a rock or a sturdy stick (some hikers carry a special trowel for this purpose), take care of your business, and cover the whole mess over so that no disturbance is apparent.

HIKING ORGANIZATIONS

The umbrella organization for hiking in New Jersey is the New York–New Jersey Trail Conference (NYNJTC), a nonprofit federation of 10,000 individuals and 100 hiking and environmental organizations working to build and maintain trails and to preserve open space. Its trail network includes more than 2,000 miles of foot trails. Formed in 1920, the Conference built the first section of the Appalachian Trail in 1923.

The Conference is supported by dues, publication sales, and donations—along with thousands of hours of volunteer time. Members receive the quarterly news journal *Trail Walker*, and can purchase maps and guides at a 25 percent discount, avail themselves of the Conference library, and obtain a 10 percent discount on purchases at many outdoors stores. At present, dues are $30 for individuals and $25 for seniors. A single life membership is $1,000; a joint life membership (for two adults residing at the same address) is $1,500.

We encourage you to support the people who maintain the trails. The NYNJTC office is located at 156 Ramapo Valley Road (on US 202 just north of NJ 17), Mahwah, NJ 07430. You can also call 201-512-9348, or visit their Web site, www.nynjtc.org.

There are also many fine hiking clubs in New Jersey, catering to all grades of hikers in many areas of the state. These clubs are an excellent way to meet people who share your love of the outdoors. The clubs are your ticket to the special natural sections of your area and will help you learn the ins and outs of hiking in the Northeast. For a listing, go to the Trail Conference's Web site, www.nynjtc.org.

Volunteers maintain many of the trails described in this book. Respect their work and their tender loving care, and do not cut corners on switchbacks or otherwise erode the trail unnecessarily. If you'd like to help maintain a trail, contact the New York–New Jersey Trail Conference.

MAP KEY

USGS
Free USGS topo maps are available online: store.usgs.gov.

NYNJTC
The New York–New Jersey Trail Conference publishes and sells waterproof, color topographic maps, usually in sets. Four map sets cover trails in New Jersey: Hudson Palisades, North Jersey, Kittatinny, and Jersey Highlands. About half of the hikes in this book can be found on these maps, which are printed on nearly indestructible Tyvek. To obtain copies of these maps, contact the Trail Conference at 156 Ramapo Valley Road, Mahwah, NJ 07430, call 201-512-9348, or find them on the Web at www.nynjtc.org.

DEP
Free maps are available from the various state park and forest offices. Or, write to the New Jersey Department of Environmental Protection, Division of Parks and Forestry, P.O. Box 402, Trenton, NJ 08625; call 1-800-843-6420. The quality of these maps varies, and some of them do not clearly show hiking trails.

NPS
National Park maps, usually free, are available from individual park offices. Addresses are in the hike text.

Ridge and Valley

1

South of High Point

Total distance: 6.3 miles

Hiking time: 4 hours

Vertical rise: 500 feet

Rating: Moderate to strenuous

Maps: USGS Port Jervis South; NYNJTC Kittatinny Trails #123; DEP High Point State Park map

Trailhead GPS Coordinates: N 41° 18' 10" W 74° 40' 04"

South of High Point Monument and the popular Lake Marcia is a section of High Point State Park (1480 State Route 23, Sussex, NJ 07461; 973-875-4800; www.njparksand forests.org) that is wild, expansive, scenic, and lightly used. In contrast, the portion of the park that is north of NJ 23 is heavily used. The Appalachian Trail (AT) passes through this southern section, and the Rutherford Shelter, one of the few New Jersey AT trail shelters, is also found here. A warning is in order. If you have not had any experience with this section of the AT, or if your feet are particularly sensitive, be prepared for a rocky path that will test your boots. The first 2 miles of this hike will be demanding on your feet and on your balance. Most people prefer to do the hike in the direction described below, because the second leg of the hike is on a flat woods road. That way, you can first do the more challenging portions of the hike and then return on a relatively easy route.

HOW TO GET THERE

The trailhead is just east of the High Point State Park Visitor Contact Station in Sussex County. Take NJ 23 to the visitors center at the top of Kittatinny Ridge, on the south side of the highway. Stop in at the office for a map (or a permit if you are camping and leaving your car overnight). Park at the AT parking area, which is on the same side of NJ 23, about 0.3 mile east of the visitors center. (It is the second active driveway when heading east on NJ 23 from the visitors center.)

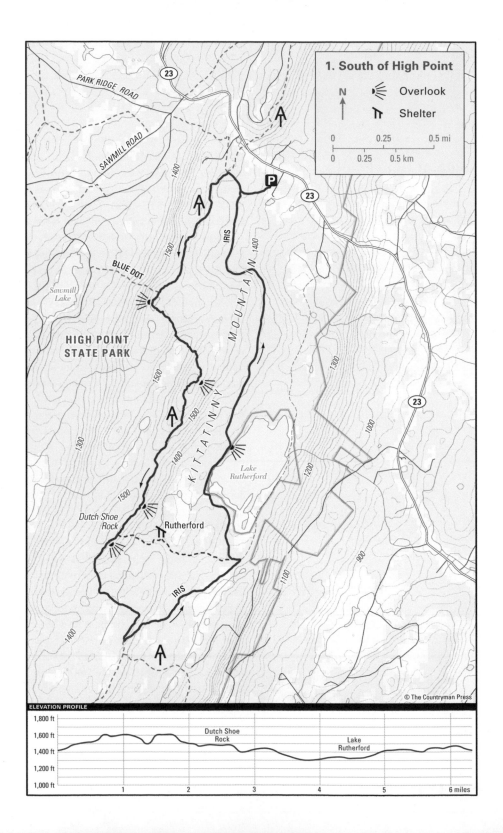

1. South of High Point

N

Overlook

Shelter

| 0 | 0.25 | 0.5 mi |
| 0 | 0.25 | 0.5 km |

PARK RIDGE ROAD

SAWMILL ROAD

23

P

23

1400

IRIS

1400

1500

BLUE DOT

Sawmill Lake

HIGH POINT
STATE PARK

1300

1300

1000

K I T T A T I N N Y

M O U N T A I N

1500

1500

1400

Lake Rutherford

1200

1500

Dutch Shoe Rock

Rutherford

1100

IRIS

1400

900

23

© The Countryman Press

ELEVATION PROFILE

1,800 ft						
1,600 ft			Dutch Shoe Rock		Lake Rutherford	
1,400 ft						
1,200 ft						
1,000 ft	1	2	3	4	5	6 miles

THE TRAIL

From the southwest corner of the parking area, follow a blue-blazed trail that leads for about a quarter of a mile to the red-on-white-blazed Iris Trail. Turn right and follow both blue and red-on-white blazes for another 0.2 mile to a junction with the AT at a four-foot-high drainpipe. Turn left at this junction and begin to follow the white-blazed AT.

After a short distance, the AT begins to climb, with a large cliff on your right as you ascend along an embankment. The next section of the AT is a beautiful stretch of trail. In places, pine needles cover the rocky trail, which winds through huge fern fields under oak, maple, and large white pines. The trail follows the eastern side of a ridge for a while, then swings over to the western side. Your feet will notice that the rocks are particularly jagged in this section, a characteristic of the AT in Pennsylvania and New Jersey. You'll pass a junction with the Blue Dot Trail, which descends steeply to the right and reaches Sawmill Lake below in about 0.5 mile. Viewpoints along the trail in this section overlook the lake, as well as the Delaware River and Pennsylvania beyond. The AT next turns away from this ridge and descends steeply over rocks into a valley.

After climbing a parallel ridge to the east, the AT again turns south, reaching a series of rocky outcrops vegetated only sparsely with pitch pines and scrub oaks. For the next mile the trail is quite rugged and very rocky in places as it passes through first this ragged forest and then an oak-and-maple woods. After a long and gradual descent, the trail arrives at a series of clearings offering some of the best views on this hike.

Lake Rutherford from the Appalachian Trail　　　　DAN BALOGH

Lake Rutherford

Here is Dutch Shoe Rock, a long, glacially polished rock slab of Silurian sandstone that offers a spectacular east-facing view. Lake Rutherford and a large marsh are just to your left. In the distance are Pochuck Mountain and Wawayanda Mountain, both traversed by the AT farther north. As you walk south on the AT, the vistas from the enormous slab continue. The best viewpoint is located about 150 feet north of a trail junction, where a blue-blazed trail leads down the slope to the Rutherford Shelter.

You have two options at this point. The first, which will add about 0.5 mile to your hike, is to continue following the AT south for another 0.8 mile to its junction with the red-on-white-blazed Iris Trail. Turn left here and follow the Iris Trail along an old woods road that will feel positively soft after those

first few miles on the jagged rocks of the AT. Keep left at a junction, staying with the red-on-white markers, and soon you will arrive at the west shore of Lake Rutherford. The trail description from there follows below.

Your other choice is somewhat more adventurous but definitely worth considering—especially if you are backpacking. You can take the blue trail down to the shelter, then pick up an old woods road that leads east out to the Iris Trail. From the AT, follow the blue markers down the steep slope and then along a footpath to the shelter. You'll cross over a small stream and pass a rock-lined spring that feeds a small brook along the way. The Rutherford Shelter is one of the more remote AT shelters in New Jersey. The presence of large lilac bushes around it indicates that it was built on land that was once farmed. In back of the shelter are a number of attractive campsites at the edge of the marsh you saw earlier. This remote area is a good place for lunch or a snack, and of course for primitive camping.

To continue on the hike, leave the shelter, following a path that exits the small clearing in front of the shelter. This path, actually an old woods road, is not heavily used, nor is it maintained. Parts of it are grassy and mossy, parts are quite wet, and there may be a few blowdowns blocking the path. At first, to your left, you will see the large marsh in back of the shelter. The path rises gradually, crests a small ridge, descends, and reaches the red-on-white-blazed Iris Trail in about 0.5 mile. Turn left here and walk another 0.5 mile or so to the west shore of Lake Rutherford. On the way, you will cross over one of the small brooks that feed the lake. Here the bright red cardinal flower, a type of *Lobelia*, blooms during the summer.

Regardless of which option you chose, you are now on the west shore of Lake Rutherford, a reservoir that provides water to the town of Sussex. Where the Iris Trail comes closest to the lake, look for a side trail that will take you to a rocky overlook near the shore of the lake. Lake Rutherford is quite large and, except for one distant building, is uninhabited and quite wild. Unfortunately, swimming is not permitted.

From the lake, continue northward on the Iris Trail through a dark and dense forest. The trail, now covered with fine gravel, gradually widens in this section and is used in the winter by snowmobiles and cross-country skiers. Low rock outcrops line the trail in places. Forest birds, such as the rufous-sided towhee, are often seen hopping in the bushes. The seldom seen Swainson's thrush, with its ethereal call, also inhabits these woods. The trail gradually rises through a more open forest filled with lowbush blueberry bushes, then descends through a mixed-oak forest with an understory of ferns. After crossing a small brook on a footbridge, the trail heads uphill and eventually arrives at the junction where you began the loop. Turn right here and follow the blue blazes back to your car.

2

Rattlesnake Swamp to Catfish Pond

Total distance: 5 miles	
Hiking time: 3 hours	
Vertical rise: 500 feet	
Rating: Moderate	
Maps: USGS Flatbrookville; NYNJTC Kittatinny Trails #121; NPS Millbrook Area Trails map; NY-NJ Appalachian Trail Guide map #4	
Trailhead GPS Coordinates: N 41° 03' 29" W 74° 57' 54"	

This loop hike in the heart of the Kittatinnies skirts the edge of a swamp, passes a lake, and then climbs to an excellent overlook from the ridge. The area is still not heavily used, and if you are hiking during the week, your chance of encountering others is minimal. Though you probably will not see any rattlesnakes (which are on the endangered species list), prepare for a very rocky trail by wearing sturdy boots with good ankle support. An overnight option is the AMC's Mohican Outdoor Center.

The Appalachian Mountain Club (AMC) is a Boston-based hiking club that has a strong presence in the White Mountains of New Hampshire and several other areas in New England. The club was founded in 1876 and was a model for the Sierra Club, founded in 1892. The AMC's Mohican Outdoor Center (formerly Camp Mohican) might be called a guide center: It is part nature center, part hotel, and part conference center. Workshops are held on weekends, covering topics such as backpacking, canoeing, and birding. Hikers may stay overnight for a fee in one of their cabins or at a walk-in campsite. Since the AMC has been at Camp Mohican, the trails in the area have been well maintained. On the second weekend of each summer month, volunteers do trail work in exchange for lodging. The Mohican Outdoor Center is at 50 Camp Road, Blairstown, NJ 07825-9655. Call 908-362-5670, or check their Web site, www.outdoors.org/lodging /mohican/. Call ahead for rates and availability if you plan to stay overnight.

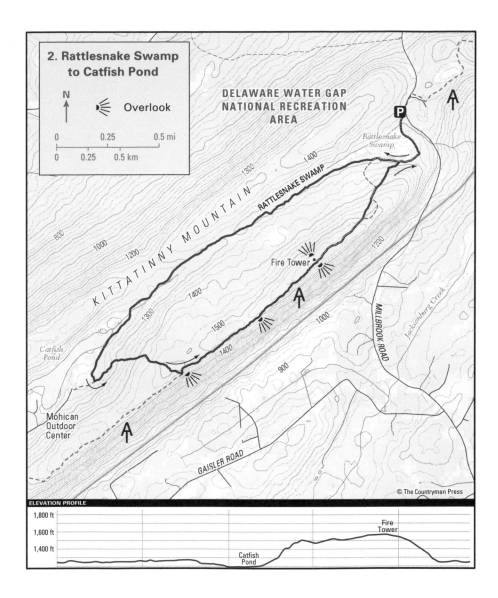

**2. Rattlesnake Swamp
to Catfish Pond**

N

🖝 Overlook

0   0.25   0.5 mi

0   0.25   0.5 km

DELAWARE WATER GAP
NATIONAL RECREATION
AREA

*Rattlesnake
Swamp*

RATTLESNAKE SWAMP

K I T T A T I N N Y   M O U N T A I N

*Catfish
Pond*

Fire Tower

MILLBROOK ROAD

Jacksonburg Creek

Mohican
Outdoor
Center

GAISLER ROAD

© The Countryman Press

ELEVATION PROFILE

1,800 ft

1,600 ft

1,400 ft

Fire
Tower

Catfish
Pond

HOW TO GET THERE

Take I-80 to Exit 12 (Blairstown, Hope) and proceed north on County Route 521, following the sign to Blairstown. After about 5 miles, you'll come to a junction with NJ 94.

Make a left here and, in another 0.2 mile, turn right at the light. Continue straight ahead on Bridge Street. (Do not make the sharp right onto County Route 521.) When you reach the end of Bridge Street at the top of a

Catfish Fire Tower DANIEL CHAZIN

sharp rise, turn sharply right onto Millbrook Road and then make the next left. You are now on Millbrook-Blairstown Road (County Route 602). Continue ahead for 6.2 miles to the top of the ridge, where the Appalachian Trail (AT) crosses the road. You'll see the ridge and the fire tower looming in front of you about a mile before you reach the crest of the ridge. Parking for a few cars can be found near the gate on the left side of the road (don't block the gate). Additional parking is located on the right, about 150 yards west in a small area just off the road.

THE TRAIL

Begin by hiking south from the gate on a gravel road, following the white blazes of the Appalachian Trail (AT). Pass an AT trail sign, cross a small brook, and proceed through a dense rhododendron thicket. Take note where the AT turns left off the gravel road, leading uphill through the rhododendron. Continue straight ahead on the gravel road, past this junction and Rattlesnake Spring (50 feet ahead on the left). A short distance beyond, a sign marks the start of the orange-blazed Rattlesnake Swamp Trail. Bear right, leaving the gravel road, and continue on a footpath. The footing, typical of trails on the Kittatinny Ridge, is quite rocky.

The Rattlesnake Swamp Trail continues to the left of and slightly above Rattlesnake Swamp, with its hemlocks, ferns, mosses, and skunk cabbage. Some sections are deep and dark, dominated by hemlock and other shade plants, while other areas, with dead trees and high ostrich ferns, are open to the sun. At one point, the trail detours to the left, climbing a little farther up the hill to avoid a wet section of the former trail route. As you leave the swamp, the trail, now traversing a thick growth of mountain laurel, enters a deep hemlock grove. Farther along, the footing becomes mossy and in places quite wet. Cross over a small brook (the inlet of Catfish Pond) and begin to climb toward higher ground and more open forest.

Don't be surprised if you startle a deer in this section, sending it crashing through the brush. After a stretch of less dense woods, the trail descends and crosses the brook three more times. About 45 minutes to an hour into the hike, Catfish Pond appears through the trees on your right.

As you walk past the northern end of the pond, enjoy the views of lily-covered water against the steep western banks, some of which are bare of foliage because of rockslides. The sounds of frogs fill the air in spring and summer. The trail follows a rocky old road lined with both low- and highbush blueberries. The highbush blueberries, ripe in late July and early August, are particularly delicious. Catfish Pond is adjacent to Mohican Outdoor Center, the site of a former Boy Scout camp. The federal government acquired the camp in the 1960s as part of the Tocks Island dam project. After the project was abandoned, the camp was leased to the Appalachian Mountain Club, which now operates it as the Mohican Outdoor Center.

The Rattlesnake Swamp Trail gradually veers away from the pond and soon reaches a junction—just past a concrete slab—where a sign indicates a turn to the left. (A right turn here leads to the Mohican Outdoor Center.) To continue the hike, turn left, following the orange blazes. The trail now begins a gradual climb of the Kittatinny Ridge on a woods road. After a while, the grade steepens, and the trail narrows to a footpath. You'll climb over large rocks and through clumps of laurel. Soon, there is a temporary respite where the trail levels off before it resumes climbing, this time not so steeply. After meandering through another level section, the trail climbs once more, leading to the flat, level summit of the Kittatinny Ridge. Here, among dense huckleberry bushes, a vast vista of forest and farmland opens up through the trees. Just a few steps ahead is a junction with the AT and a magnificent east-facing view over the Great Valley from open rock ledges.

After resting from the climb and enjoying the spectacular view, head north, now following the white blazes of the AT. The trail

East-facing view over the Great Valley from rock ledges at junction of AT with Rattlesnake Swamp Trail

winds along the east face of the broad summit through a parklike, open area of trees and grass. To the right are vistas out to the eastern horizon. After about a half hour of walking, arrive at the Catfish Pond fire tower, which is operational during the fire season. Climb the tower for views in all directions. On a clear day even the distant Catskills to the north are visible.

Continue straight ahead on the AT, which now follows the service road that provides vehicular access to the fire tower. Watch for a turn where the AT heads left, leaving the road, and descends a little more steeply through bushes and ferns. The AT rejoins the road, now gravel, for a few hundred feet before turning right, back into the woods on a footpath. After descending on a rocky trail under a power line, you'll reach another junction where the AT joins the gravel road once again—this time near Rattlesnake Spring, which you passed near the beginning of the hike. Turn right and follow the AT along the gravel road back to your car.

3

Mount Tammany

Total distance: 3.5 miles

Hiking time: 3 hours

Vertical rise: 1,200 feet

Rating: Moderately strenuous

Maps: USGS Portland, Bushkill; NYNJTC Kittatinny Trails #120; NPS Kittatinny Point Area Trails map; NY–NJ Appalachian Trail Guide map #4

Trailhead GPS Coordinates: N 40° 58' 17" W 75° 07' 31"

Overlooking the Delaware River on the New Jersey side of the Delaware Water Gap stands Mount Tammany. This mountain, at the southern tip of the Kittatinny Ridge and located within Worthington State Forest and the Delaware Water Gap National Recreation Area (Bushkill, PA 18324; 570-426-2452; www.nps.gov/dewa), offers one of the steepest climbs in all of New Jersey, as well as spectacular views from its summit. Because of its easy access from I-80, the trail to the summit is heavily used year-round, especially in summer. Also in the area are Dunnfield Creek, with its many falls and cascades, the Appalachian Trail (AT), and Sunfish Pond, making this location a major natural area in the state.

The Delaware Water Gap, certainly one of the scenic wonders of New Jersey, is a 1,200-foot-deep gorge carved by the waters of the Delaware River through the long, wall-like Kittatinny Ridge. Back in Cretaceous times, roughly 100 million years ago, the water gap did not exist. The entire area, which was once very mountainous, had been worn down by erosion to a flat plain that sloped gently toward the Atlantic Ocean some 40 miles away. The streams that drained the land meandered through this landscape on their way to the sea. In the late Cretaceous Period the land began to rise, and the streams began cutting deeper channels.

As the land rose, the ancestral Delaware River found itself confronted with a major barrier—the relatively resistant rock that makes up the Kittatinny Ridge. This rock, made of the tough sandstone and

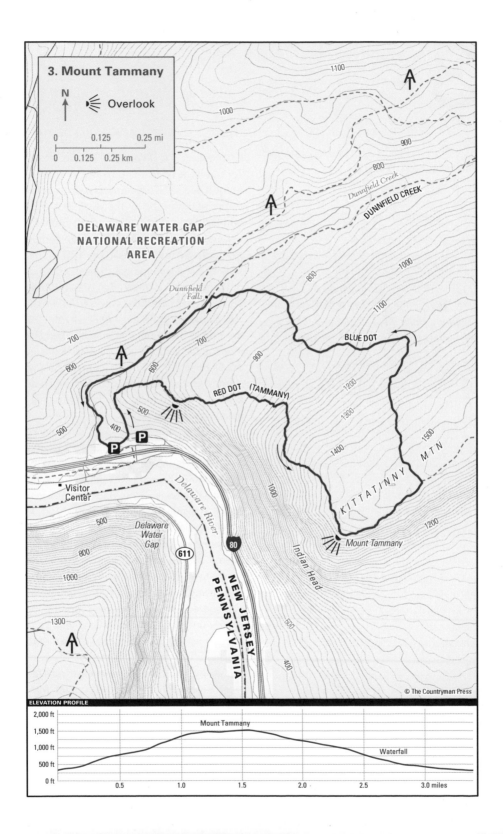

3. Mount Tammany

N

◀▦ Overlook

| 0 | 0.125 | 0.25 mi |
| 0 | 0.125 | 0.25 km |

1100

1000

900

800

Dunnfield Creek

DUNNFIELD CREEK

DELAWARE WATER GAP
NATIONAL RECREATION
AREA

800

1000

Dunnfield Falls

1100

BLUE DOT

700

900

700

1200

RED DOT (TAMMANY)

800

1300

600

500

1500

500

400

M T N

P P

1400

K I T T A T I N N Y

Visitor Center

1200

500

Delaware River

Delaware Water Gap

611 80

1000

Indian Head

Mount Tammany

800

1000

NEW JERSEY
PENNSYLVANIA

500

1300

400

© The Countryman Press

ELEVATION PROFILE

2,000 ft				Mount Tammany			
1,500 ft							
1,000 ft						Waterfall	
500 ft							
0 ft							
	0.5	1.0	1.5	2.0	2.5		3.0 miles

Delaware River from viewpoint on Red Dot Trail

DANIEL CHAZIN

conglomerate of the Shawangunk Formation, dips to the north at the entrance to the gap. These rocks and the red rocks that overlie them are warped into many folds. The cross-section of the ridge exposed by the gap is a geology lesson in itself. Right at the gap, the Kittatinny Ridge is fractured, its long continuity broken. Because of this structural weakness, the Delaware River has successfully maintained its course through this section of the Kittatinny Ridge. Today, the river continues to cut and remove rock as the land continues to rise slowly.

HOW TO GET THERE

Take I-80 west to the Delaware Water Gap. Immediately beyond milepost 1, take the exit for "Dunnfield Creek/Appalachian Trail" and bear left at the fork. Continue past the underpass on the left and turn right into a parking area at signs with "P" and "hiker" symbols.

If you miss the turnoff, take the next exit off the highway—the last exit in New Jersey—and follow signs to the Delaware Water Gap National Recreation Area Kittatinny Point Visitor Center. To reach the parking area where the hike begins, go past the visitors center, cross back under I-80, bear left, then turn right into a parking area at signs with "P" and "hiker" symbols.

THE TRAIL

Begin the hike on the Red Dot Trail (also known as the Tammany Trail), which leaves the parking area near its entrance. The trail, marked with red-on-white blazes, climbs wooden steps and soon merges with a branch of the trail that leads up from another parking area. The trail then begins to climb—a foreshadowing of things to come. After this brief elevation gain, the trail levels off, briefly paralleling Dunnfield Creek, well below on the left. Where the trail turns sharply right, it begins a steady climb on a well-used, rocky path lined with evergreens, hemlocks, and rhododendrons. The sounds of the falls on Dunnfield Creek, even farther below now, are still in the distance. Watch for where the trail turns right, climbing over tilted but parallel beds of sedimentary rock.

After this last climb, you'll arrive at the first of several overlooks. Here, at the edge of a steep cliff and exposed to the elements, cedar trees struggle for survival. Below, looking south, the Delaware Water Gap opens in front of you. Mount Minsi on the Pennsylvania side is to the right and Mount Tammany to the left. Mount Minsi, which rises 1,463 feet above sea level, is named after the Native Americans who lived in the area. Mount Tammany, at 1,527 feet, is named after the Lenni-Lenape chief Tamenund.

After skirting a few more viewpoints, the trail crosses a brook and passes a reliable spring on the left. After this brief respite, it once again begins seriously climbing the mountain ridge. Because of the rocky terrain, climbing this section is difficult in any season, but it can be particularly challenging and even dangerous in icy conditions. First you cross a boulder field; then, through a beautiful forest of hemlock and rhododendron, you must navigate a steep rock slab. Use both your feet and your hands when you need to, while still paying attention to the markers so

View from summit of Mount Tammany

DANIEL CHAZIN

Ridge and Valley

as not to lose the trail. After leveling off temporarily through a more open forest, the trail begins climbing again on a rocky footpath high on the ridge. From here to the summit, the forest is sparse, offering little protection from the winds. Along the way, you will find a cedar-lined viewpoint on the right.

Just before you reach the summit, notice that the forest to the left is more open; a fire burned this area some years ago. Thick laurel is replacing the former oak forest. Finally you reach the summit. Here the oak forest stops at the edge of a 1,200-foot cliff overlooking the Delaware River. Only scrub oak and pitch pine survive in this rocky, exposed environment. At the summit area, walk to the right and down over the exposed rocks, which offer you an expansive view west to Mount Minsi and the Blue Mountain Ridge behind it. The Pocono Plateau of Pennsylvania stretches north to the horizon. To the south you see the plains of the Great Valley, and beyond that, the Reading Prong section of the Highlands extends to the horizon. If you walk down the exposed rocks of the summit you will see the Indian Head profile—located on a portion of the cliff below and to the north (upriver) of the viewpoint—staring out over the river.

When you're rested from the climb, retrace your steps to the trail. Just ahead, you'll see a triple-blue blaze that marks the start of the Blue Dot Trail. Follow this trail, which heads northeast along the ridge of Mount Tammany on a rocky but relatively level path. Upon reaching the actual summit (1,549 feet), it turns sharply left at a wooden sign for the Blue Trail and soon begins a rather steep descent on a rocky, eroded woods road.

After a long, steady descent from the ridge over rocks, the trail swings to the left and finally reaches a junction with the green-blazed Dunnfield Creek Trail. Turn left and follow the joint blue and green blazes parallel to Dunnfield Creek. Just ahead, you'll notice an open area on the right with a bench that overlooks an attractive waterfall. Continue ahead a short distance until you reach a wooden footbridge that spans the creek. Here, a short unmarked trail on the right leads to the base of the waterfall.

When you're ready to continue, cross the footbridge and follow along the trail, which parallels the creek on a wide path. Here in this dark hemlock gorge are numerous cascades and plunge pools, the white water creating a sharp contrast to the dark rock it glides over. Along with some spectacular rock, water, and plant scenery, you may encounter many people, including families with small children, who have stopped in their travels along I-80 to explore this scenic ravine. For some, this may be their first experience with a natural area.

In another quarter mile, the Blue Dot and Dunnfield Creek Trails end, and you continue ahead along the creek, now following the white-blazed Appalachian Trail. Soon, the trail bears left, leaving the wide path, and crosses Dunnfield Creek on a steel bridge with a wooden deck. Just ahead, you'll reach the parking area where the hike began.

4

Appalachian Trail Backpack

Total distance: 28.2 miles
Hiking time: 17 hours—allow 3 days, 2 nights
Vertical rise: 2,750 feet
Rating: Strenuous
Maps: USGS Portland, Bushkill, Flatbrookville, Culvers Gap; NYNJTC Kittatinny Trails #120, #121, and #122; NY–NJ Appalachian Trail Guide map #4.
Trailhead GPS Coordinates: N 40° 58' 17" W 75° 07' 31"

Most hikers know that the Appalachian Trail (AT) is a marked footpath extending 2,185 miles from Springer Mountain, Georgia, to Mount Katahdin, Maine. The first stretch of trail was built in the 1920s in Bear Mountain–Harriman State Parks in New York State. A crew from the Civilian Conservation Corps cut the last section on a remote ridgeline in Maine between Spaulding and Sugarloaf Mountains in the summer of 1937. Trail markers are white rectangles; side trails to water, viewpoints, and shelters are marked in blue.

This backpacking trip begins at the Delaware Water Gap and follows the ridge of the Kittatinny Mountains generally north through Worthington State Forest and the Delaware Water Gap National Recreation Area. The terrain is rocky, and we recommend that you wear sturdy hiking boots instead of sneakers.

Squirrels and chipmunks are numerous and are always attracted to campsites where food scraps are available. Their sharp teeth can do a tremendous amount of damage to tents and packs. You must protect your food from bears as well as from smaller animals. The numbers of black bears in New Jersey have escalated in recent years, making it essential to use proper bear-resistant hanging procedures. Please read the section on bears in the introduction to this book.

Most natural water sources along the trail are liable to be contaminated, so you should purify all water by boiling, filtering, treating it with chemicals, or using a combination. Open ground fires are not permitted in the Delaware Water Gap National Recreation

Lower Yards Creek Reservoir from the Appalachian Trail   DANIEL CHAZIN

Area, so a portable camp stove is essential. Camping is permitted along the trail, with certain restrictions, and you should check on regulations with the ranger at the Delaware Water Gap National Recreation Area Kittatinny Point Visitor Center before setting out.

This hike requires transportation at each end. If you are willing to do some investigation on where cars should be placed, you could walk the following three sections of the AT as day hikes.

HOW TO GET THERE

Leave one car at Culvers Gap—the end point of this hike—at the parking lot on Sunrise Mountain Road. To reach this lot from US 206, head northeast on Upper North Shore Road just north of Culvers Lake, 3.4 miles northwest of Branchville, then immediately turn left onto Sunrise Mountain Road. The lot is at the first bend on the left (west) side of the road.

With the second car, drive south to the Delaware Water Gap. You can park either at the Delaware Water Gap National Recreation Area Kittatinny Point Visitor Center south of I-80 at the gap, or at the Dunnfield Creek Natural Area. The latter lot, which is east of the information center, is often crowded. It can be reached by turning left at the underpass under I-80, then making another left onto a paved road. Go to the parking lot on the right with the sign DUNNFIELD CREEK NATURAL AREA. For more information, contact the Delaware Water Gap National Recreation Area Kittatinny Point Visitor

Center, Bushkill, PA 18324; 570-426-2452; www.nps.gov/dewa.

THE TRAIL

First Day

*Delaware Water Gap
to Catfish Fire Tower
Total distance first day: 12.6 miles
Hiking time: 7 hours
Vertical rise: 1,000 feet*

Hoist your backpack and enter the woods at the far end of the Dunnfield Creek Natural Area parking lot. Soon, the trail crosses a substantial wooden bridge and parallels the stream on the opposite side. The trail leads steadily upward, through a mixture of deciduous and coniferous trees and ferns. Look to the right: You can see distinct layers of rock on the opposite bank. Look down as you climb high above the stream to see numerous pools and waterfalls and enjoy this delightfully cool section.

About a half mile from the start of the hike, the woods road forks. Bear left at the fork and head uphill through small sweet chestnut trees, which will probably never reach maturity because of blight; the disease practically destroyed these trees in the 1930s. Dunnfield Creek is visible below.

Still climbing, the woods road soon becomes a rocky trail, and at 1.5 miles, it reaches an intersection where the yellow-blazed Beulahland Trail begins on the left and the red-blazed Holly Springs Trail begins on the right. Continue ahead on the AT, which climbs some more before leveling off, paralleling the ridge of Mount Tammany on the right.

After traversing a rocky trail with tall mountain laurel, you will reach an intersection with the blue-blazed Douglas Trail. A backpacker campsite is located near the junction. No fires are permitted, and a stay of only one night is allowed but, because this site tends to be overcrowded, you will not use it as an overnight stop on this trip.

In a little over half a mile, you'll reach the southern tip of Sunfish Pond. This glacial lake is 1,370 feet above sea level and is considered a natural geological oddity. Just to the left of the trail here is a stone monument dated 1970. Walk straight ahead to the shore of Sunfish Pond, then turn left to follow the trail around the western shore. The no-camping regulation is strictly enforced at Sunfish Pond.

The trail is now rocky and narrow. It soon crosses the pond's outlet stream, climbs, turns right, and descends again to the water's edge. Many rocky areas on the shore of the pond invite the traveler to rest. In one area, we came across a stony beach where industrious folk had built many Stonehenge-like edifices. This nondestructive graffiti must have kept someone busy for many hours.

At the northern end of Sunfish Pond, the trail moves deeper into the woods, as the Turquoise Trail begins on the right. A short distance beyond, the orange-blazed Garvey Springs Trail begins on the left. The spring is on the left side of the trail, about 600 feet from the AT, although the water supply is dependable only in the springtime.

The AT now bears left and climbs to the crest of the ridge. In about two-thirds of a mile, it reaches two panoramic west-facing viewpoints. After descending a little to cross a stream, the trail climbs again and soon begins to run along the crest of the Raccoon Ridge. About 6 miles from the start, a power line crosses the trail, with views on both sides of the ridge. A short distance beyond, there are even better views from an open area with a large pile of rocks. The best views of the Delaware River below and Pennsylvania beyond are from rock ledges to the left

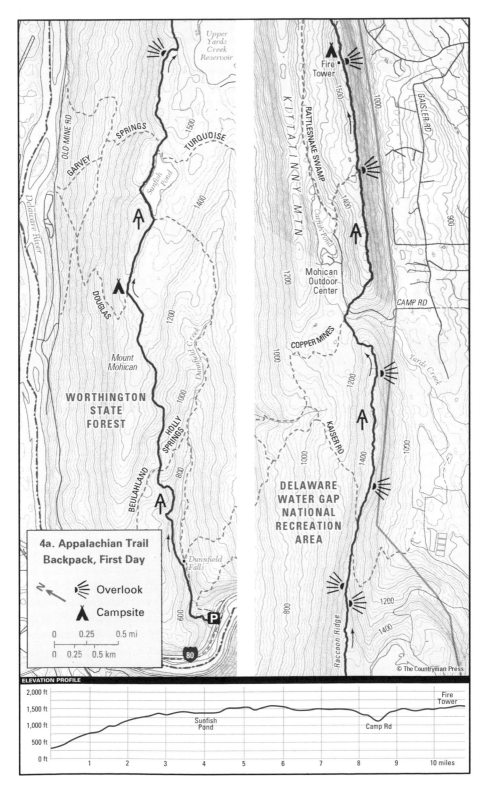

Upper Yards Creek Reservoir

OLD MINE RD

GARVEY SPRINGS

TURQUOISE

Sunfish Pond

DOUGLAS

Delaware River

Mount Mohican

WORTHINGTON STATE FOREST

Dunnfield Creek

HOLLY SPRINGS

BEULAHLAND

Dunnfield Falls

1500

1400

1200

1000

800

600

P

80

KITTATINNY MTN

RATTLESNAKE SWAMP

Fire Tower

Catfish Pond

Mohican Outdoor Center

COPPER MINES

CAMP RD

GAISLER RD

Yards Creek

KAISER RD

DELAWARE WATER GAP NATIONAL RECREATION AREA

Raccoon Ridge

1500

1000

900

1200

1000

800

1400

1000

1200

1400

© The Countryman Press

4a. Appalachian Trail Backpack, First Day

N

☀ Overlook

⛺ Campsite

| 0 | 0.25 | 0.5 mi |
| 0 | 0.25 | 0.5 km |

ELEVATION PROFILE

2,000 ft

1,500 ft

1,000 ft

500 ft

0 ft

Sunfish Pond

Camp Rd

Fire Tower

1   2   3   4   5   6   7   8   9   10 miles

of the trail. Directly ahead is the Catfish Fire Tower, and to the right you can see the Yards Creek–pumped water-storage ponds.

The Yards Creek Pumped Storage Electric Generating Station began operation in 1965. The upper reservoir was created from two small swampy areas on the mountaintop, and the lower, about a mile east and approximately 700 feet below, is located on Yards Creek. An auxiliary reservoir, now part of a Boy Scout camp, is just to the north of the Lower Yards Creek Reservoir.

As you head north along the crest of the ridge, you can see the Walpack Bend in the Delaware River. On a clear day, the Catskills are also visible. Just as the trail begins to descend, you'll pass a large sign that marks the boundary between Worthington State Forest and the Delaware Water Gap National Recreation Area.

Soon, the blue-on-white-blazed Kaiser Road Trail, an old woods road, joins from the right. The Kaiser Road Trail runs concurrently with the AT for 0.3 mile until it leaves to the left. In another mile, the trail becomes rockier as it descends steeply through mountain laurel. At the base of the descent, the red-blazed Coppermines Trail begins on the left. Just beyond, the AT crosses Yards Creek, a dependable water source, and reaches Camp Road (formerly known as Mohican Road). Fifty yards to the left, on Camp Road, is the Appalachian Mountain Club's Mohican Outdoor Center, where cabins and tent sites are available for rent. For information, contact the Mohican Outdoor Center, 50 Camp Road, Blairstown, NJ 07825-9655; 908-362-5670; www.outdoors.org/lodging/mohican. You have now walked about 9 miles, and as it will soon be time to make camp, you should collect water here for overnight use.

The AT crosses Camp Road and climbs rather steeply to regain the Kittatinny Ridge. The next section of the trail is spectacular—it runs along the side of the ridge through cedar and scrub pines. There is a sharp drop-off on the right, and if you look back, Yards Creek Reservoir is visible in the distance. In about a mile and a half from Camp Road, the trail emerges onto open rock ledges at the edge of the escarpment, with panoramic east-facing views over the Great Valley. Here, the orange-blazed Rattlesnake Swamp Trail, which descends the western side of the ridge, begins on the left.

After the trail leaves the ledges, it passes areas that could be used for camping, but we recommend you proceed just beyond Catfish Fire Tower. This tower, built in 1922, is 60 feet high, and it is well worth climbing the stairs for the splendid 360-degree view if the tower is open. The elevation here is 1,565 feet. You can see Sand Pond just to the north, and on a clear day, the Catskills are visible in the distance. From Catfish Fire Tower, the trail descends on an old woods road toward Millbrook–Blairstown Road. There are some ideal campsites just past the fire tower, both left and right of the woods road. It is your responsibility to comply with camping regulations.

Second Day

Catfish Fire Tower to Junction with
Trail to Buttermilk Falls
Total distance second day: 7.8 miles
Hiking time: 5 hours
Vertical rise: 1,000 feet

Still heading north, the AT turns left, leaving the woods road, and descends slightly on a rocky footpath until it rejoins the woods road. Then it turns right, once again leaving the woods road, and descends through mountain laurel and rhododendron to emerge on a gravel road. Rattlesnake Spring is about 50 feet south, on the left side of the road. This spring is delightful and is a dependable

View from the Catfish Fire Tower

source of water—after purification, of course—for today's hike. The next water is approximately 5 miles ahead.

Walk back to where the AT joins the wide gravel road and continue along the road, following the white blazes of the AT, until you reach paved Millbrook–Blairstown Road. Turn left onto it, go about 500 feet, then turn right and reenter the woods at a small parking area. Soon, the trail skirts around a beaver pond. A drain has been installed to lower the level of the pond and prevent the trail from flooding, but the beavers sometimes outwit the humans who installed the drain. The trail turns left to skirt the northern end of the pond and soon bears right, climbs a rocky slope, and emerges onto a power-line clearing, from where the Wallkill Valley and Pocono Plateau are visible.

The AT continues across the clearing and reenters the woods. Just beyond, a short side trail leads to a rock outcrop with a panoramic east-facing view. Sand Pond and Camp No-Be-Bo-Sco of the Boy Scouts of America, Northern New Jersey Council, are visible below. The AT now heads north on a footpath along the crest of the ridge, passing several viewpoints.

About a mile and a half from the power-line crossing, the trail reaches an old woods road that it follows to the north. This road was constructed as part of a proposed housing development that was abandoned when the property was acquired by the federal government in the 1960s for the proposed Tocks Island Dam (which was never built). Then, in another mile and a half, just before reaching paved Blue Mountain Lakes Road,

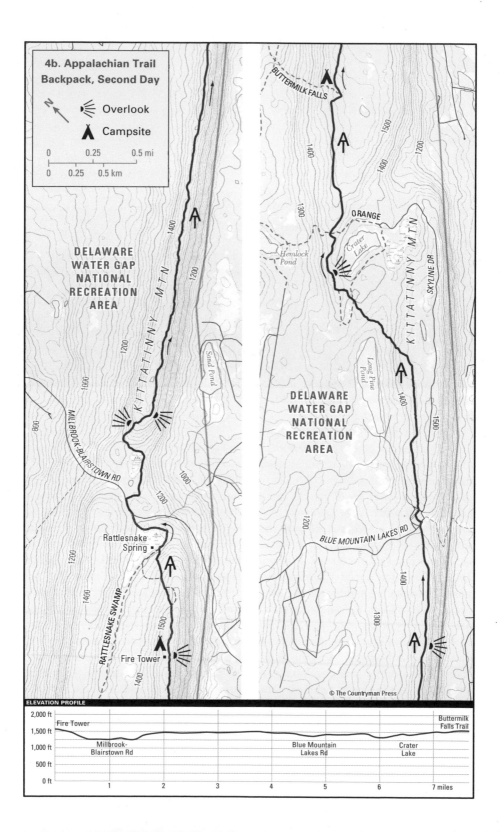

4b. Appalachian Trail Backpack, Second Day

N

● Overlook

⛺ Campsite

0   0.25   0.5 mi

0   0.25   0.5 km

BUTTERMILK FALLS

ORANGE

Crater Lake

Hemlock Pond

DELAWARE WATER GAP NATIONAL RECREATION AREA

KITTATINNY MTN

SKYLINE DR

Sand Pond

Long Pine Pond

DELAWARE WATER GAP NATIONAL RECREATION AREA

MILLBROOK-BLAIRSTOWN RD

Rattlesnake Spring

RATTLESNAKE SWAMP

Fire Tower

BLUE MOUNTAIN LAKES RD

© The Countryman Press

ELEVATION PROFILE

2,000 ft	Fire Tower						Buttermilk Falls Trail
1,500 ft							
1,000 ft	Millbrook-Blairstown Rd			Blue Mountain Lakes Rd		Crater Lake	
500 ft							
0 ft	1	2	3	4	5	6	7 miles

look for a water pump on the left. (If you miss it, there is also a spring contained in a metal pipe about 0.1 mile down the hill on Blue Mountain Lakes Road, on the right side of the road.) When you reach the road, turn right, walk a few steps down the road, and turn left into an area of small white pines. A short distance beyond, you'll pass a trail register on the left (please sign).

The trail traverses a pretty area here, and is narrower and cut through mountain laurel. In about a mile, it descends steeply on rock slabs until it reaches a rock-strewn bog on the right. If you look back and to the left through the trees, you can see Long Pine Pond. Various lakes and ponds in the vicinity are all potential sources of water, though all water should be treated before drinking. Cross a gravel road by bearing slightly to the right, reenter the woods on the left, and climb a steep rock outcrop. At the top, you'll cross another gravel road. Just beyond, a blue-blazed side trail on the right leads 150 feet to a viewpoint over Crater Lake.

The AT now heads north along a level woods road, with an orange-blazed trail leading downhill on the left to Hemlock Pond. The trail is on a ledge, with the ground dropping down to the left and rising to the right—a rock-slab slope dotted with white pines. About 3 miles north of Blue Mountain Lakes Road, the blue-blazed Buttermilk Falls Trail begins on the left.

Stay for the night at one of the many secluded and attractive campsites in this area. You can find a prime site by proceeding down the AT approximately 100 yards from the Buttermilk Falls sign and turning left onto a wide, grassy woods road. Within a minute you will find a delightful, flat, grassy opening with a beautiful white pine at each end. After setting up camp, water and a refreshing wash are available by taking a side trip (1.6 miles each way) to Buttermilk Falls. The trail to the

falls is very steep, but—except in dry weather—it is not necessary to go all the way to the falls for water. After about a half mile along the trail, you'll cross Woods Road, and in another few minutes, you'll hear the sound of water. Where the trail goes downhill and makes a sharp left turn, go straight ahead to a group of two or three pools of water. If these pools are dry, follow the streambed down until you find a suitable water-gathering spot. On the way down, the trail passes through several open blueberry patches, which in season might provide a snack.

If you prefer not to add this side trip to the day's walk and want to camp closer to a water supply, continue for approximately another mile and a half until the trail descends to a stream crossing. (Water is also available farther along, about 200 feet down a blue-blazed trail to a dependable spring.) The beautiful campsite at the head of the Buttermilk Falls Trail (described above), however, might make the extra effort to get water very worthwhile.

Third Day
Buttermilk Falls Trail to NJ 206 at Culvers Gap
Total distance third day: 7.8 miles
Hiking time: 5 hours
Vertical rise: 800 feet

About a third of a mile north of the trailhead of the Buttermilk Falls Trail, the gravel road bends to the right, but you should continue ahead on the white-blazed AT, which bears left and enters the woods on a footpath. In another two-thirds of a mile, an unmarked trail on the left leads to a western-facing viewpoint from rock slabs. The trail now descends steeply through a rocky section. At the base of the descent, it bears right and crosses a stream (this is the location of the alternate camping spot past the Buttermilk

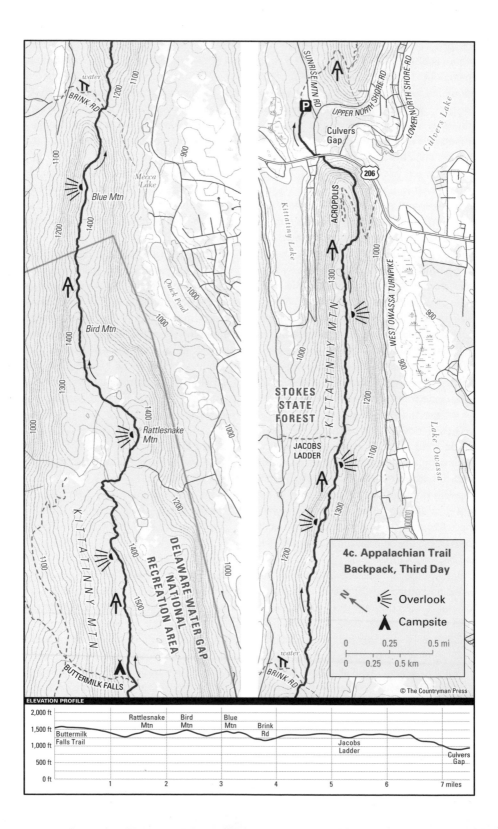

water
BRINK RD
1200
1100
1100
1200
1400
Blue Mtn
1400
Bird Mtn
1300
1000
1400
Rattlesnake Mtn
1200
K I T T A T I N N Y   M T N
1100
1400
1500
BUTTERMILK FALLS

900
Mecca Lake
Quick Pond
1000
1000
1000
1200
DELAWARE WATER GAP NATIONAL RECREATION AREA

SUNRISE MTN RD
UPPER NORTH SHORE RD
LOWER NORTH SHORE RD
Culvers Lake
P
Culvers Gap
206
ACROPOLIS
Kittatiny Lake
K I T T A T I N N Y   M T N
1300
STOKES STATE FOREST
JACOBS LADDER
1000
1000
1100
1200
1300
1200
WEST OWASSA TURNPIKE
900
900
Lake Owassa
water
BRINK RD

4c. Appalachian Trail Backpack, Third Day

N

💥 Overlook

⛺ Campsite

0   0.25   0.5 mi

0   0.25   0.5 km

© The Countryman Press

ELEVATION PROFILE

2,000 ft
1,500 ft — Rattlesnake Mtn — Bird Mtn — Blue Mtn — Brink Rd
Buttermilk Falls Trail
1,000 ft — Jacobs Ladder — Culvers Gap
500 ft
0 ft
1   2   3   4   5   6   7 miles

Falls area).

The trail now goes through a mature hemlock and laurel grove. It soon turns left and begins to climb Rattlesnake Mountain. In less than a half mile, you'll reach the summit (1,492 feet) and find panoramic west-facing views over the Wallkill Valley and the Pocono Plateau. You can see the Normanook (Culver) Fire Tower and High Point to the north.

Continue northward, gently descending on a narrow, rocky trail through many small pine trees, until you cross a small stream on rocks near a swampy area. The AT now climbs to the summit of Bird Mountain, where it turns right onto an old dirt road and begins to descend again. This section offers views of Quick Pond and Mecca Lake, below on the right.

When the road bears left at the base of the descent, the AT turns right and begins to climb through white pines. Soon, you'll cross the boundary between the Delaware Water Gap National Recreation Area and Stokes State Forest (marked by a sign). There are views to the left from the rock ledges and, at the top of the ridge, extensive views of the Wallpack Valley and the Poconos, before the trail moves back into the woods on rocky terrain. This high area is commonly known as Blue Mountain, and the larger area of water you glimpse through the trees is Lake Owassa. You will see this lake more clearly later.

The trail now begins a steady descent and, about 4 miles from the Buttermilk Falls Trail, reaches dirt Brink Road. Here, a blue-blazed side trail leads west 900 feet to the Brink Road Shelter. Water is available from a spring 350 feet beyond the shelter. The AT crosses Brink Road and climbs through a pretty area, with tall mountain laurel, white pines, massive rhododendrons, and hemlock. Soon, the trail regains the crest of the ridge, and it heads north along the ridge. A little over a mile from Brink Road, an unmarked side trail on the left leads to a west-facing viewpoint. A short distance beyond, an unmarked trail on the right leads to a viewpoint over Lake Owassa.

The trail now reaches a junction with the blue/green-blazed Jacob's Ladder Trail, which descends to the west. The AT continues to follow undulating terrain along the crest of the ridge. In 0.7 mile, the trail emerges onto a large cleared area. From this vantage point, the Normanook (Culver) Fire Tower, Culvers Lake, and US 206 are visible straight ahead, and Lake Owassa is behind you. The trail now reenters the woods, reaches another clearing, with US 206 visible on the right, and emerges onto a gravel road. Soon, the trail turns right, leaving the gravel road, and descends steadily to US 206, crossing the gold/brown-blazed Acropolis Trail along the way. When you reach US 206, turn left and continue to Upper North Shore Road (County Route 636). At the northwest corner of this intersection, follow the AT as it turns right onto a footpath. Continue for 0.2 mile, then turn right onto a short side trail that leads the parking lot on Sunrise Mountain Road, where you left the first car.

Highlands

5

Schuber Trail, End to End

Total Distance: 6.5 miles

Hiking time: 5 hours

Vertical rise: 800 feet

Rating: Strenuous

Maps: USGS Wanaque, Ramsey; NYNJTC North Jersey Trails #115. Sketch map available at www.nynjtc .org/map/ramapo-valley-county- reservation-brochure-map

Trailhead GPS Coordinates: N 41° 02' 52" W 74° 15' 06"

The Schuber Trail traverses the rugged Ramapo Mountains from Skyline Drive to US 202 (Ramapo Valley Road), crossing streams, climbing to viewpoints, and using parts of older trails and woods roads. When hiked from south to north, its trend is gradually downhill, though this tendency is not obvious because of the many uphill sections. The Schuber Trail is named after William "Pat" Schuber, who served as Bergen County's first County Executive and worked to preserve some of the land through which the trail passes. The trail was dedicated as part of a National Trails Day ceremony on June 1, 2002.

The trail connects Ramapo Mountain State Forest with Ramapo Valley County Reservation. On the way, it passes through Camp Glen Gray, a former Boy Scout camp, established in 1917 and acquired by Bergen County in 2002. The camp is now open to the public and is managed by the Friends of Glen Gray. For more information, or to make a reservation for weekend camping, call 201- 327-7234 or go to www.glengray.org. The Schuber Trail also skirts Camp Yaw Paw, an active Boy Scout camp of the Northern New Jersey Council, and it traverses the former Camp Tamarack.

For more information on Ramapo Mountain State Forest, contact Ringwood State Park, 1304 Sloatsburg Road, Ringwood, NJ 07456; 973-962-7031; www.njparksand forests.org. For more information on Ramapo Valley County Reservation, contact Bergen County Parks, One Bergen County Plaza, Hackensack, NJ 07601; 201-336-7275

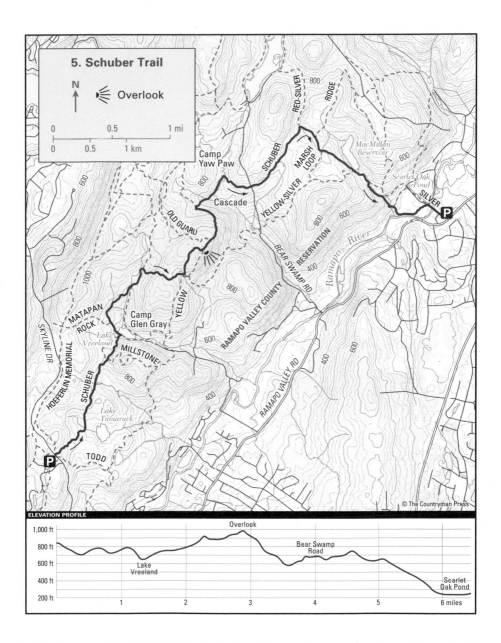

5. Schuber Trail

N ↑ ≣ Overlook

0   0.5   1 mi
0   0.5   1 km

ELEVATION PROFILE

(main office) or 201-327-3500 (park office); www.co.bergen.nj.us/parks.

The state acquired Ramapo Mountain State Forest through the use of Green Acres and federal funds in 1976. The land that eventually became Ramapo Valley County

Reservation was purchased from the Native Americans in 1720 by Samuel Laroe. Though the principal use of the land was farming, it also housed a gristmill, a sawmill, and later a bronze foundry. The land changed hands several times until its 1872

View of Manhattan skyline from the Schuber Trail   DANIEL CHAZIN

purchase by Alfred Burbank Darling, a native of Burke, Vermont and owner of many other properties, including the Fifth Avenue Hotel in Manhattan. It was his country estate, and the area became known as Darlington. The name Ramapo means "round ponds."

HOW TO GET THERE

This one-way hike requires a car shuttle. Begin by driving two cars to the Ramapo Valley County Reservation. To reach the reservation from NJ 17 in Mahwah, head south on US 202 (Ramapo Valley Road) for 1.9 miles. The parking area is on the right side of the road. Leave one car here and with the second car turn right (south) onto US 202 and drive 4.5 miles to a traffic light. Continue ahead and, at the next light (Courthouse Place), turn right onto I-287 South. Take the next exit (Exit 57), bear right at the fork, and proceed uphill on Skyline Drive for 1.4 miles to the crest of the hill. Park in the dirt parking area on the left side of the road.

THE TRAIL

Cross Skyline Drive. On the opposite side of the road, adjacent to a gravel road, you'll notice several trail markers on a nearby tree. Triple blazes mark the trailheads of the Schuber (orange) and Todd (white) Trails, and yellow blazes indicate the route of the Hoeferlin Memorial Trail. You will be following the orange-blazed Schuber Trail for the entire hike. Begin the hike by crossing the gravel road diagonally to the right and entering the woods, then head downhill on a winding, rocky footpath.

At the base of the descent, the trail turns right, immediately bears left, and crosses a stream on cinder blocks. After climbing over a small knoll, it crosses a second stream on stepping stones. The white-blazed Mill-stone Trail crosses the Schuber Trail just over a mile into the hike. Continue on the orange-blazed Schuber Trail, which descends to Lake Vreeland in Camp Glen Gray, passing the Explorer Cabin on the way. Near the lakeshore, about 1.3 miles from the start, the Millstone Trail briefly joins. The Schuber Trail turns left at the lakeshore, passing a shelter, and begins to climb on a wide gravel road.

The red-square-on-white-blazed Matapan Rock Trail veers off to the left five minutes from the lake, while the Schuber Trail continues ahead to cross a branch of North Brook on a wooden bridge. After passing more cabins and campsites, the trail approaches a former archery range, now a campsite, which it bypasses through the woods to the left.

The Schuber Trail passes by remnants of the historic Sanders Farm and briefly parallels North Brook before crossing it on a wooden footbridge. On the other side of the brook, the Old Guard Trail—marked with green-tulip-tree-leaf-on-white blazes—joins the Schuber Trail, and both trails run jointly for the next quarter of a mile. The trails now leave the camp and continue to parallel the brook. When the two trails split, bear right to continue on the Schuber Trail, which climbs away from the stream and soon crosses a wide woods road, the historical route of the Cannonball Road.

The Schuber Trail continues ahead on a wide gravel road, which climbs over a knoll and descends to a gate and a wooden bridge crossing a culvert—the outlet of Sanders Pond (on the left). A sign on the right identifies the area as an old foundry site, and stone ruins are visible. Then, about 2.3 miles into the hike, you'll reach the trailhead of the Yellow-Silver Trail. Here, the Schuber Trail turns left and climbs to a junction with the Yellow Trail (yellow diamond blazes), marked by a wooden signpost with blazes. Continue ahead a short distance to a panoramic viewpoint on the east side of the ridge. The east-facing vista encompasses the hills of the Ramapo Valley County Reservation, suburban Bergen County, and on a clear day, the Manhattan skyline on the horizon to the right.

After enjoying the view, return to the trail junction and turn right, now following the route of the joint Yellow/Schuber Trails downhill. In a few minutes, you'll pass the trailhead of the Old Guard Trail on the left, and the Schuber Trail soon bears left and descends steeply through deep woods. After the trails level off, the two trails diverge, and you should follow the Schuber Trail as it makes a sharp right turn. Watch carefully for this turn, after which the trail crosses a seasonal stream, passes a derelict lean-to (a former Camp Yaw Paw outpost) on the right, and crosses a larger watercourse on large rocks. You may wish to take a break at this crossing to enjoy the beautiful cascades (when the water is high).

The Schuber Trail now follows along Bear Swamp Brook, a wide stream, to your right, and it is tempting to stop to admire its cascades and canyons. When you reach the paved road that leads left to Camp Yaw Paw, you have hiked 3.6 miles. Turn right onto this road, cross Bear Swamp Brook on a wide wood-plank bridge, and continue ahead across paved Bear Swamp Road to reenter the woods. The trail now begins to climb on switchbacks.

In another mile (4.7 miles into the hike), you'll come to a junction with the Red-Silver Trail, which leaves to the left. Here, the Schuber Trail bears right and descends gradually on a woods road. In about five minutes, you'll pass the trailhead of the blue-blazed Ridge Trail on the left, and in another few minutes you'll see the red-blazed Marsh Loop beginning on the right. The MacMillan Reservoir can be glimpsed down to the left. Soon, you'll reach the dam at the end of the reservoir, where the Yellow-Silver Trail begins on the right. It is always interesting to pause a few minutes at the reservoir and to enjoy the exuberance of the dogs relishing their outing. You probably will encounter

MacMillan Reservoir

more walkers here than you have seen all day.

After crossing two stone bridges on the park road, follow the Schuber Trail as it turns right, leaving the road, and continues on a footpath. (The Silver Trail begins here and continues downhill along the park road.) The outlet of the reservoir, with its cascades, pools and waterfall, is visible down in the gorge on the left of the trail. At the base of the descent, the ruins of a stone cabin (built for a camp that formerly was located here) are to the right. Here, the trail bears left, crosses a footbridge over a stream, and soon reaches a junction where the green-on-white Halifax Trail begins on the left. Follow the orange blazes of the Schuber Trail, which bear right and then left, and begin to run on a footpath along the shore of the Ramapo River.

This trail section, located in the floodplain of the river, is often muddy.* The footpath soon crosses a grassy area and reaches the wide park road bordering Scarlet Oak Pond (the route of the Silver Trail). Turn right, cross the steel truss bridge over the Ramapo River, and climb the steps to reach the northern terminus of the Schuber Trail at the parking lot where you left the first car.

* If you find that the Schuber Trail is impassible because of flooding, use the following high-water route. After crossing the wooden footbridge beyond the abandoned stone cabin, turn left onto the green-on-white Halifax Trail and follow it for 0.2 mile. Then turn right onto the Silver Trail and take it across the steel truss bridge and up the steps to the parking area.

6

Ramapo Lake, Ramapo Mountain State Forest

Total distance: 5.1 miles

Hiking time: 3.5 hours

Vertical rise: 700 feet

Rating: Moderate

Maps: USGS Wanaque; NYNJTC North Jersey Trails #115

Trailhead GPS Coordinates:
N 41° 01' 57" W 74° 15' 08"

The 3,000-acre Ramapo Mountain State Forest is part of a rugged ridge straddling the Bergen–Passaic County boundary. Added to New Jersey's public lands in the mid-1970s, much of it had been the estate of the late William MacEvoy, a wealthy public works contractor. The centerpiece of the forest is the attractive Ramapo Lake, formerly known as Lake LeGrande, and before that Rotten Pond. Swimming is not permitted, but fishing is a popular pastime. A few privately owned inholdings remain, with their owners using several dirt access roads which are closed to public vehicular use (but open to hikers and bicyclists). These and other former estate roads have made this a popular area for mountain bikers, especially on weekends.

Miles of marked hiking trails lace the forest and lead to viewpoints and rock outcrops. This hike loops to one of the best of these outcrops and adds an out-and-back side trip to the interesting remains of one of the more prominent estates. Parking areas can fill up early on weekend days. However, on weekdays the area is often an island of tranquility—just a stone's throw from busy I-287. Ramapo Mountain State Forest is administered by Ringwood State Park (1304 Sloatsburg Road, Ringwood, NJ 07456; 973-962-7031; www.njparksandforests.org).

HOW TO GET THERE

To reach the lower parking area on Skyline Drive in Oakland, take I-287 to Exit 57. If you are coming from the north (heading south), bear right at the fork on the exit ramp to proceed onto Skyline Drive. If traveling from the

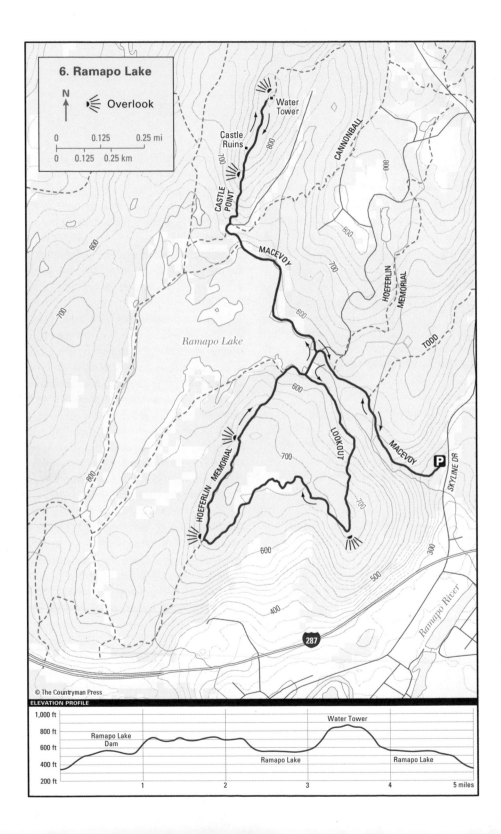

6. Ramapo Lake

N

Overlook

| 0 | 0.125 | 0.25 mi |
| 0 | 0.125 | 0.25 km |

Water Tower

Castle Ruins

Castle Point

MACEVOY

Ramapo Lake

CANNONBALL

HOEFERLIN MEMORIAL

TODD

HOEFERLIN MEMORIAL

LOOKOUT

MACEVOY

P

SKYLINE DR

Ramapo River

287

ELEVATION PROFILE

1,000 ft			Water Tower	
800 ft				
600 ft	Ramapo Lake Dam			
400 ft		Ramapo Lake		Ramapo Lake
200 ft				
	1	2	3	4	5 miles

south, make a left at the bottom of the exit ramp and continue under I-287 onto Skyline Drive. The parking area is a short distance ahead on the left, at milepost 0.3.

THE TRAIL

The blue-marked MacEvoy Trail, which will take you up to the lake, starts from the southwest corner of the parking area, near a bulletin board and several portable toilets. The trail passes stone ruins and continues along a wide woods road, with a stream below on the left. The grade is moderate, with an occasional short, steep pitch. About halfway to Ramapo Lake, the white-blazed Todd Trail begins on the right, and a short distance beyond, the yellow-blazed Hoeferlin Memorial Trail joins from the right. Stay on the blue-blazed MacEvoy Trail, which descends to a paved estate road, with the lake visible to the left. Leave the MacEvoy Trail, turn left, and follow the yellow blazes across the concrete dam and spillway.

About 100 feet beyond the dam, the red-blazed Lookout Trail begins on the left. Turn left onto it, heading away from the lake and following a rocky footpath along a stream—the other side of the same stream you saw along the MacEvoy Trail. Soon, the trail bears right and begins a steady climb up the ridge. Near the crest of the rise, the trail levels off and passes a huge boulder on the left.

A short distance beyond, the trail turns sharply right. Here, an unmarked trail heads to the left. Bear left and follow it for about 300 feet to an expansive viewpoint, which looks over Oakland and beyond to High Mountain. On a clear day, you can see the New York City skyline in the distance. Unfortunately, I-287 is visible directly below, and the sights and sounds of its traffic are intrusive.

Retrace your steps to the red-blazed Lookout Trail, bear left, and continue as it

The water tower at Foxcroft   DANIEL CHAZIN

meanders up and down, sometimes steeply, for less than a mile to a T-junction with the yellow-blazed Hoeferlin Memorial Trail. You'll continue the hike by turning right and following the joint Lookout/Hoeferlin Memorial Trails (yellow and red blazes). However, first take a moment to wander over to the left of the junction. This is a particularly scenic place to rest: a large rock ledge with a splendid pitch pine and a nice view across the Wyanokies.

Return to the trail, follow the yellow and red blazes across the ridge, and begin the descent to the lake. You'll pass several more viewpoints, with Ramapo Lake getting closer and looking more serene as you reach each spot.

When you reach the lake (where the

The ruins of the Foxcroft mansion   DANIEL CHAZIN

beyond, a rock outcrop on the left offers a broad view over the lake.

At a trail junction at the northwest corner of the lake, turn right, uphill, continuing to follow blue blazes and passing between two concrete posts. Soon, the blue trail will turn left off the road you've been following. Here, a triple-white blaze marks the start of the Castle Point Trail. Continue straight ahead along the road, but just ahead, as the road bends to the right, follow the white blazes as they turn left, leaving the road, and continue uphill on a steep, rocky footpath.

Near the top of the ridge, a rock outcrop on the left affords a panoramic view of Ramapo Lake and the Wyanokies. Just beyond, the trail goes over a stone wall and soon reaches the remains of the Foxcroft Estate, also known as Van Slyke Castle. The first ruin you'll encounter is of the mansion itself, built around 1910 by William Porter, a stock-broker. He died soon after it was finished, but his widow occupied the house until her death around 1940. Sadly, it fell into ruin and was burned by vandals in the 1950s. Continuing up the trail, you will pass the remains of an in-ground swimming pool. A bit later, you'll spot a massive stone tower. This most-attractive water tower served the estate. A detailed history, including pictures, awaits you at www.users.nac.net/axtell. Just beyond, another rock outcrop offers excellent views of the Wyanokies, to the west.

After enjoying the view, retrace your steps back to your car. To do so, follow the white trail past the mansion and down to the road, descend on the road to the lake, then turn left and follow the blue trail along the lakeshore and back to your car.

Lookout Trail ends), turn right along the road and walk back across the dam. If you would like to shorten the hike, turn right and follow the blue blazes back to your car. Otherwise, turn left and follow the blue MacEvoy Trail blazes along the lakeshore. You'll pass a large house on the right—one of the private inholdings previously mentioned—as well as an attractive cascade. A short distance

7

Ringwood Manor Circular

Total distance: 3 miles
Hiking time: 2 hours
Vertical rise: 250 feet
Rating: Easy
Maps: USGS Greenwood Lake (NY/NJ); NYNJTC North Jersey Trails #115; DEP Ringwood State Park
Trailhead GPS Coordinates: N 41° 08' 21.5" W 74° 15' 13.5"

Ringwood Manor, part of Ringwood State Park, is located in northeast Passaic County. The history of the area is closely tied to the local iron industry, which started at Ringwood in 1740. The products of the forges and furnaces were of much importance to the colonies during the Revolutionary War. Troops were stationed here, and George Washington made Ringwood his headquarters on several occasions. Robert Erskine, manager of the mines, served General Washington as surveyor general and prepared many of the maps for the campaign against the British.

Peter Cooper purchased the property in 1853. Cooper, a New York philanthropist, is best known as the founder of Cooper Union for the Advancement of Science and Art. Abram Hewitt, a family friend of the Coopers who later married their daughter Sarah Amelia, became a business partner of Peter Cooper, and the firm became known as Cooper, Hewitt & Co. It was always a summer house; the family spent winters in New York City.

Most of the present manor house was built between 1854 and 1910, during the Hewitt period. However, the earliest part of the house dates to 1807, when it was owned by the Ryerson family. During Peter Cooper's lifetime, title to the property was transferred to Abram Hewitt.

In 1936, Abram Hewitt's son Erskine Hewitt donated the manor house and 95 acres to the State of New Jersey. His nephew, Norvin Green (namesake of nearby Norvin Green State Forest), made an additional gift to bring the total to 579 acres.

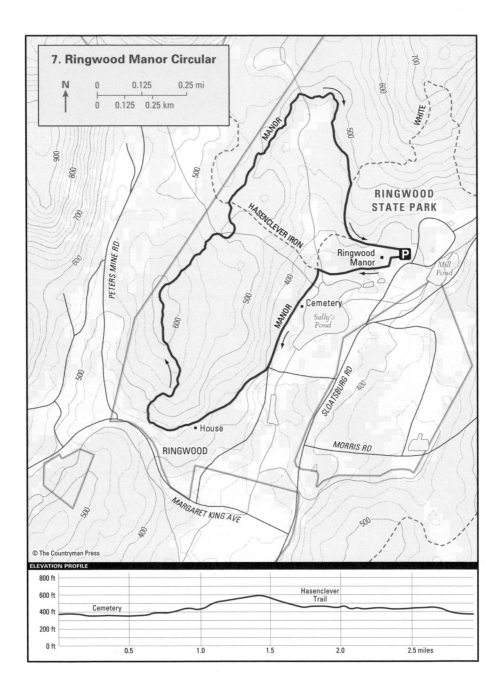

7. Ringwood Manor Circular

N

0   0.125   0.25 mi

0   0.125   0.25 km

MANOR

WHITE

700

600

700

500

500

RINGWOOD
STATE PARK

900

800

700

HASENCLEVER IRON

Ringwood
Manor

P

Mill
Pond

PETERS MINE RD.

800

400

Cemetery

Sally's
Pond

500

MANOR

600

500

SLOATSBURG RD.

400

500

House

RINGWOOD

MORRIS RD.

500

MARGARET KING AVE.

400

500

© The Countryman Press

ELEVATION PROFILE

800 ft

600 ft   Hasenclever
                                              Trail

400 ft   Cemetery

200 ft

0 ft

0.5   1.0   1.5   2.0   2.5 miles

Later purchases, using Green Acres funds, continued until as recently as 1978. The park now extends east into Bergen County, connecting with Ramapo Mountain State Forest and Ramapo Valley County Reservation to form a large network of public lands.

Volunteers coordinated by the New York–New Jersey Trail Conference developed an extensive network of trails in the area in the 1970s.

For more information on the park, contact Ringwood State Park, 1304 Sloatsburg Road, Ringwood, NJ 07456; 973-962-7031; www.njparksandforests.org. For more information on Ringwood Manor, go to www.ringwoodmanor.com.

HOW TO GET THERE

If coming from the south, take Skyline Drive to its northwestern end at Greenwood Lake Turnpike (County Route 511). Turn right and proceed north for 1.5 miles to Sloatsburg Road. Turn right onto Sloatsburg Road and continue for 2.4 miles to the entrance to Ringwood Manor, on the left side of the road. If coming from the north, take NY 17 to Sterling Mine Road (County Route 72), just south of Sloatsburg, and continue for 4.5 miles to the entrance to Ringwood Manor, on the right (the entrance is 1.0 mile south of the New York–New Jersey state line). Park in the parking area adjacent to the manor house. A parking fee is charged from Memorial Day to Labor Day. New Jersey residents ages 62 and older can obtain a pass that allows free parking at all state parks and forests (see the Introduction).

THE TRAIL

History is everywhere at Ringwood Manor, and it is a fine idea to combine your hike with a tour of the manor house. Call ahead (973-962-2240) to determine the house tour schedule, usually Wednesday through

Ringwood Manor

DANIEL CHAZIN

Sally's Pond

Sunday year-round. As this book went to press (spring 2014), the manor house was closed for restoration of damage caused in January 2012 by a malfunctioning furnace that spread a layer of soot through portions of the first two floors. The grounds remain open, and the trails are accessible to hikers.

The hike commences at the park office, where maps and brochures are usually available. Walk around the front of the manor house. When you reach the western end of the porch, you'll notice a pair of wrought-iron gates standing by themselves on the lawn below. Head down to these gates, with the large Sally's Pond on your left (the USGS maps label this pond as Ringwood Mill

Pond). The pond is stocked with bass and pickerel, and fishing is permitted, but subject to state fishing regulations.

Proceed west (away from the Manor House) across the lawn. Initially, you'll notice yellow blazes that mark the route of the Hasenclever Iron Trail, but the yellow blazes soon turn right on a gravel road. Here, there is a blue blaze on a telephone pole to the left. Turn left onto the gravel road, the route of the blue-blazed Manor Trail. You will be following this trail for the remainder of the hike.

Continue along the gravel road, with the pond on your left. As you cross a bridge over a small stream, note the rust-colored rocks, indicative of the iron ore present throughout

Highlands

the area. Beyond the bridge, you'll notice a small cemetery on the left, with headstones bearing the Morris, Erskine, and Hewitt family names. Many of the graves are those of small children, who often died young in the 18th and 19th centuries. Cedar trees add to the tranquility of the area.

The large Victorian mansion visible across the pond was built in 1861 by Edmund Miller of New York, a prominent farmer and politician. In 1878, Abram Hewitt purchased the property and gave it to his daughter Amy as a wedding present when she married Dr. James O. Green. Their son Norvin Green donated the property to the Capuchin Sisters in 1930, and it served as the Mount St. Francis Retreat Center until its closing in 2011.

After passing the southern end of Sally's Pond, the trail goes around a gate. Just beyond, you'll come to a fork in the road. Bear right and follow the blue blazes uphill on a gravel road. In a short distance, you'll pass a house on the left (the residence of a park employee). Beyond the house, the road becomes rougher, and the sounds of traffic become louder. At the next fork, bear right again (the road to the left, partially blocked by boulders, leads out to Margaret King Avenue).

The trail continues uphill on a woods road, first rather steeply, then more gradually. Note the rusted cables embedded in the trailbed. Park historians surmise that they may have been used as part of a conveyor system to transport iron ore from nearby mines, but they don't know for sure. In spring, flowers abound: jack-in-the-pulpit, rue anemone, spring beauty, and trout lily, to name just a few.

At the top of the climb (about 45 minutes into the hike), you'll see a power line ahead. The marked trail turns right *before* reaching the power line, but you might want to take the short jog out to it for this hike's only view. The valley below was the site of several iron mines, including the Hope and Peters Mines.

Return to the trail, turn left at the fork, then immediately turn left again onto a narrower route. The trail now descends steadily to a lovely stream. It follows the stream for a short distance, then turns left and crosses it on rocks. The stream crossing can be a little tricky when the water is high.

In a few minutes, you'll come to a junction with the yellow-blazed Hasenclever Iron Trail. You've now hiked about 2 miles. A right turn onto this yellow-blazed trail will take you directly back to the manor house, shortening your hike. But if you want to continue, hike ahead on the blue-blazed Manor Trail, which follows a pleasant, relatively level footpath through the woods. There is little evidence of civilization in this isolated area.

The trail descends to skirt a wet area and continues along undulating terrain, with some minor ups and downs. In about 15 minutes from the junction with the Hasenclever Iron Trail, you'll pass a large water-filled depression—an old mine pit—on the left. Just beyond, the trail crosses a wide stream on rocks. Soon, you'll parallel another stream for a short distance and then cross it (and a tributary) on rocks. The trail now joins a wide woods road and passes through an area where the thick vegetation forms a canopy overhead. After a short climb, you'll reach a T-intersection with another woods road. The White Trail begins on the left and can be used as an alternative return route that adds about 0.7 mile to the hike (it ends at the Ramapo River, just upstream of the manor house). But to continue on the route of the hike, bear right at the junction and follow the blue blazes downhill.

At the next junction, the blue blazes head in both directions. Turn left, and you'll soon pass behind the manor house. Continue ahead to the parking lot where the hike began.

8

Skylands Manor

Total distance: 5.4 miles
Hiking time: 4 hours
Vertical rise: 1,000 feet
Rating: Moderate
Maps: USGS Ramsey; NYNJTC North Jersey Trails #115
Trailhead GPS Coordinates: N 41° 08' 10" W 74° 13' 56"

This hike combines portions of the Ringwood-Ramapo (red), Halifax (green), Crossover (white), Cooper Union (yellow), and Cupsaw Brook (blue) Trails. It affords an opportunity to linger in the New Jersey Botanical Garden and to walk past the Skylands Manor House. The peacefulness of the hike may be somewhat spoiled by the noise of the Thunder Mountain shooting range, but the sound is less intrusive along certain sections of the hike and at certain times of day. Many of the trails in the park are multi-use, and at most trailheads there are signs indicating the trail's designated use. For more information, contact Ringwood State Park, 1304 Sloatsburg Road, Ringwood, NJ 07456; 973-962-7031; www.njparksandforests.org.

HOW TO GET THERE

Take Skyline Drive to its northwestern terminus at Greenwood Lake Turnpike (County Route 511). Turn right, continue for 1.5 miles, and turn right onto Sloatsburg Road. Continue for 2.1 miles and turn right onto Morris Road. Alternatively, from NY 17, just south of the village of Sloatsburg, take the Sterling Forest exit. Follow Sterling Mine Road (County Route 72) west for 3.5 miles to the New Jersey state line. Continue ahead (the road becomes Sloatsburg Road) for another 1.5 miles and turn left onto Morris Road at the sign for Thunder Mountain.

Follow Morris Road for 1.3 miles. Just before the entrance to the Skylands section of Ringwood State Park (marked by two stone eagles), turn left onto Shepherd Lake Road and proceed for 0.8 mile to Shepherd Lake.

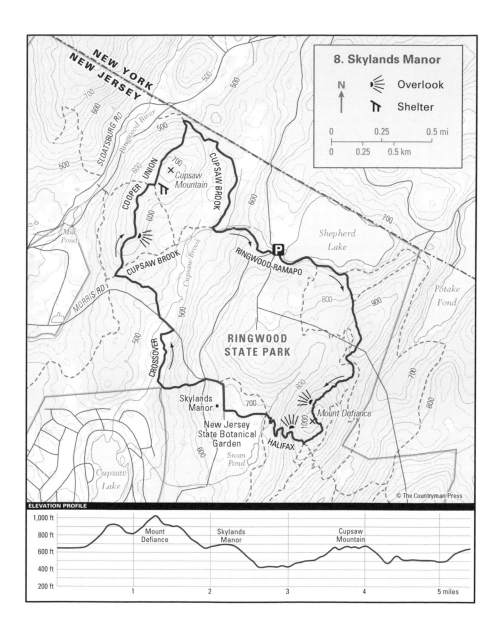

ELEVATION PROFILE

Mount Defiance — Skylands Manor — Cupsaw Mountain

Past the entrance booth, bear left and park in the designated parking area (a parking fee is charged from Memorial Day to Labor Day).

Note: Shepherd Lake is a popular destination on summer weekends, and the parking area can fill up early in the day.

THE TRAIL

From the parking area, follow the paved path down to the beach on Shepherd Lake. Continue through the boat launch parking area and past the boat house, with the lake to your left. You will notice the red-on-white blazes of the Ringwood-Ramapo Trail, which you will follow for the first part of the hike. After passing a kiosk, where the orange-blazed Shepherd Lake Loop Trail begins, continue on a gravel road along the lake, following both red-on-white and orange blazes and soon passing between two stone pillars.

In about a third of a mile, both trails turn right, leaving the road. Continue to follow the blazed trails, which head uphill on a footpath. At an intersection with a woods road, the orange-blazed trail turns left, but you should continue ahead, now following only the red-on-white blazes of the Ringwood-Ramapo Trail.

The trail climbs to the top of a rise (from where, in winter, you can see the long ridge of Mount Defiance on the right, through the trees), then descends to cross a mountain bike trail about a mile into the hike. A short distance beyond, the trail curves to the right, crosses a pipeline and, just beyond, climbs through boulders. Soon, the trail begins to climb again. Just before reaching the summit of Mount Defiance (1,040 feet), you'll pass a limited viewpoint to the north, with a view of Cupsaw Lake to the left. After a short but steep descent, the trail follows just below the crest of the ridge, paralleling impressive cliffs on the right and passing an interesting split boulder. At the end of the cliffs, you'll reach a junction with the green-on-white-blazed Halifax Trail. You're now about 2 miles into the hike.

Turn right onto the Halifax Trail, which climbs over a small rise and then levels off. Just before the trail begins a steady descent, follow an unmarked path to the right that leads up to a rock outcrop with a view over the gardens of Skylands Manor and Cupsaw Lake. Here, there is a beautiful cedar tree that may be visible when you walk past the manor house later on in the hike.

Return to the Halifax Trail, which now descends quite steeply in a series of switchbacks. This section of trail was constructed many years ago as a bridle path (note the impressive stonework supporting the downhill side of the path). At the base of the descent, a triple-green blaze marks the end of the Halifax Trail. Turn right onto a gravel road, the route of the white-blazed Crossover Trail, but almost immediately turn left onto a woods road between two large rocks. Walk past a large stand of evergreens, take the right fork, and proceed through the gate ahead into the New Jersey Botanical Garden.

The site of the New Jersey State Botanical Garden was originally a working farm assembled from pioneer farmsteads by Francis Lynde Stetson, a prominent New York lawyer. In addition to outbuildings and gardens, it included a vast lawn used as a nine-hole golf course. Many famous people—including President Grover Cleveland, actress Ethel Barrymore, industrialist Andrew Carnegie, and financier J. P. Morgan—were guests at Skylands Farms. The estate was sold in 1922 to Clarence McKenzie Lewis, an investment banker and a trustee of the New York Botanical Garden, who demolished the mansion built by Stetson and replaced it with the Tudor mansion now on the site.

Once through the gate and past the small stream, bear right on the grass toward two wooden benches. The second bench has a small plaque, dated 1991 and dedicated to Humbert "Al" Cincotti, a Skylands volunteer. Turn right; before you reach another gate, turn left and admire the stone birdbath, then continue toward another gate. Go through that gate into an open field, with the manor house visible to the right. Walk straight ahead toward Maple Avenue, the paved auto road, passing underneath an arbor on the way, and turn right when you reach the road. Look up to the right as you walk; if there are no leaves on the trees, you may be able to

Gatehouse at Skylands Manor

see the cedar tree and rocky outcrop at the viewpoint on Mount Defiance you visited earlier in the hike.

Maple Avenue takes you past Skylands Manor House, on the left. This house was designed by John Russell Pope and built from stone quarried from Pierson Ridge. The building's weathered facade and the sags and ripples in its slate were deliberately introduced to make it appear older. Clarence Lewis collected plants from all over the world—including New Jersey roadsides—resulting in the fine collection now in the botanical gardens. He also planted most of the trees framing the house. The state of New Jersey bought Skylands Gardens in 1966.

This property was the first purchased under the Green Acres program, and was later designated the state's official botanical garden.

Although the manor house is usually closed to the public, it is open (and often decorated) on certain days during the year, such as Mother's Day and during the Christmas season. Sixty gardeners worked here during Mr. Lewis's ownership, but volunteers now help out. The New Jersey Botanical Garden/Skylands Association is a non-profit organization founded in 1976 to assist with the preservation and restoration of the gardens and manor house. For information on volunteering and membership, call 973-962-9534, or go to www.njbg.org.

View from Mount Defiance

Continue down Maple Avenue, past the restrooms on the right, until you reach Parking Lot A. Stay on the paved road outside Parking Lot A and bear left at the fork in the paved road. The two stone eagles you passed in the car just before you arrived are on either side of this road. They adorned the since-demolished Pennsylvania Station in New York City and were moved here after the station was torn down in 1963. If you need to shorten the hike at this point, turn right and walk down the road to the Shepherd Lake parking lot and your car.

To continue, proceed downhill on the paved road, then almost immediately turn left onto the white-blazed Crossover Trail, which bears left, reenters the woods, and descends steadily. This trail section tends to be muddy, especially in spring. At the end of the descent, the trail turns right and heads out to Morris Road, crossing the route of a pipeline a short distance before reaching the road.

Turn left onto the road, cross a stone bridge over Cupsaw Brook, and in about 100 feet, turn right before a large evergreen tree and reenter the woods. The trail passes stone ruins on the right, begins a gradual climb, then continues over undulating terrain to reach a junction with the yellow-blazed Cooper Union Trail.

Turn right onto the Cooper Union Trail, which climbs steadily on a woods road. Soon, you'll come to a junction where the blue-blazed Cupsaw Brook Trail begins on the right. You may shorten the hike by taking the Cupsaw Brook Trail to the Ringwood-Ramapo Trail, and thence to your car. The route of this hike, however, continues uphill on the Cooper Union Trail, and in about 10 minutes reaches a high point (elevation 680 feet) with several cedars and a good view of Mount Defiance from a rock ledge to the right of the trail (when there are no leaves on the trees).

Beyond the viewpoint, the trail continues along the crest of the ridge. After a while, you'll be able to see the Cooper Union Shelter downhill to the right. Just beyond, the red-on-white-blazed Ringwood-Ramapo Trail comes in from the left. Turn right and follow the joint Ringwood-Ramapo/Cooper Union Trail for a short distance. When the Ringwood-Ramapo Trail leaves to the right, follow the red-on-white markers down to the shelter for a short break. This wooden shelter

was built by the "Hiking, Eating, Arguing and Puzzle-Solving Club of the Cooper Union." The land on which the shelter is located, purchased by the state of New Jersey in 1978, was formerly part of the Green Engineering Camp of the Cooper Union for the Advancement of Science and Art, of New York City. Although camping is no longer permitted at the shelter, and it is not well maintained, it is still the site of an annual gathering of the Cooper Union Alumni Association. After taking a break at the shelter, backtrack to the junction and continue ahead on the wide Cooper Union Trail, which climbs a little and then heads steadily downhill.

After a steeper downhill stretch, watch carefully for a triple-blue blaze indicating the start of the Cupsaw Brook Trail. Turn right and follow this blue-blazed trail, which climbs back up the ridge of Cupsaw Mountain, then descends rather steeply. At the base of the descent, the trail turns right onto a woods road, which levels off.

The trail briefly approaches Cupsaw Brook, then moves away from it. If the leaves are off the trees, Cupsaw Mountain can be seen to the right. After some more level walking, you'll reach the junction where the Cupsaw Brook Trail intersects the red-on-white-blazed Ringwood-Ramapo Trail. Turn left onto the Ringwood-Ramapo Trail and cross a wooden footbridge over Cupsaw Brook. You'll continue to parallel the brook, with attractive cascades in the brook if the water is high. Soon, the trail begins to ascend, and after a short climb, you'll emerge onto a woods road. Turn left and follow the red-on-white blazes back to the parking area where the hike began.

9

Lake Sonoma and Overlook Rock

Total distance: 4 miles

Hiking time: 3 hours

Vertical rise: 700 feet

Rating: Moderate

Maps: USGS Wanaque, Greenwood Lake (NJ/NY), Sloatsburg (NJ/NY); NYNJTC North Jersey Trails #115

Trailhead GPS Coordinates: N 41° 05' 28" W 74° 19' 16"

This hike traverses the northwestern area of Norvin Green State Forest. It goes along Lake Sonoma and climbs to two panoramic viewpoints: Overlook Rock and Manaticut Point.

The area surrounding Lake Sonoma was once owned by Maitland B. Bleecker, an American inventor and author who was instrumental in modern helicopter design. In the late 1920s, he developed and constructed a prototype helicopter known as the Curtiss-Bleecker SX, which flew successfully. When he retired in 1945, he purchased 1,500 acres in West Milford, where he dammed a tributary of Burnt Meadow Brook to create Lake Sonoma, started a trout hatchery, and operated the Tapawingo Fishing Preserve.

Prior to his death in 2002 at the age of 99, Bleecker sold the property to the State of New Jersey, and it became a part of Norvin Green State Forest. Beginning in 2007, several trails were constructed in the area by the North Jersey Trails Committee of the New York–New Jersey Trail Conference, under the leadership of John Moran. Volunteers scouting out the trails discovered the spectacular Overlook Rock and routed the trails to pass this vista.

HOW TO GET THERE

Take Skyline Drive to its northwestern terminus at Greenwood Lake Turnpike (County Route 511). Turn left and proceed south for 1.6 miles to West Brook Road. Turn right onto West Brook Road and cross the Wanaque Reservoir on a causeway. At the next

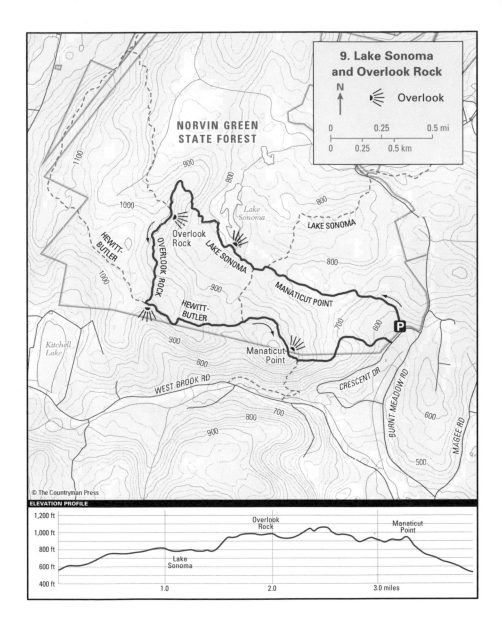

9. Lake Sonoma and Overlook Rock

N

Overlook

0   0.25   0.5 mi

0   0.25   0.5 km

NORVIN GREEN
STATE FOREST

Lake
Sonoma

LAKE SONOMA

Overlook
Rock

HEWITT-
BUTLER

LAKE SONOMA

MANATICUT POINT

HEWITT-
BUTLER

Kitchell
Lake

Manaticut
Point

WEST BROOK RD

CRESCENT DR

BURNT MEADOW RD

MAGEE RD

© The Countryman Press

ELEVATION PROFILE

1,200 ft
1,000 ft
800 ft
600 ft
400 ft

Overlook
Rock

Manaticut
Point

Lake
Sonoma

1.0   2.0   3.0 miles

T-junction, turn left and proceed for 0.8 mile to Magee Road. Turn right onto Magee Road and take the first left onto Burnt Meadow Road. Continue for 0.9 mile and turn left at the second intersection with Crescent Drive. Continue for 0.2 mile until you reach a huge boulder on the right side of the road, just beyond a curve. Park along the side of the road.

THE TRAIL

To the left of the boulder, a triple yellow blaze marks the start of the Manaticut Point Trail. Head into the woods on this trail, which

Cascade along the Lake Sonoma Trail

Highlands

View from Overlook Rock

follows an attractive route through a valley. Soon, you'll cross two branches of a stream on rocks and pass a cliff. A short distance beyond, you'll cross another stream below an interesting V-shaped rock formation and continue uphill, parallel to the stream.

About a mile from the start, the orange-blazed Lake Sonoma Trail joins from the right. The two trails run jointly for a short distance, but when they diverge, continue ahead on the orange-blazed Lake Sonoma Trail. The trail crosses the inlet stream of Lake Sonoma, turns right, and soon reaches a viewpoint over the lake. The trail parallels the lake for a quarter mile.

After re-crossing the woods road, the trail briefly parallels a stream, then crosses it below an attractive cascade. It immediately turns left and begins a steady climb.

At the top, it bears left, briefly descends, then turns sharply left at a switchback and climbs gently to reach a junction with the white-blazed Overlook Rock Trail, which joins from the right. When the trails diverge in 150 feet, follow the Lake Sonoma Trail as it makes a short, steep climb to its terminus at Overlook Rock—a massive exposed rock face with a panoramic east-facing view. Lake Sonoma is directly below, Windbeam, Bear, and Board Mountains are beyond, and the Ramapo Mountains may be seen in the distance. You've now gone about 2 miles from the start, and you'll want to take a break and enjoy the spectacular view.

When you're ready to continue, backtrack a short distance on the Lake Sonoma Trail and turn left onto the white-blazed Overlook Rock Trail. In a half mile, after crossing an intermittent stream and climbing gradually, the Overlook Rock Trail ends at a junction with the blue-blazed Hewitt-Butler Trail. This spot, marked by a single cedar tree, offers views to the southwest.

Turn left onto the Hewitt-Butler Trail, which descends briefly, then climbs steeply to the crest of the ridge. The trail heads southeast along the ridge, passing a viewpoint to the right over the privately owned Saddle Mountain, and descends gradually. At the base of the descent, you'll see a small pond on private property to the right.

The Hewitt-Butler Trail now climbs through a cleft in the rock and reaches a junction with the yellow-blazed Manaticut Point Trail, which joins from the left. Continue ahead, following both blue and yellow blazes. After descending slightly, the trail climbs steadily to an open rock ledge known as Manaticut Point, which offers a panoramic view. Windbeam Mountain is directly ahead (east), with Bear and Board Mountains to its left. To the south, you can see a quarry on Saddle Mountain, and on a clear day, the New York City skyline on the horizon. This is another good spot to take a break.

After taking in the view, follow the blue and yellow blazes, which head very steeply downhill. Watch carefully for a double yellow blaze, and follow the yellow-blazed Manaticut Point Trail as it turns left and continues to descend more gradually. It soon joins a grassy woods road, which it follows downhill, bearing left at a fork along the way. When you reach the trailhead at Crescent Drive, turn left and follow the road a short distance back to your car.

10

Wyanokie Circular

Total distance: 7.2 miles
Hiking time: 6.5 hours
Vertical rise: 1,500 feet
Rating: Moderately strenuous
Maps: USGS Wanaque; NYNJTC North Jersey Trails #115
Trailhead GPS Coordinates: N 41° 04' 12" W 74° 19' 20"

The Wyanokie Ridge, which forms part of the New Jersey Highlands, dates back to the Precambrian Period, and many of the rocks in the area are more than 600 million years old. These hills were here long before there was a Wanaque Reservoir or a New York skyline to be seen from the viewpoints on this hike. Blue iron ore was abundant, and villages grew up around the iron mining operations and charcoal furnaces scattered throughout the area. Construction of the Wanaque Reservoir, which is visible from several high points in the area, was started in 1920, and the reservoir was filled by 1930. Wanaque and Wyanokie are both variants of the Native American word meaning "sassafras."

This hike offers spectacular views, pleasant walking in the woods, some rock scrambling, waterfalls on Blue Mine Brook, and two mines in rugged territory. Located in Norvin Green State Forest (c/o Ringwood State Park, P.O. Box 1304, Ringwood, NJ 07456; 973-962-7031), the hike traverses an area with one of the largest concentrations of trails in New Jersey.

In season, one attractive possibility is to swim after your hike in the freshwater Highlands Natural Pool, adjacent to the Weis Ecology Center. A provisional membership is available. For more information, go to www.highlandspool.com.

HOW TO GET THERE
Norvin Green State Forest is accessible from County Route 511, reached from the east by way of Skyline Drive or from the south by NJ 23.

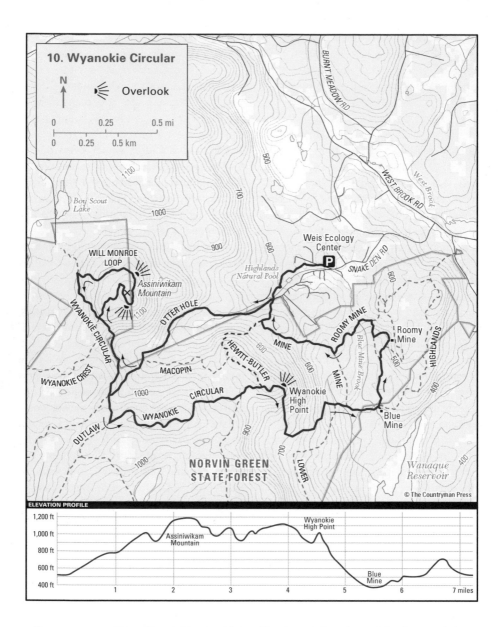

10. Wyanokie Circular

N

Overlook

| 0 | 0.25 | 0.5 mi |
| 0 | 0.25 | 0.5 km |

ELEVATION PROFILE

Turn west onto West Brook Road, which is 1.6 miles south of the western end of Skyline Drive. The road soon crosses the reservoir on a causeway, then parallels the reservoir on the left. At the end of the reservoir, you reach a junction with Stonetown Road. Bear left to continue on West Brook Road, and after about 0.5 mile, turn left onto Snake Den Road. In 0.3 mile, bear left at a fork, and continue for another 0.3 mile to a large dirt parking area on the right side of the road, just before the entrance to the Weis Ecology Center.

The Weis Ecology Center, which contains

a number of buildings, was formerly operated by the New Jersey Audubon Society. As of this writing, the buildings are closed, but the parking area and the trails remain open.

THE TRAIL

The hike begins at the western end of the parking area, where a gatepost with a triple light-green blaze marks the start of the Otter Hole Trail, which you will follow for the first part of this hike. Several short trails, such as the "L" Trail and the "W" Trail, are co-aligned for part of the way. The Otter Hole Trail turns left, just before the ball field, and then, almost immediately, turns right. This pleasant entryway parallels Blue Mine Brook on the left, with a row of large Norway spruce trees on the right. Just ahead, the lower end of the Highlands Natural Pool can be seen on the left, and a bulletin board is on the right. Soon, the trail bears right to skirt the pool. The trail briefly joins a dirt road, then bears left and ascends on a footpath, passing the weir that regulates the supply of water to the pool.

After crossing a footbridge over the brook, the Otter Hole Trail proceeds through a rocky area and reaches a wide woods road—the continuation of Snake Den Road. Turn right and follow this road, which soon dips down to cross Blue Mine Brook at an old bridge abutment. The next 2 miles are mostly a steady climb until you reach the summit of Assiniwikam Mountain.

In about a quarter of a mile, as the woods road bends to the left, watch carefully for a right turn, where the Otter Hole Trail leaves the road, passing through a gap in a rock wall, and continues on a footpath parallel to the road. It soon descends to rejoin the woods road. A short distance beyond, the white-blazed Macopin Trail begins on the left, but you should continue ahead on the Otter Hole Trail.

After about 1.3 miles on the Otter Hole Trail, you'll reach an intersection with the red-dot-on-white-blazed Wyanokie Circular Trail. Turn right onto the Wyanokie Circular Trail, which soon begins to descend, winding past some interesting boulders. After crossing a woods road, the trail climbs to reach a junction where the yellow-blazed Wyanokie Crest Trail begins on the left and the pink-blazed Will Monroe Loop begins on the right. Turn right onto the Will Monroe Loop, which leads to the summit of Assiniwikam Mountain.

Professor Will S. Monroe was the original Wyanokie trailblazer during the 1920s. Among the trails he blazed was a route over Assiniwikam Mountain, which traversed private property. In the late 1990s, the landowner closed the trail to hikers. But several years later, the one-mile Will Monroe Loop, entirely on state land, was blazed to enable hikers to enjoy the great views from this peak. The trail includes some interesting ups and downs on rock slabs and passes some outstanding rock formations. Unfortunately, some stands of trees have been killed by recent droughts and by gypsy moth caterpillar infestations, but in spring, the blooming shadbush—also called downy serviceberry—makes a wondrous sight. Tradition claims that these trees bloom at the same time that shad ascend the rivers to spawn.

A great spot to take a break and enjoy one of the many views is at a large boulder perched on smaller rocks at an open rock outcrop. Over to the right is the Wanaque Reservoir, and straight ahead are the Pine Paddies, which are now unfortunately closed to hikers. On the way down, you'll pass an interesting split boulder with a tree growing out of a crack in the rock.

After completing the Will Monroe Loop, turn left onto the red-dot-on-white-blazed Wyanokie Circular Trail. When you reach the

View from Wyanokie High Point

junction where you began the loop, continue ahead on the Wyanokie Circular Trail, now briefly retracing your steps. You'll cross both a woods road and the Otter Hole Trail. The Wyanokie Circular Trail then climbs to reach a large boulder, where the orange-blazed Outlaw Trail begins on the right. Turn left here to continue on the Wyanokie Circular Trail, which climbs to a peak with limited views and then descends to a junction with the blue-blazed Hewitt-Butler Trail (also the route of the teal diamond–blazed Highlands Trail).

After crossing a seasonal stream, the trails begin a short, sharp climb to another junction. If you've had enough hiking for the day, you can bear left to continue on the Hewitt-Butler Trail, which heads down to the Otter Hole Trail (to return to your car, cross the dirt road and proceed ahead on the green-blazed Otter Hole Trail). But to continue on the hike, turn right (following the sign to Hi-Point) and proceed steeply uphill, following both red-dot-on-white and teal-diamond blazes. The last part of the short climb is over bare rock, with the trail marked by blazes painted on the rock.

The summit of Wyanokie High Point offers a magnificent 360-degree view. The Wanaque Reservoir is to the southeast. Beyond the reservoir, you can see a long bridge carrying I-287 over a low area and, on a clear day, the New York City skyline may be seen on the horizon. To the north and west are Saddle, Assiniwikam and Buck Mountains.

When the time comes to leave this superb viewpoint, find the trail that leads toward the reservoir, and follow the red-dot-on-white and teal-diamond blazes as they descend steeply from the summit, passing more views of the reservoir along the way. Many trees in this area have died as a result of droughts and gypsy moth infestations, so the blazes are painted on rocks and occasional tree stumps.

The trail eventually goes back into the woods and bears left, with the descent becoming less steep. At the base of the descent, the white-blazed Lower Trail begins on the right and, soon afterwards, the yellow-on-white Mine Trail joins from the left. Proceed ahead, now following three different trail blazes: red dot on white, teal diamond, and yellow on white.

A short distance ahead, on the left, you'll notice the ruins of a stone shelter, constructed by members of the Green Mountain Club in the 1930s. The trail now approaches Blue Mine Brook. Just before reaching the brook, there is a circular mine pit to the right of the trail, with a small pile of tailings (discarded waste rock) to its left. The trail crosses the brook on a wooden footbridge, built as an Eagle Scout project in 2002, with the assistance of volunteers from the New York–New Jersey Trail Conference.

On the other side of the bridge, turn right to see the entrance to the Blue Mine, so called because of the dark blue color of the local ore. Now filled with water, it was once known as the Iron Hill, London, or Whynockie Mine. Until 1855, most of the ore was processed at a hot-blast charcoal furnace called the Freedom Furnace. For a short period after the Blue Mine's reopening in 1886, the mine produced about 300 tons of ore per month.

Water in the mine was obviously a problem, and the mine was "de-watered" several times. This operation was quite difficult. Mine workers stood on a raft that sank lower as the water was pumped out. Their job was to remove the debris left clinging to the walls of the mine and to shore up the timbers in the sides of the shaft, while keeping their balance on the raft. After another de-watering operation in 1905, the mine was not worked again. The concrete pad in front of the mine was once used as a base for steam-operated equipment, and by exploring the surroundings you can detect other evidence of mining operations.

Return to the bridge, but do not cross it. Just beyond, the teal diamond–blazed Highlands Trail diverges to the right, but you should continue ahead on the joint Mine (yellow on white) and Wyanokie Circular (red dot on white) Trails, which follow a rocky woods road. Bear left at a fork and continue ahead for about a quarter of a mile until the two trails separate. Here, you should turn right and follow the yellow-on-white blazes of the Mine Trail, which climbs on a narrow woods road, once used to access the Roomy Mine. At the top of a rather steep pitch, the Mine Trail turns sharply right, but you should continue ahead on the old road, now following the orange blazes of the Roomy Mine Trail.

At the top of the rise, the entrance of Roomy Mine (formerly known as the Laurel or Red Mine) is on the right. Named for Benjamin Roome, a local land surveyor, the mine opened shortly after 1840 and worked until 1857. The ore was compact and mostly free of rock. The vein was about 4 feet thick, with a pitch of 58 degrees, dipping sharply to the southeast. The mine shaft extends about 60 feet into the hillside, but it is presently closed to the public to prevent the spread of white nose syndrome, a fungal infection which attacks the bats hibernating in the cave.

Blue Mine

Continue to follow the orange blazes of the Roomy Mine Trail along the mine road. Soon, the trail bears right onto another road (the red-on-white-blazed Wyanokie Circular Trail ends here). A short distance ahead, at a huge boulder marked with orange blazes, turn left and continue to follow the Roomy Mine Trail, which climbs over a rise and passes interesting rock outcrops.

After a jog to the right, the trail crosses Blue Mine Brook above a waterfall, briefly follows the brook, then turns left and continues to a junction with the yellow-on-white-blazed Mine Trail. Here, the Roomy Mine Trail ends, and you should turn right onto the Mine Trail.

The trail is level at first, then climbs steadily. Near the top, you'll pass some interesting jumbled boulders and rock outcrops on the right.

At the top of the climb, turn right, joining the blue-blazed Hewitt-Butler Trail. Now following both blue and yellow-on-white blazes, descend steeply to a kiosk at Snake Den Road, here a dirt road. The Hewitt-Butler and Mine Trails end here, but you should cross the road and continue ahead on the green-blazed Otter Hole Trail, retracing your steps past the Highlands Natural Pool and along Blue Mine Brook and ending at the parking area where the hike began.

11

Carris Hill

Total distance: 4 miles	
Hiking time: 4 hours	
Vertical rise: 800 feet	
Rating: Moderately strenuous	
Maps: USGS Wanaque; NYNJTC North Jersey Trails #115	
Trailhead GPS Coordinates: N 41° 02' 45" W 74° 21' 02"	

Although this hike is only 5 miles long, the rugged terrain and possibly difficult water crossings make for an exciting and challenging day hike. Carris Hill is not the highest point in Norvin Green State Forest (c/o Ringwood State Park, 1304 Sloatsburg Road, Ringwood, NJ 07456-1799; 973-962-7031; www.njparksandforests.org), but it includes a strenuous climb and an arduous descent. Good footwear is necessary, and take special care if you attempt this hike in winter—certain sections are on steep slopes of bare rock that could be difficult to navigate when covered with snow and ice. Posts Brook, which you will cross at the start of the hike, is usually easily crossed on rocks. After a snowmelt or heavy rain, however, it becomes a raging torrent and can present serious problems.

HOW TO GET THERE
From I-287, take Exit 53 (Bloomingdale) and turn left onto Hamburg Turnpike. Upon entering Bloomingdale, the name of the road changes to Main Street. In 1.3 miles (from I-287) you will reach a fork in the road. Bear right, and in another 0.1 mile turn right (uphill) onto Glenwild Avenue, following the sign to West Milford. Continue ahead for 3.2 miles to a parking area on the right side of the road.

THE TRAIL
For the first part of this hike, you will be following the blue-blazed Hewitt-Butler Trail, which heads north into the woods from the eastern end of the parking area. Soon you

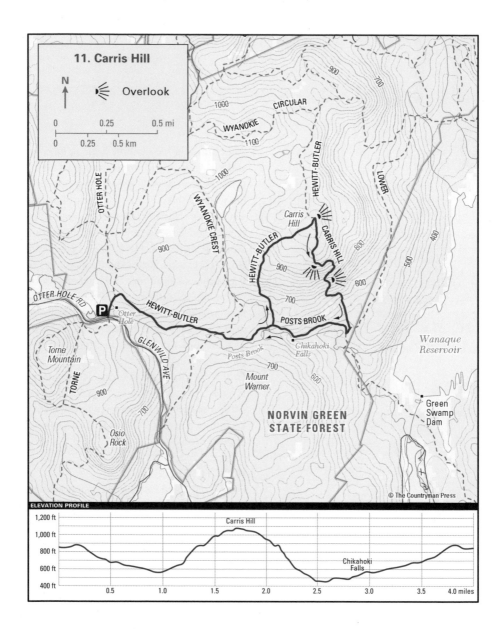

11. Carris Hill

N

Overlook

| 0 | 0.25 | | 0.5 mi |
| 0 | 0.25 | 0.5 km | |

OTTER HOLE

WYANOKIE

CIRCULAR

WYANOKIE CREST

HEWITT-BUTLER

Carris
Hill

HEWITT-BUTLER

CARRIS HILL

LOWER

OTTER HOLE RD

HEWITT-BUTLER

P

Otter
Hole

GLENWILD AVE

POSTS BROOK

Chikahoki
Falls

Posts Brook

Wanaque
Reservoir

Torne
Mountain

TORNE

Mount
Warner

Osio
Rock

**NORVIN GREEN
STATE FOREST**

Green
Swamp
Dam

© The Countryman Press

ELEVATION PROFILE

Carris Hill

Chikahoki
Falls

1,200 ft
1,000 ft
800 ft
600 ft
400 ft

0.5   1.0   1.5   2.0   2.5   3.0   3.5   4.0 miles

will arrive at Otter Hole, a small cascade and falls on Posts Brook. It is normally possible to cross the brook on large boulders, but if this is impractical or dangerous, you should abort this hike and try another one. (Just across the road the Hewitt-Butler Trail

ascends Torne Mountain, a summit with several fine views; see Hike 12.)

After crossing the brook, continue ahead to an intersection with the green-blazed Otter Hole Trail. Bear right to continue on the blue-blazed Hewitt-Butler Trail, which is joined by the teal diamond–blazed Highlands Trail. You'll now head uphill and roughly parallel to Posts Brook, following a rocky woods road. When you reach the next Y-intersection, take the right fork, following the sign for Chik Falls. The trail continues to ascend for a short distance and then begins a steady descent.

In about half a mile, the trail turns left, leaving the woods road, and continues to descend. About 15 to 20 minutes from the start of the hike, the yellow-blazed Wyanokie Crest Trail joins from the right. The two trails run jointly for only 75 feet, and when the Wyanokie Crest Trail leaves to the left, continue ahead, following the blue blazes. Just ahead, the trail approaches Posts Brook and then crosses a tributary stream on a log bridge. A short distance beyond this stream crossing,

the Hewitt-Butler Trail turns left. (The white-blazed Posts Brook Trail, which proceeds straight ahead, will be your return route.) The steady uphill climb to the summit of Carris Hill begins here.

At first, the trail gains elevation very slowly as it winds through the woods. Soon the footing gets rockier, although there is a temporary reprieve along the bed of an abandoned gas pipeline. The trail then bears right, and the climb begins in earnest. Eventually, the ascent becomes less steep, and the footpath meanders through an area characterized by blueberry bushes, moss, occasional glacial erratics, and numerous exposures of bedrock. This terrain is typical of the Precambrian gneiss and granite of the New Jersey Highlands. A slight descent into an area that is sometimes wet brings

Chikahoki Falls

Carris Hill

Wanaque Reservoir from Carris Hill　　　　　　　　DANIEL CHAZIN

needed relief, but almost immediately the climb resumes.

The trail now passes through mountain laurel and traverses the first of a series of bare rock outcrops contoured with green moss and tall grasses. The first evergreens (hemlocks) are encountered here, and pitch pines appear, often heavily laden with clumps of pine cones. The trail descends slightly into a dense heath forest before it continues, now fairly gradually, up to bare rock and the first of a few small false summits. Look behind you. The views of Torne Mountain, Osio Rock, and beyond are steadily improving. After another slight descent into a laurel depression, the trail winds through scrub pine

to the true summit with views to the south, west, and north. There is a real feeling of accomplishment from reaching this heavily glaciated summit. Wyanokie High Point is to the north, and from this vantage point it looks like a small cluster of bare rocks. Beyond it and to the right is Windbeam Mountain. To the immediate west are Assiniwikam Mountain, Buck Mountain, and Torne Mountain.

At the summit, look on the rocks for the yellow blazes of the Carris Hill Trail. Follow this trail, which begins here, along the broad, flat summit of Carris Hill through mountain laurel thickets to another viewpoint, where you'll find pitch pines on bare rock outcrops and a large glacial erratic. The expansive views are to the south and southeast. To the left of the large boulder, follow the yellow blazes downhill. Soon, you will reach yet another viewpoint, this one overlooking the Wanaque Reservoir, nearby Green Swamp Dam, and the more distant Raymond Dam.

From here, the trail begins a steeper descent. The footing can be difficult until you reach a rock formation not unlike a wall. The trail turns right, following to the right of the wall. If you scramble up the ledge on your left you'll find an even broader view of the reservoir and beyond. Then head south and down, descending rather steeply in places. A few cedars line the trail, which winds around a deep and jagged cliff. In some sections you have to be very careful, and you'll need careful planning and proper equipment (crampons) in icy or slippery conditions.

Once off the main part of the hill, the going is much more manageable, though still quite steep. Continue following yellow blazes steadily downhill over rocky ground. Eventually you will reach a small brook; crossing might be difficult in times of high water. (If this is a problem, keep to the west of the brook, bushwhack downstream to Posts Brook, and turn right onto the white-blazed Posts Brook Trail.) Soon the yellow-blazed Carris Hill Trail ends at a junction with the white-blazed Lower Trail. Turn right here, following white blazes, with a low rock outcrop on your left.

In a short distance, you'll reach a junction with the white-blazed Posts Brook Trail. Turn right onto the Posts Brook Trail, which crosses a wet area, then climbs and heads away from the brook. Soon, you'll again descend to the level of the brook and reach Chikahoki Falls—a 25-foot sluiceway of water, split in two as the water tumbles into a huge plunge pool. The falls are most impressive in spring or after a rain. Beyond the falls, the trail climbs steeply and continues to parallel the brook, passing attractive cascades. In just a few minutes you will reach the junction with the blue-blazed Hewitt-Butler Trail and the teal diamond–blazed Highlands Trail that you encountered earlier in the hike, where the climb to Carris Hill began. Follow the blue and teal diamond blazes straight ahead—the way you came. Most of the way back is a gradual uphill climb. After about a half hour, turn left, cross over Posts Brook at Otter Hole, and return to your car.

12

Torne Mountain–Osio Rock

Total distance: 2.3 or 3.7 miles

Hiking time: 2.5 or 3.5 hours

Vertical rise: 425 to 650 feet

Rating: Moderate

Maps: USGS Wanaque; NYNJTC North Jersey Trails #115

Trailhead GPS Coordinates:
N 41° 02' 45" W 74° 21' 02"

Although this hike starts at a popular trailhead, most hikers head north into the main section of Norvin Green State Forest. This hike heads south into a less-used section of the forest where you are likely to find greater solitude. The main section of this hike (2.3 miles) is a "lollipop"-loop, while the optional extension is an out-and-back climb to a yet another fine viewpoint.

Members of the local chapter of the Green Mountain Club planned and constructed many of the trails in Norvin Green in the 1920s, and the trails were subsequently maintained by the Nature Friends. Their former camp is now the Weis Ecology Center, a few miles to the north (see Hike 10, Wyanokie Circular, and Hike 11, Carris Hill). This area must have seemed pretty remote 90 years ago.

HOW TO GET THERE

To get to the trailhead, take I-287 to Exit 53 (Bloomingdale) and turn left onto Hamburg Turnpike. Upon entering Bloomingdale, the name of the road changes to Main Street. In 1.3 miles (from I-287), you will reach a fork in the road. Bear right, and in another 0.1 mile, turn right (uphill) onto Glenwild Avenue (following the sign to West Milford). Continue ahead for 3.2 miles to a parking area on the right side of the road. If this lot is full, there is space for more cars a little farther down the road.

THE TRAIL

Cross the road at the eastern end of the parking area (at the sign that reads WELCOME

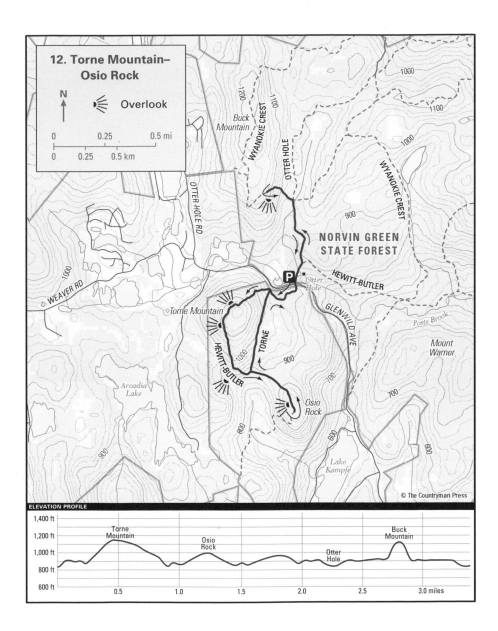

12. Torne Mountain–Osio Rock

N

≥ Overlook

| 0 | 0.25 | 0.5 mi |
| 0 | 0.25 | 0.5 km |

Buck
Mountain

WYANOKIE CREST

OTTER HOLE

1200

1100

1000

1100

1000

OTTER HOLE RD

WYANOKIE CREST

900

NORVIN GREEN
STATE FOREST

WEAVER RD

1000

P

Otter
Hole

HEWITT-BUTLER

Torne Mountain

GLENWILD AVE

Posts Brook

TORNE

HEWITT-BUTLER

1000

900

700

Mount
Warner

Arcadia
Lake

800

Osio
Rock

700

700

600

Lake
Kampfe

600

© The Countryman Press

ELEVATION PROFILE

1,400 ft						
1,200 ft	Torne Mountain		Osio Rock			Buck Mountain
1,000 ft				Otter Hole		
800 ft						
600 ft	0.5	1.0	1.5	2.0	2.5	3.0 miles

TO BLOOMINGDALE) and enter the woods at a blue-blazed post marked "HB." Follow the blue-blazed Hewitt-Butler Trail, which climbs on a rocky footpath. Soon, it will seem that you have left civilization behind—well, except for some road noise! After a short dip, the climb resumes, and then you descend a little into a ravine, where you cross the red-blazed Torne Trail, with Glenwild Avenue just to the right. Make a mental note of this spot, because you'll return to it after completing the loop.

Glacial erratics at viewpoint on Torne Mountain DANIEL CHAZIN

Proceed straight ahead on the blue-blazed Hewitt-Butler Trail and begin a steady ascent of Torne Mountain, climbing steeply at times. After 15 minutes or so, you'll reach a large rock ledge with a panoramic vista to the west and north. If there are no leaves on the trees, you'll get a good view of Buck Mountain, just to the north. Buck Mountain is the destination of the optional extension of the hike. Continue ahead, taking care to follow the blue blazes (there are a number of unmarked paths in this area) as the trail contours around the edge of Torne Mountain (1,120 feet). A short hike through the woods brings you to a second open area, marked by a cairn, which features a view to the west through the trees. Soon, you'll reach yet a third open area—this one marked by a larger cairn.

Continue to follow the blue-blazed trail along the crest of the mountain. Soon, you'll reach another open area, where you'll find a single cedar tree and two balanced glacial erratics. There are views both to the west and to the south from here. You can see both Osio Rock and a peak covered with pine trees (known as the West Torne) to its right.

Proceed ahead on the blue-blazed trail, which soon reaches a junction. A black-dot-on-blue-blazed side trail begins here, but you should bear left and continue to follow the blue-blazed Hewitt-Butler Trail, which begins to descend. In a short distance, you'll emerge onto a panoramic viewpoint, from which the New York City skyline may be seen in the distance on a clear day. After passing another viewpoint, the trail descends on a

View from Torne Mountain

switchback and comes out on open rocks, with a view of Osio Rock to the southeast.

Continue to descend on the blue-blazed Hewitt-Butler Trail, passing the other end of the black-dot-on-blue-blazed side trail on the right. When you reach the low point between Torne Mountain and Osio Rock, you'll notice a triple-red blaze on the left that marks the start of the Torne Trail, your route back to your car. You'll be returning along this trail, but for now, turn right and continue to follow the blue blazes. After a relatively steep climb, the trail levels off, then resumes a more gradual climb. On the way, you'll pass a group of large glacial erratics on the right.

The summit of Osio Rock, some 15 or 20 minutes from the low point, offers a fabulous 360-degree vista. This is a great place for lunch. The large body of water visible in the distance to your left is the Wanaque Reservoir, and the curved elevated roadway in the distance is I-287. The little lake below is Lake Kampfe, which is privately owned. Some pathetic graffiti mars the summit itself.

Retrace your steps to the low point and continue ahead on the red-blazed Torne Trail, which climbs steeply up a boulder-filled ravine, paralleling a stream. You'll have to squeeze your way between some huge boulders to negotiate this stretch of the trail. Soon, the trail levels off and continues through a beautiful valley, then gently descends back to the blue/red trail junction near Glenwild Avenue. You were here earlier in the hike. Continue ahead to the road, turn right, and walk back to your car along the shoulder of the road. You should reach your car in about two minutes.

You've hiked 2.3 miles and climbed (and descended) 425 feet. Ready for more?

From the eastern end of the parking area, head north on the blue-blazed Hewitt-Butler Trail (do not cross the road). Soon you'll be rock-hopping across a wide part of Posts Brook. If the water is high or the rocks icy, leave this part of the hike for another day. This section is known as Otter Hole. Sorry, there are no otters, but there is a lovely series of pools and cascades.

Just beyond the crossing, you'll reach a trail junction. Note the three green blazes that mark the start of the Otter Hole Trail, occasionally marked as well with the teal diamonds of the Highlands Trail. Follow the green blazes to the left on a rocky woods roads for 10 or 15 minutes. Watch for a yellow blaze that will alert you to an upcoming junction where the Wyanokie Crest Trail crosses. Here, you turn left onto the yellow trail, now and then also marked with teal diamond blazes.

After a short descent to cross a stream on rocks, the steady 200-foot climb up Buck Mountain begins. Follow the blazes carefully because the route can be unclear in the brushy areas of the slope. As you climb, the pitch gets steeper, and you'll have to scramble up a steep rock face (with some nice views behind you).

At last the slope gets gentler and you'll emerge at a viewpoint rock guarded by a wonderfully sculptured pine tree. The view across the valley is of Torne Mountain and Osio Rock.

Retrace your steps to the parking area. It should take about half an hour.

13

Terrace Pond

Total distance: 4.5 miles
Hiking time: 3.5 hours
Vertical rise: 350 feet
Rating: Moderate
Maps: USGS Wawayanda, Newfoundland; NYNJTC North Jersey Trails #116
Trailhead GPS Coordinates: N 41° 08' 34.5" W 74° 24' 27"

This hike in Wawayanda State Park (885 Warwick Turnpike, Hewitt, NJ 07421; 973-853-4462; www.njparksandforests.org) is on land called the Sussex Woodlands when it was owned by Fred Ferber, a Depression-era immigrant from Austria. Ferber was not a lover of state parks; he objected to hunting and to restaurants, toilets, and campsites—facilities normally found in state parks. His ambition was to keep his property as wilderness, untouched by such facilities. But gradually, as he ran into debt over the years, he sold portions of his land to the state. Bearfort Ridge, which contains Terrace Pond, was one of the last tracts sold, in 1973.

This hike uses portions of the yellow-blazed Terrace Pond South Trail, the Yellow Dot Trail, the Terrace Pond Red Trail, the white-blazed Terrace Pond Circular Trail, and the blue-blazed Terrace Pond North Trail. The terrain is varied, and all sections are superb. At first the hike is gentle, but the approach to Terrace Pond—the climax of the hike—is reminiscent of a roller coaster.

HOW TO GET THERE

The trailhead is on the east side of Clinton Road, which runs north from NJ 23 to Warwick Turnpike. Look for it 1.7 miles south of the junction with Warwick Turnpike, or 7.3 miles north of NJ 23. There is a parking area on the west side of the road, just north of the entrance to the Wildcat Environmental Center (Project U.S.E.). This parking area is designated as P7 on the New York–New Jersey Trail Conference maps.

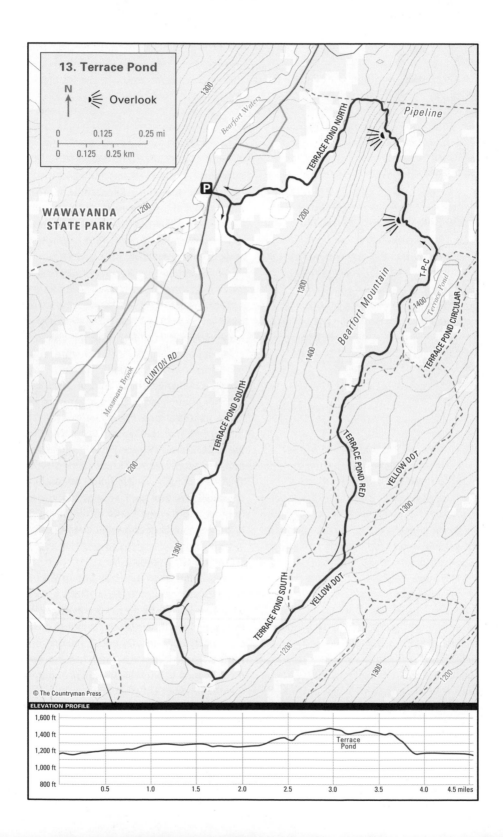

13. Terrace Pond

N

◀ Overlook

| 0 | 0.125 | 0.25 mi |
| 0 | 0.125 0.25 km | |

WAWAYANDA
STATE PARK

Bearfort Waters

Pipeline

TERRACE POND NORTH

1300

1200

1200

P

1300

Mossmans Brook

CLINTON RD

TERRACE POND SOUTH

1400

Bearfort Mountain

T-P-C

1400

Terrace Pond

TERRACE POND CIRCULAR

TERRACE POND RED

YELLOW DOT

1300

1200

TERRACE POND SOUTH

YELLOW DOT

1200

1300

1200

© The Countryman Press

ELEVATION PROFILE

1,600 ft									
1,400 ft									
1,200 ft						Terrace Pond			
1,000 ft									
800 ft	0.5	1.0	1.5	2.0	2.5	3.0	3.5	4.0	4.5 miles

THE TRAIL

Cross the road and enter the woods at a trailhead with a triple-blue blaze and a triple-yellow blaze. These mark the start, respectively, of the Terrace Pond North Trail and the Terrace Pond South Trail. Follow the yellow blazes, which almost immediately bear right (the blue trail, which goes off to the left, will be your return route) and proceed over a small hill through mountain laurel and white pine. Volunteers from the New York–New Jersey Trail Conference continue their work to improve the trail through wet sections by installing puncheons (bog bridges). Soon, the trail winds around a swampy area to the left, then parallels a small stream.

In about half a mile, the trail goes through a magnificent rhododendron grove, with the large rhododendrons forming an arch over the trail in places. Soon after you leave the rhododendron grove, the laurel and evergreens end, and you proceed through a second-growth forest of deciduous trees. A short distance beyond, the trail heads across an interesting whaleback rock and crosses two low stone walls. Before the walls, there is a pleasant place to take a break on a large rock to the left, which looks down over a tiny, elongated lake. Just beyond the stone walls, the yellow trail turns left onto a woods road. You'll be following woods roads, with gentle grades, for the next 1.3 miles.

Soon, the yellow blazes bear left again onto another woods road lined with barberry bushes, indicating that this area was once farmed. Then, after half a mile, take care to follow the yellow blazes as they bear very

Conglomerate rock outcrop along the Terrace Pond Red Trail   DANIEL CHAZIN

Terrace Pond

sharply left at a junction of woods roads. A short distance ahead, the yellow trail passes a swamp (with many dead trees) on the left. A quarter of a mile beyond the sharp turn, the yellow trail bears left at the top of a rise, with another woods road going off to the right.

The trail again begins to run along the swamp, on the left. Towards the end of the swamp, the yellow-blazed trail twice bears right, bypassing flooded sections of the woods road and crossing the outlet of the swamp on rocks. Between the two detours, the trail crosses a large concrete pipe, with much beaver activity visible in the swamp. Two miles into the hike, the yellow-blazed

Terrace Pond South Trail leaves to the left and three blazes resembling fried eggs (a yellow circle on a white background) indicate the beginning of the Yellow Dot Trail. Continue straight ahead on this wide woods road for 0.2 mile. Leave the Yellow Dot Trail here—it continues straight ahead—and turn left onto the red-blazed Terrace Pond Red Trail, which follows a rugged, rocky footpath.

The trail flattens out briefly, but then climbs through more rugged terrain before descending into an attractive valley, where it crosses a stream. It crosses several low ridges and proceeds along the base of a large slab of puddingstone rock, which it climbs and continues across the top. After approximately 45 minutes walking on the Terrace Pond Red Trail, the footpath descends to a junction with the yellow-blazed Terrace Pond South Trail, which you followed at the start of this hike. For a short distance, you follow both red and yellow blazes, but when the yellow blazes leave to the right, bear left, continuing to follow the red blazes of the Terrace Pond Red Trail.

The Terrace Pond Red Trail climbs along another rock outcrop, then steeply climbs over rocks to reach a seasonal viewpoint to the east, through the trees. Just beyond, Terrace Pond itself may be seen below to the right (when there are no leaves on the trees). Finally, the Terrace Pond Red Trail descends steeply over rocks to end at a junction with the white-blazed Terrace Pond Circular Trail. The Terrace Pond Circular Trail circles Terrace Pond, but if you make a right turn, you'll eventually have to cross the outlet of the pond, and this crossing is sometimes difficult to negotiate. So to continue along the route of the hike, turn left and follow the white blazes along the west side of Terrace Pond.

A short distance ahead—just beyond another rock scramble—you'll reach an open area along the lakeshore. This is a great spot to take a break and enjoy the beauty of this secluded glacial lake. In about a quarter of a mile, you'll come to a T-junction with the blue-blazed Terrace Pond North Trail. Here, you'll notice a triple white blaze (indicating that the Terrace Pond Circular Trail technically begins and ends here). Turn left and follow the blue blazes of the Terrace Pond North Trail, which crosses several wet areas on planks, logs, and rocks. After a short climb, you'll emerge onto a large open rock outcrop. Just to the left of the trail, there are panoramic west-facing views from the top of a rounded peak of conglomerate rock. This is another good spot for a break.

After refreshing your spirit with the beautiful panorama, continue on the blue-blazed trail, which passes alternately through woody, wet areas and rock outcrops. Some of the descents, although short, are steep and can be slippery. The main direction is downhill, but there are a few short climbs. Quite suddenly, the trail comes upon the ugly slash of a pipeline.

Turn left and follow the pipeline downhill for about 500 feet, keeping to the left of the gash on the hill and looking for the blue blazes to confirm that you are still on the trail. Just as the pipeline levels off, you will reach a very distinct, blue-blazed woods road. (If you miss it, follow the pipeline to Clinton Road, turn left, and walk 0.4 mile along the road to the parking lot.) Turn left, following the blue blazes, which follow a relatively level route for the next half mile, crossing several wet areas on rocks, and lead back to the trailhead. Cross the road to reach the parking area where the hike began.

14

Bearfort Ridge

Total distance: 7 miles
Hiking time: 5.5 hours
Vertical rise: 1,200 feet
Rating: Moderately strenuous
Maps: USGS Greenwood Lake (NY/NJ); NYNJTC North Jersey Trails #116; DEP Hewitt State Forest map
Trailhead GPS Coordinates: N 41° 09' 20.5" W 74° 21' 46"

This hike is in Abram S. Hewitt State Forest, administered by Wawayanda State Park (885 Warwick Turnpike, Hewitt, NJ; 973-853-4462; www.njparksandforests.org) as a day-use area; no camping or swimming is permitted. Bearfort Mountain, which this hike traverses, may still even have a few bears—they have been seen in nearby Wawayanda—and it is assumed that this is the derivation of the name.

HOW TO GET THERE

From the large shopping center—which contains a post office and an A&P superstore—on the southwestern shore of Greenwood Lake, where County Route 511 meets County Route 513, (just west of Browns Point Park in West Milford) continue west 0.1 mile on County Route 513 to a fork in the road. Take the right fork (Warwick Turnpike) going uphill. Cross a small concrete bridge and park on the right side of the road just after the bridge. If you reach a junction with White Road, you've gone too far.

THE TRAIL

The trail begins on the north side of the road, just to the east of the bridge. Three white paint blazes indicate the start of the Bearfort Ridge Trail. You'll also notice a sign for the Jeremy Glick Trail, named to honor a local hero of the tragic events of September 11, 2011. Glick was one of the passengers who tried to regain control of Flight 93, which crashed in Pennsylvania. The trail that has been (unofficially) named in his honor will be your return route.

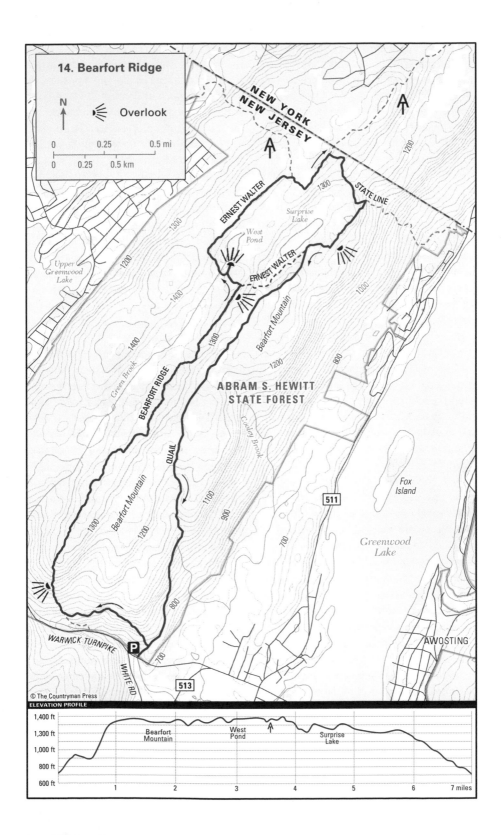

14. Bearfort Ridge

N

≋ Overlook

0   0.25   0.5 mi
0   0.25   0.5 km

NEW YORK
NEW JERSEY

ERNEST WALTER

STATE LINE

Surprise Lake

West Pond

ERNEST WALTER

1300

1200

Upper Greenwood Lake

1200

1300

Bearfort Mountain

1400

1300

BEARFORT RIDGE

Green Brook

1400

1200

1200

ABRAM S. HEWITT STATE FOREST

QUAIL

Conley Brook

800

1000

1100

900

1300

Bearfort Mountain

1200

800

700

511

Fox Island

Greenwood Lake

700

800

WARWICK TURNPIKE

P

WHITE RD

513

AWOSTING

© The Countryman Press

ELEVATION PROFILE

1,400 ft
1,300 ft
1,000 ft
800 ft
600 ft

Bearfort
Mountain

West
Pond

Surprise
Lake

1   2   3   4   5   6   7 miles

Starting uphill through a pretty grove of hemlocks and rhododendrons, the trail briefly traverses the slope before joining a woods road. Following the white blazes, proceed left along the woods road and, after a short distance, turn left again, uphill and off the road. The woods road, called the Quail Trail, is marked with orange blazes and continues northward to Surprise Lake. Note this spot, as it will be on your return route.

The Bearfort Ridge Trail is well marked with white blazes. It climbs moderately uphill, with some steep pitches, through a mixed hardwood forest consisting of red, black, and white oak, and some maple, ash, beech, and birch. The forests here were heavily timbered for charcoal production during the area's iron-producing period. This forest is therefore the second—or even third—growth of trees.

After crossing a stream in a small hollow, the trail continues ahead along the side of a slope. Except for some road noise from nearby Warwick Turnpike, there is a feeling of isolation in deep woods. You may or may not notice a blue-blazed side trail to the left, which is a short link to Warwick Turnpike and the Terrace Pond North trailhead. As you proceed, gaining elevation, the road noise quickly fades, and the real beauty of this area becomes evident. Passing through some tall and lush rhododendrons— magnificent in June when they bloom—the climb begins to steepen. After you ascend around rocks and along the base of a ledge, there is a good south-facing viewpoint off the trail to the right. The steep, bare-faced peak across the road is another part of this same mountain. Continuing ahead and upward, you soon reach the first of the pitch pines that dominate the main part of the hike.

As the trail turns right onto the ledge, a scramble up the large rock on the left of the trail yields another fine view. The water in the distance is a small section of Upper Greenwood Lake. This viewpoint is also a good place to take note of the rock formation that composes much of Bearfort Ridge. A collection of white quartz pebbles embedded in a red puddingstone, it is considered similar to the Shawangunk conglomerate found in Mohonk and Minnewaska. These rocks generally provide secure footing, but, as usual, take extra care when they are wet or icy.

Continue on the trail as it climbs up onto the ledges. Once reaching the top of the ridge, the Bearfort Ridge Trail follows a relatively level route along puddingstone conglomerate outcrops, with several dips back into the woods to cross small hollows and streams. There are some sudden but well-marked turns; if you lose the white blazes, retrace a short way back and pick up the turn. The elevation is generally 1,300 feet or more, and the climb up has been more than 600 feet. The views from this section of the Bearfort Ridge Trail are not as sweeping as those behind you or to come, but the charm of the landscape surrounds you. Note the fine array of mosses along—and occasionally even in—the footpath, indicative of the surprisingly light use this trail receives. The boulders strewn along the way have been moved to these spots by glaciers, remaining from the ancient ice sheets as they melted and retreated north. Striations on the rock surface can also be attributed to this period.

One of the nicest spots in all of New Jersey is about a half-hour hike along this ridgetop. Here, a large section of rock has split away from the base, leaving a deep crevice just to the left of the footpath. On the far side of the split is an attractive swamp. The separation of rock here possibly commenced as water seeped into cracks and then expanded with repeated freezings. Time and erosion have widened it to more dramatic dimensions. This is a good spot for a break.

This narrow wedge of bedrock split away from the main ledge, leaving a deep crevice   DANIEL CHAZIN

Continuing ahead, pass a rather large boulder. After a while, cross a stream, then climb up through a rock notch. The ridge soon becomes less pronounced, with fewer rock outcrops, and rhododendron and mountain laurel reappearing. As the trail gently rises out of the woods, a symmetrical cedar tree dominates the skyline. In another 100 feet, three white paint blazes on the top of a small rock mark the end of the Bearfort Ridge Trail, about 2.5 miles (and about 2 hours) from the hike's start.

The view is extensive, including Surprise Lake, with only small traces of civilization visible. Off to the right in the distance is a section of the Monksville Reservoir. The hike now begins a loop that starts and ends on the yellow-blazed Ernest Walter Trail, named for a dedicated hiker and trailblazer.

The yellow blazes lead both right and left. Proceed left, following the loop in a clockwise direction. The trail steeply descends a rock face and continues along a narrow footpath. Because it crosses "against the grain" on the ridge, the route undulates pleasantly through the woods and rock outcrops, soon crossing Green Brook, the outlet stream of West Pond. This section of trail is particularly rugged, with many short but steep ups and downs. At the bottom of the second steep descent, you'll come to a T-intersection. A yellow arrow on a tree points right to a view.

West Pond

Turn right and follow a side trail for about 500 feet to a rock outcrop overlooking pristine West Pond. You'll want to spend a little time enjoying the view at this special spot.

When you're ready to continue, retrace your steps to the trail junction and continue ahead, heading west along the Ernest Walter Trail. You'll soon come to a third, very steep descent, at the base of which the trail crosses Green Brook, the outlet stream of West Pond. The trail now proceeds through an attractive forest of hemlocks, pines, and deciduous trees. You'll pass a junction with an unofficial trail (blazed green at this writing) that goes off to the left, but you should continue to follow the yellow blazes of the Ernest Walter Trail.

About half a mile from Green Brook, the trail crosses a small stream, the outlet of a wetland to the left. Just beyond, a rock outcrop to the left of the trail affords a view over the wetland. An unusual huge split boulder adds interest to this spot, which is another good place to take a break.

Soon, the trail traverses a long, narrow, smooth rock. A short distance beyond, it turns right and descends to end at a T-junction with the white-blazed Appalachian Trail (AT). See Hike 4, Appalachian Trail Backpack, for background information on this National Scenic Trail. Turn right onto the AT, which almost immediately climbs a steep ledge. You're now heading east, again crossing several sharp ridges. At a limited viewpoint to the east, the trail turns left and heads north.

A short distance beyond, you'll reach another limited viewpoint, with both east- and west-facing views from an open rock ledge. The AT now descends a long, sloped rock and reaches a junction with the blue-and-white-blazed State Line Trail (the junction is marked by paint blazes on a rock). Turn right and follow the blue blazes downhill off the ridge.

After about 15 or 20 minutes going generally downhill on the State Line Trail, you will encounter another junction. This spot is the other end of the U-shaped Ernest Walter Trail. Make a sharp right turn onto it and climb steeply up to a promontory overlooking Greenwood Lake.

Surprise Lake is now about 20 minutes away, but the journey may take longer because the views on this rise are outstanding and invite lingering. Much of the two-state area of Greenwood Lake is visible. The large island in the middle is Fox Island and across the lake are the mountains of Sterling Forest State Park in New York and Long Pond Ironworks State Park in New Jersey. Area hikers were a major (arguably *the* major) supporting force in a successful campaign to bring these lands into the park systems of the two states.

Leave the ridge and turn right into the woods, passing a pile of shale ruins. Just before the shore of Surprise Lake, there are a few unmarked side trails, so keep a close watch on those yellow blazes. Your impressions of this graceful lake may be determined by how many people are there or the litter and debris they may have left. It sees heavy warm-weather use.

Here you have a choice. You can continue following the yellow Ernest Walter blazes for a half-mile climb to its end at the previously encountered junction with the Bearfort Ridge Trail. From there you would retrace your steps on the Bearfort Ridge Trail back to your car. This adds about a mile to the hike, but the trail looks surprisingly different when you're traveling in the opposite direction.

For the most direct return route (and to avoid retracing your steps), look for the orange-blazed Quail Trail. The orange and yellow trails split about 100 feet from the lake, the yellow-blazed Ernest Walter Trail turning sharply right and the orange-blazed Quail Trail going straight ahead.

The 2.5-mile-long Quail Trail is an old woods road that at times can be wet underfoot. However, it is mostly easy walking and passes by some lovely rock and cliff formations on both sides of the trail.

Just under 2 miles from the lake, the trail heads steeply downhill for a short stretch, then passes a distinct woods road heading sharply off to the left.

Two or three minutes further along, you'll see the last orange blaze at the previously encountered junction with the Bearfort Ridge Trail. Continue ahead, now following the white blazes back to your car, just a few minutes away.

15

Pequannock Watershed

Total distance: 8 miles (9.5 miles without car shuttle)

Hiking time: 6 hours

Vertical rise: 400 feet

Rating: Moderately strenuous

Maps: USGS Newfoundland; NYNJTC North Jersey Trails #116; Pequannock Watershed trails map

Trailhead GPS Coordinates: N 41° 04' 30" W 74° 26' 46"

This outstanding hiking area is named for the Pequannock River. Pequannock is an Algonquin word said to mean "battlefield." The river is fed by the streams, lakes, and reservoirs of this mountainous and particularly scenic section of western Passaic County. Owned and managed by the city of Newark, this natural area just south of Wawayanda State Park supplies much of Newark's drinking water. Under the auspices of the New York–New Jersey Trail Conference, a network of about 25 miles of hiking trails has been blazed in this largely uninhabited area, and the land is open for recreational use by permit only. At the time of this writing, the fee is $12 per year. For more information, or to obtain a hiking permit, contact the city of Newark, by mail at P.O. Box 319, Newfoundland, NJ 07435; or in person at their office, 223 Echo Lake Road, West Milford, NJ 07480; 973-697-1724.

This hike takes you on a grand tour of some of the watershed's more scenic and interesting features. Though it is long, the walking is not difficult, and much of it is along the shores of ponds and reservoirs. You will traverse some deep hemlock forests typical of this area, and there are a few overlooks, as well as the Bearfort Fire Tower, from which you can survey the area. Part of the hike follows the Bearfort Ridge, with its pink-to-purple sandstones and conglomerates. This ridge, composed of Paleozoic (Silurian and Devonian) sedimentary rock, occurs in the midst of the much older Precambrian Highlands formation. Apparently, Bearfort Mountain is the remains of the sand

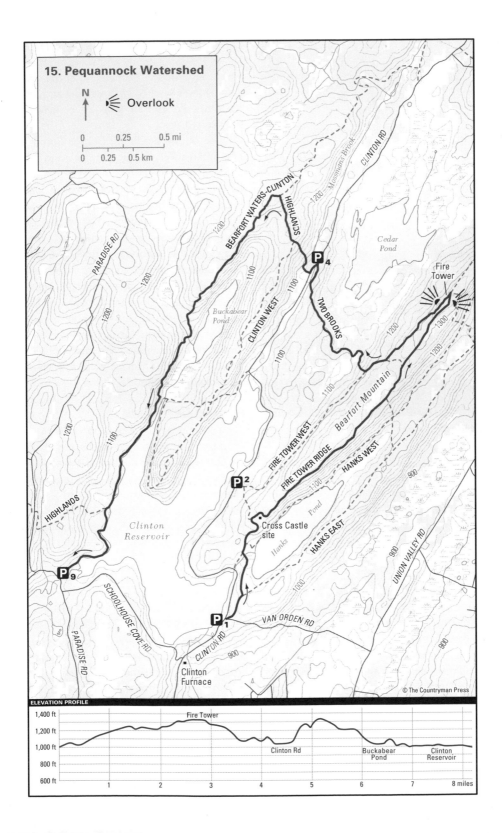

15. Pequannock Watershed

N

☀ Overlook

| 0 | 0.25 | 0.5 mi |
| 0 | 0.25 | 0.5 km |

PARADISE RD

BEARFORT WATERS–CLINTON

HIGHLANDS

Massmans Brook

CLINTON RD

Cedar Pond

P 4

Fire Tower

TWO BROOKS

Buckabear Pond

CLINTON WEST

Bearfort Mountain

FIRE TOWER WEST

FIRE TOWER RIDGE

HANKS WEST

P 2

Hanks Pond

HIGHLANDS

Clinton Reservoir

Cross Castle site

HANKS EAST

Hanks

P 9

SCHOOLHOUSE COVE RD

P 1

VAN ORDEN RD

UNION VALLEY RD

PARADISE RD

CLINTON RD

Clinton Furnace

© The Countryman Press

ELEVATION PROFILE

Fire Tower

1,400 ft

1,200 ft

1,000 ft

800 ft

600 ft

Clinton Rd

Buckabear Pond

Clinton Reservoir

1   2   3   4   5   6   7   8 miles

Bearfort Fire Tower　　　　DANIEL CHAZIN

and silt deposits of a long, narrow inland sea or sound that penetrated the older Highlands. Notice the distinct change of bedrock as you hike from Bearfort Mountain to Buckabear Pond, the latter being entirely in the Highlands with its typical gray Precambrian gneiss.

Of special interest on this hike is the site of the former Cross Castle (also known as Bearfort House), a large mountain estate built by Richard James Cross about in 1907. Cross, a native of England, made a fortune in banking and later erected a fantastic but short-lived mansion. The 365-acre estate featured a three-story castle with views in all directions, hot and cold running water, numerous fireplaces, stables, carriage houses,

guest cottages, and a boathouse on Hanks Pond. The foundations and walls of stone—which survived the dismantling of the mansion by the city of Newark when it acquired the property in 1919—were demolished in the late 1980s.

Also of interest is the Clinton Furnace, one of the very few furnaces surviving from the region's iron-making era. The furnace, located just off Clinton Road near its intersection with Schoolhouse Cove Road, is still in fairly good shape. Iron-smelting furnaces were always built near running water, necessary for the waterwheel-driven bellows. As you would expect, a substantial series of waterfalls is located immediately adjacent to Clinton Furnace. Once the furnace was fired up and loaded with iron, it would burn for months at a time. Its location at the base of a sharp drop facilitated the loading of iron from the top of the furnace via a ramp known as a "charging bridge."

HOW TO GET THERE

The hike can be done as a loop or cars can be parked at each end and a shuttle arranged to avoid an additional 1.5 miles of road walking. The walk along the road is not at all unpleasant and will only add about a half hour to your hike. If you choose to do the extra walking, park at Parking Area P9 and walk to P1. If you have two cars, leave one car at P9 and drive another to P1 to begin the hike.

To reach Parking Area P9 from NJ 23, take Clinton Road north for 1.2 miles and turn left on Schoolhouse Cove Road, a gravel road with good views of Clinton Reservoir. After 1 mile, make a right turn onto Paradise Road; you will find the small parking area on the right in 0.1 mile. After parking, walk or drive down Schoolhouse Cove Road the way you came to Clinton Road. At this intersection, directly in front of you—though it may be obscured by foliage in the summer—are the Clinton Furnace and the falls described earlier. Turn left at the intersection, and walk or drive 0.3 mile north on paved Clinton Road to where Van Orden Road (gravel) comes in on the right. This is Parking Area P1, and you will begin your hike from here.

A number of instances of vandalism to cars parked in these parking areas have been reported, so be certain not to leave any valuables in your car.

THE TRAIL

The hike begins at a gate on the north side of Van Orden Road, just east of Clinton Road. Here, a triple-white blaze marks the start of the Hanks East Trail. Follow this trail, which heads north on a wide woods road. Soon, you'll come to a fork. Bear left onto a blue-blazed connector trail, which leads past some old foundations and crosses the outlet of Hanks Pond. After passing the start of the blue/white-blazed Hanks West Trail, the connector trail reaches a junction with the red/white-blazed Fire Tower Ridge Trail. Turn right and follow the red/white blazes, which lead uphill on a grassy woods road to the site of the former Cross Castle.

After exploring the site, continue north on the Fire Tower Ridge Trail. Follow the red /white markers, passing the stone water-storage tower that supplied water to the castle. About three-quarters of a mile from the site of the castle, the woods road turns left and makes a steep but brief climb to a rock outcrop studded with cedar and white pine. Here, the woods road ends. The trail bears right and continues on a footpath along the ridge, following a series of interesting out-crops of conglomerate rock. White pine, mountain laurel, and an occasional cedar make this section of trail especially scenic. Continue following the red/white blazes over slabs of glaciated conglomerate bedrock,

then downhill over a small stream and into deeper woods. The blue-blazed Newark Connector Trail joins from the right, runs concurrently with the Fire Tower Ridge Trail for about 0.2 mile, then leaves to the left.

As you rise to the broad summit area of Bearfort Mountain, which contains oaks, lau-rels, and patches of grass, you'll see that the mountaintop is actually a series of parallel, narrow ridges separated by swamps and wet areas. Some of these ridges are well worth exploring. After less than an hour of walking from the Cross Castle site (and about 2.5 miles from the start of the hike), you'll come to a clearing, picnic tables, and the fire tower—a good place for a snack or lunch. Take the time to climb the five flights of steps to the top of the fire tower. You will be rewarded by views of the entire watershed.

When you're ready to continue, head south from the tower. In about 50 feet, you'll notice the teal diamond blazes of the High-lands Trail to the right. Turn right (west) and follow this trail, which almost immediately turns left and heads south along the ridge, joined by the yellow-blazed Fire Tower West Trail. At the next fork, bear right to continue on the joint Highlands/Fire Tower West Trails.

You are now heading south through hemlock and laurel and will soon reach a viewpoint near a large glacial erratic. Cedar Pond, a natural glacial lake, is below to the north. Continuing, the trail traverses some beautiful woodland, with large pudding-stone rock outcrops framed with white pine. In another half mile, when the blue-blazed Newark Connector Trail begins on the left, you should continue ahead on the joint Fire Tower West/Highlands Trail. But at the next junction, bear right, leaving the Fire Tower West Trail, and follow the Highlands Trail, along with the white-blazed Two Brooks Trail (which begins here), as they head downhill, off the mountain.

View from Bearfort Fire Tower

Soon you will come to a small clearing. Follow the Highlands/Two Brooks Trail through ferns and deep hemlocks and then out to a brook, which is crossed on rocks. If you look around, you may find beaver-gnawed trees in this area. After crossing the brook, the trail turns sharply to the right through tall and dense hemlocks. Continue over rocks and pine needles and then out to another brook with a log bridge. The trail now turns left and heads uphill. It then descends slightly through moss, pine, beech, maple, and especially hemlock, which gets thicker as the trail approaches Mossman's Brook. After a pleasant walk on hemlock needles through a primeval forest along the brook, the trail comes out to Clinton Road at P4. Here, the Two Brooks Trail ends, and you continue on the Highlands Trail.

Turn left onto Clinton Road and head south. In 300 feet, follow the teal diamond blazes of the Highlands Trail as they turn right onto a woods road. The white-blazed Clinton West Trail begins here, and you will now be following both white and teal diamond blazes. Another right turn comes up almost immediately as the trail briefly heads north. In a short distance, it swings left and heads steeply uphill. This climb is the longest of the hike. Notice that the rock in this area is different from that on which you have been walking. The rock here is Precambrian gneiss, a much older rock than the purple sedimentary sandstones and puddingstone conglomerates that are found on Bearfort Mountain.

When you reach the top of the rise, you will arrive at a junction. The white-blazed Clinton West Trail leaves to the left, but you should proceed straight ahead, continuing to follow the teal diamond–blazed Highlands Trail. Soon, you'll come to another junction, where you turn left, now following both the Highlands Trail and the yellow-blazed Bearfort Waters–Clinton Trail.

The Bearfort Waters–Clinton Trail used to closely parallel the shore of Buckabear Pond. However, in recent years, beavers have enlarged the dam at the southern end of the pond, resulting in a rising water level and the flooding of sections of the trail along the shore. Volunteers have relocated a 1.5-mile section of the trail so that it now runs high above the pond, eliminating the flooding problem. As the trail approaches the southern end of the pond, it descends gradually until reaches the southern tip of the pond at the beaver dam.

Continue to head south on the yellow-blazed Bearfort Waters–Clinton Trail and the teal diamond–blazed Highlands Trail, now following a wide woods road (formerly a horse trail) built by the Civilian Conservation Corps (CCC) in the 1930s. Soon you will see Clinton Reservoir, the largest body of water on this hike, on your left. The trail parallels the reservoir for about a mile, then bears right and heads away from the reservoir. Watch for a junction where the Bearfort Waters–Clinton Trail turns left, leaving the woods road and the Highlands Trail. Follow the yellow blazes, which head back toward the reservoir on a footpath.

The trail now hugs the shoreline with good views of water, islands, and hills, and again turns left and downhill where a rocky woods road comes in. In this vicinity, on the right and uphill, you will find a number of plaques set in boulders and rock outcrops commemorating the lives of hikers and trail builders of the past. Still following the shoreline, the trail passes a cove popular with Canada geese, which frequently forage there. Just a short walk ahead you will emerge from the woods at Parking Area P9, where you parked your car.

Note: Shorter explorations of this scenic but vast area are possible. Consider the following options: Park at P9 and walk along the shore of Clinton Reservoir for a mile or two and then turn back. Park at P1 and explore the shoreline of Hanks Pond. For a 4.5-mile loop hike, park at P2 and follow the yellow-blazed Fire Tower West Trail to the fire tower. To return, head south on the red/white Fire Tower Ridge Trail to the Cross Castle site, then turn right, following a blue-blazed connector trail that leads to the yellow trail. A left turn here will lead to your car.

16

Wawayanda State Park

Total distance: 7.5 miles

Hiking time: 4 hours

Vertical rise: 530 feet

Rating: Easy to moderate

Maps: USGS Wawayanda; NYNJTC North Jersey Trails #116; DEP Wawayanda State Park

Trailhead GPS Coordinates: N 41° 11' 17" W 74° 25' 31"

Wawayanda State Park (885 Warwick Turnpike, Hewitt, NJ 07421; 973-853-4462; www .njparksandforests.org), which covers over 35,000 acres of forest and water, is located in Passaic and Sussex Counties, near the New Jersey–New York boundary. The park opened to the public in 1963. According to one source, the name Wawayanda is the phonetic rendition of a Lenape word meaning "water on the mountain." Another source claims it is a Munsee word meaning "winding, winding water."

Wawayanda offers a feeling of wilderness, and this hike is delightful in any season. In summer, you are protected from the heat of the sun by the leafy canopy of mature trees and are able to cool off in the lake after hiking; in fall, the same trees are a riot of color (although squirrels can bombard the unwary with acorns from above); in winter, these trails—gentle and wide—are admirably suited for cross-country skiingwhen the snow is deep enough. Because of the high elevation of the plateau, snow remains longer in Wawayanda State Park than in other areas. The terrain undulates and winds in a relaxed way, making for very pleasant walking. This hike uses the Double Pond (yellow), Cedar Swamp (blue), Banker (green), Old Coal (red), Lookout (white), Laurel Pond (yellow), and Wingdam (blue) Trails, as well as sections of Cherry Ridge Road. The hike makes a loop, meanders through areas of huge rhododendrons arching overhead, passes under tall hemlocks, and traverses the shores of several lakes.

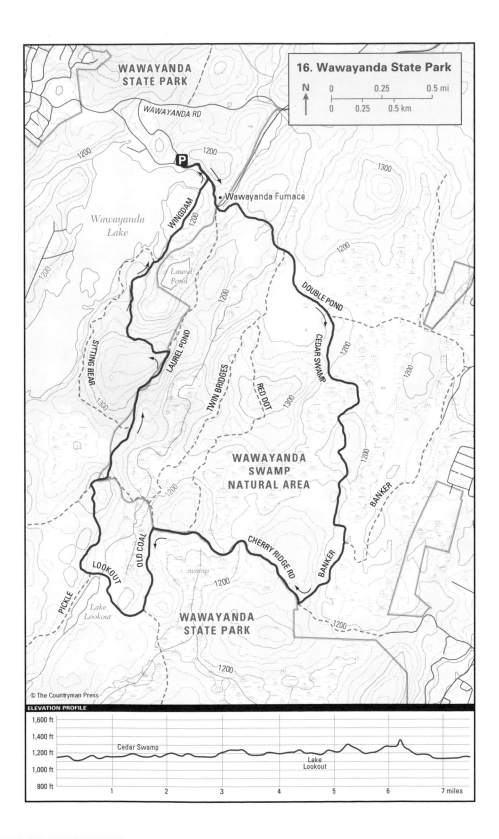

16. Wawayanda State Park

N

| 0 | 0.25 | 0.5 mi |
| 0 | 0.25 | 0.5 km |

WAWAYANDA
STATE PARK

WAWAYANDA RD

1200

1200

1300

P

Wawayanda Furnace

Wawayanda
Lake

WINGDAM

1200

1200

1200

Laurel
Pond

DOUBLE POND

1200

1200

SITTING BEAR

LAUREL POND

TWIN BRIDGES

RED DOT

CEDAR SWAMP

1300

1300

1200

BANKER

WAWAYANDA
SWAMP
NATURAL AREA

1200

1200

OLD COAL

LOOKOUT

CHERRY RIDGE RD

BANKER

PICKLE

swamp

1200

Lake
Lookout

WAWAYANDA
STATE PARK

1200

1200

© The Countryman Press

1200

ELEVATION PROFILE

1,600 ft							
1,400 ft							
1,200 ft	Cedar Swamp				Lake		
1,000 ft					Lookout		
800 ft	1	2	3	4	5	6	7 miles

HOW TO GET THERE

Wawayanda State Park is reached via Warwick Turnpike, approached from the north on NY 94 and from the south on Clinton Road. The park entrance is on the west side of Warwick Turnpike, about 1.2 miles north of Upper Greenwood Lake. Follow the entrance road for about 2.5 miles to the boating-and-fishing parking area on Wawayanda Lake (there is an entrance fee from Memorial Day weekend to Labor Day). On the way, you may wish to stop at the park office to obtain the park map and other literature. During the summer months, it is advisable to arrive before 10 AM to be assured a parking space.

THE TRAIL

With Wawayanda Lake on your right, leave the parking lot, walk left to a wide gravel road, and follow it alongside the lake. Wawayanda Lake was once two separate bodies of water called Double Pond. The narrow strip of land that divided the two ponds is still visible on the west side of Barker Island, now in the center of the lake. In winter, when the lake is frozen solid, it is pleasant to walk across to Barker Island and watch the people fishing through the ice. In 1862, the Thomas Iron Company built the stone dam at the northeastern end of the lake (as well as a wingdam), which raised the level of the lake 7.5 feet. On the lake, admire the many yellow pond lilies and white fragrant water lilies. The blue-blazed Wingdam Trail, your return route, leaves to the right within a few minutes, and very soon the remains of the old charcoal furnace come into view.

Pause here and imagine the busy scene of yesteryear when Wawayanda was the center of the New Jersey iron industry. The stone charcoal blast furnace was built by Oliver Ames and his three sons, William, Oakes, and Oliver Jr. William was in charge.

Wawayanda Furnace   DANIEL CHAZIN

His initials W. L. A. and the date 1846 are still visible on a lintel in the main arch. Iron ore from local mines was smelted here continuously from 1847 to 1857, when cheap coal became available in Pennsylvania, making it more economical to transport the ore for smelting to those hotter and more efficient furnaces. In an average day, the Wawayanda furnace produced seven tons of iron, which was poured off twice daily, at noon and at midnight. Wawayanda iron was of such superior quality that it was used to manufacture railroad wheels. During the Civil War, the Ames factories also filled government orders for shovels and swords. Nothing remains of the small village that was established in the vicinity to house the workers. The furnace building is currently supported by metal framing and protected from vandals by fencing.

When you have absorbed enough history, walk toward the two portable toilets, and turn left in front of them, crossing a small wooden bridge across a stream and walking toward a sign indicating a left turn for the Double Pond Trail. The trail passes through group campsites, and for a short distance is rocky and climbs slightly. The trail then descends to cross a wetland on a bridge, with a boardwalk along the right side. Just beyond, the Red Dot Trail begins to the right, but you should continue ahead on the Double Pond Trail, which goes through the Wawayanda Swamp Natural Area, a fascinating and ecologically significant tract. The vegetation

changes to a dense mix of hemlock and rhododendron, with rhododendron soon becoming the dominant species.

About a mile from the furnace, you'll reach a junction with the blue-blazed Cedar Swamp Trail, which begins on the right. Turn right and follow the Cedar Swamp Trail—one of the highlights of Wawayanda State Park. Huge rhododendrons arch high overhead, and hemlocks soar above these shrubs. Look for a stand of inland Atlantic white cedar trees growing in this very wet environment, but be aware that parts of the trail may be quite wet, especially after heavy rains. At one point, you'll cross a 750-foot-long boardwalk. In about a half mile, watch on the left for an old rusted car in a clearing, and follow the footpath as it makes a sharp right turn.

Wawayanda Lake

Wawayanda State Park

In about a mile and a half, the Cedar Swamp Trail ends at a junction with the green-blazed Banker Trail at an informal parking area. Turn right and follow this old road for a short distance until it ends at the unmarked Cherry Ridge Road, a wide gravel road. Here you should turn right. Follow Cherry Ridge Road past an extensive swamp on the left and cross the outlet of the swamp. In about a mile, the Red Dot Trail leaves to the right. Continue ahead on Cherry Ridge Road for a short distance until, at a curve to the right, the red-blazed Old Coal Trail begins on the left. Turn left onto the Old Coal Trail and follow it for about a half mile. At a curve to the left in the Old Coal Trail, the white-blazed Lookout Trail begins on the right. Turn right and follow this pleasant grassy woods road, which soon reaches the outlet of Lake Lookout, with its beaver dam. The peaceful and seldom-visited lake is an attractive place to take a break. After crossing the dam, the green-blazed Pickle Trail begins on the left, but you should continue ahead, following the white blazes back into the woods.

The trail now narrows to a footpath. It climbs steeply for a short distance among large boulders, then turns right and proceeds north along a valley floor, winding through a wet area lined with mountain laurel, with the heights of Cherry Ridge above on the left. In another half mile, the Lookout Trail ends at Cherry Ridge Road. Turn right onto the road, go around a gate, and in a short distance turn left onto the yellow-blazed Laurel Pond Trail, which follows a rocky woods road. You'll pass the start of the orange-blazed Sitting Bear Trail on the left, but continue ahead on the Laurel Pond Trail.

In about three-quarters of a mile, you'll reach an intersection with the blue-blazed Wingdam Trail, which begins on the left. Take this trail, which climbs at first, but soon descends and then levels off. Continue ahead on the Wingdam Trail until you reach the wingdam over the outlet of Wawayanda Lake. The water comes over this dam in a wide, swift fall and rushes on its way to feed Laurel Pond, out of sight on the left. Wildflowers abound in this lush area at most times of the year. Benches have been placed here, and you might want to take a break at this scenic location.

Continue ahead on the Wingdam Trail through a mature hardwood forest and cross the main dam at the northeastern end of the lake. Walk through the barrier of large boulders, turn left, and retrace your steps back to the parking lot, perhaps taking the time to stop at the beach and swim in the cool waters of Wawayanda Lake.

17

Appalachian Trail Stairway to Heaven

Total distance: 2.8 miles

Hiking time: 2 hours

Vertical rise: 1,000 feet

Rating: Moderately strenuous

Maps: USGS Wawayanda; NYNJTC North Jersey Trails #116; NY/NJ Appalachian Trail Guide Map #3; DEP Appalachian Trail and Wawayanda State Park maps

Trailhead GPS Coordinates: N 41° 13' 09" W 74° 27' 18"

The Appalachian Trail (AT) is our nation's first designated National Scenic Trail. It extends 2,185 miles from Springer Mountain in Georgia to Mount Katahdin in Maine. The AT is a unique partnership among 14 states, the National Park Service, the United States Forest Service, and a network of hiking clubs coordinated by the Appalachian Trail Conservancy (P.O. Box 807, Harpers Ferry, WV 25425; 304-535-6331; www.appalachian trail.org). Volunteers of the New York–New Jersey Trail Conference manage and maintain the 72 miles of the AT in New Jersey.

Entering from Pennsylvania at the Delaware Water Gap, the trail follows the crest of the Kittatinnies to High Point State Park, where it turns east along the New York–New Jersey border. After crossing Wawayanda State Park and passing through Abram S. Hewitt State Forest, the trail turns north into New York State just west of Greenwood Lake.

The main part of this hike follows an AT segment built mostly by volunteers with help from ATC trail crews, local Boy Scouts, New Jersey correctional inmates, and Wawayanda park personnel who completed their huge three-year cooperative effort in May 1991. You are about to see, appreciate, and enjoy the results of everyone's labors.

This relocation is a fine example of the concern trail builders now show for the environment. The old trail (about a half mile south) had changed little since it was first built in 1937. It shot straight up the mountain in just more than a half mile. Without a switchback, the climb was an exhausting

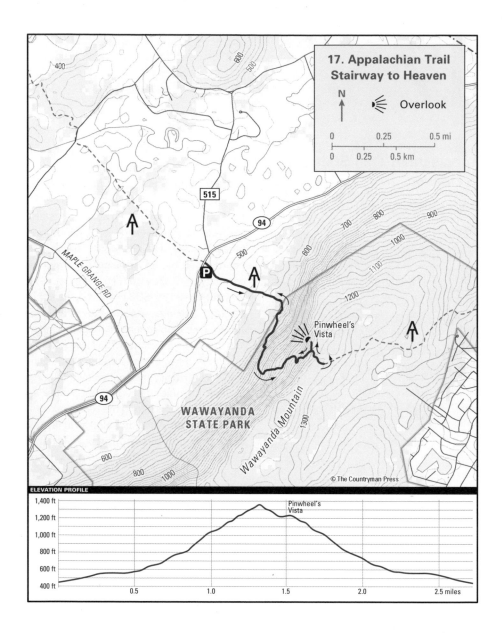

© The Countryman Press

boulder-hop and rock scramble up an ugly, erosion-scarred ditch. The new route, however, loops gracefully up the 900-foot elevation gain. Long switchbacks skirt patches of mountain laurel instead of cutting right through them. Water bars and some 300 stone steps protect the steepest sections. About two-thirds of the way up is the impressive 60-step "stairway to heaven" built in 1990. Some people walk here and actually think this all happened naturally! You know better.

HOW TO GET THERE

You can access the trail from a signed AT parking area on NJ 94, about 2.4 miles north of Vernon (0.7 mile north of the Maple Grange Road junction) and 2 miles south of the New York–New Jersey border. The parking area is on the east side of the road just south of the Amity/Pine Island directional sign and the Heaven Hill Farm Stand. There is room for about eight cars.

THE TRAIL

Your hike starts on the same side of the road as the parking area. Proceed up a small embankment on a grassy path (poison ivy abounds on the sides of the footpath), past several stone drains, and enter a large field. The path is well marked with the traditional 2-inch-by-6-inch white paint blazes of the Appalachian Trail. In this first section, often lush with wildflowers, the blazes are on wooden posts embedded in the ground. Soon you'll cross an old stone wall, enter the woods, and reach the base of Wawayanda Mountain.

After traversing an area strewn with rocks from eons of tumbledown from the heights above, the route begins the 900-foot ascent of the Wawayanda escarpment. In about a quarter mile, it ascends two small switchbacks and Annie's Bluff on the right (named for a trail builder). If you are here in the summer, especially July, many of the people you see carrying large packs are AT through-hikers, who are trying to complete the entire trail in one season. They are usually proceeding at a steady pace as they try to hike many miles, but more often than not will stop for a short chat and tell you about

View from Pinwheel's Vista

DAN BALOGH

Appalachian Trail Stairway to Heaven

their adventure. Offering some chocolate or fruit is almost always deeply appreciated and gets the conversation going.

Some 1.3 miles from your car, after the trail takes a right bend, you may notice a blue-marked trail to the left. You'll be exploring this side route on the way back. If you miss it, you'll arrive at the top of Wawayanda after about an hour's hike, with the summit marked by a hikers' register box nailed to a tree. Wawayanda is, according to one source, a Munsee word that translates to "winding, winding water," used by the Native Americans to refer to the creeks and meadows in the area. Another source indicates that Wawayanda is a phonetic translation of the Lenape term for "water on the mountain." In either case, the name was applied to the mountain before the Revolution and given to the nearby lake in 1846. You are now near the western edge of 35,000-acre Wawayanda State Park.

Turn around and proceed downhill on the AT the way you came. Soon, the trail turns right at a large rock outcrop, descends on stone steps, and then swings left. It is in this area, only a few minutes from the Wawayanda summit, that you should notice two cairns (piles of stones) to your right, and a triple-blue blaze that marks the start of a blue side trail. Follow the blue blazes for a few minutes to a rock outcrop known as "Pinwheel's Vista." "Pinwheel" was the nickname of Paul DeCoste, who helped build this section of trail. To the north, there are spectacular views of the Shawangunks and Catskills, and to the west, you can see Pochuck Mountain and the Kittatinnies beyond. You'll want to rest here and enjoy the views. When you're ready to continue, return to the AT and resume your descent. Please remember to stay on the designated footpath. Shortcutting the switchbacks leads to erosion problems and is considered very poor hiking etiquette. Retrace your steps on the AT all the way back to the parking area where you left your car.

18

Pyramid Mountain

Total distance: 3 miles

Hiking time: 2.5 hours

Vertical rise: 390 feet

Rating: Easy to moderate

Maps: USGS Boonton; NYNJTC Jersey Highlands Trails (Central North Region) #125; Morris County Park Commission Pyramid Mountain Natural Historic Area map

Trailhead GPS Coordinates: N 40° 56' 49" W 74° 23' 16.5"

At 934 feet in elevation, Pyramid Mountain is not the highest summit ridge in northern Morris County, but it has much to offer the hiker. It is crossed by foot trails that are steep and rugged in places, has several overlooks, and contains a mysterious glacial erratic that may be part of an ancient Native American calendar site. To the west and below the mountain ridge is Stony Brook and its wetland. Bear Rock, a gigantic granite monolith that towers over the brook and swamp, is found here. The land containing these wonders has been preserved, largely due to the work of an active grassroots committee, the Friends of Pyramid Mountain, together with the New Jersey Conservation Foundation, the Morris County Park Commission, the Mennen Corporation, and state agencies. Thanks to these organizations and many dedicated individuals, particularly Lucy Meyer, the next generation of New Jersey hikers will find this area as it is today—not developed with private homes.

Pyramid Mountain Natural Historic Area is a hiker's paradise. Although the area is heavily used at times, hikers can choose from many trails. There are actually two trail systems: the Pyramid Mountain section, which is the focus of the hike described below, and the Turkey Mountain section on the east side of County Route 511. Mountain bikes are not permitted in either section. A longer loop hike around the Butler Reservoir is also possible (see NYNJTC Jersey Highlands Trails Map #125).

This hike takes in the two most famous rock formations in the area, Bear Rock and Tripod Rock, as well as two vistas, Lucy's

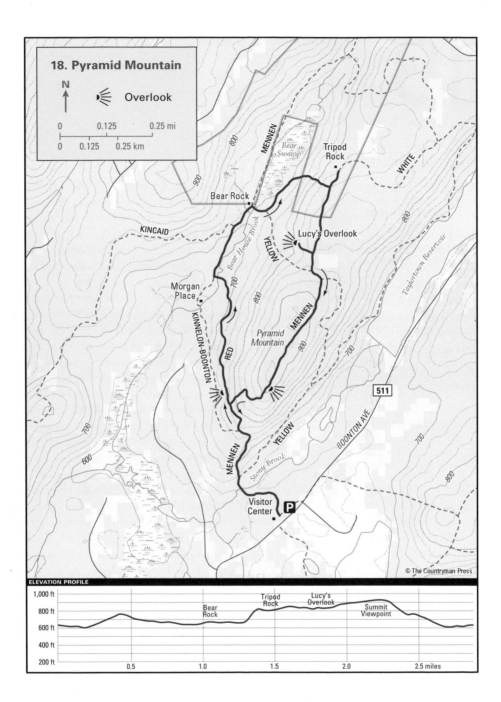

18. Pyramid Mountain

N

◀ Overlook

0   0.125   0.25 mi

0   0.125   0.25 km

MENNEN

Bear Swamp

Tripod Rock

WHITE

Bear Rock

Taylortown Reservoir

KINCAID

Bear House Brook

YELLOW

Lucy's Overlook

Morgan Place

Pyramid Mountain

MENNEN

KINNELON-BOONTON

RED

YELLOW

MENNEN

Stony Brook

BOONTON AVE

511

Visitor Center

P

© The Countryman Press

ELEVATION PROFILE

1,000 ft

800 ft

600 ft

400 ft

200 ft

Bear Rock

Tripod Rock

Lucy's Overlook

Summit Viewpoint

0.5   1.0   1.5   2.0   2.5 miles

Overlook and the summit of Pyramid Mountain. It begins at the visitors center (973-334-3130), currently open Wednesday through Sunday from 10:00 AM to 4:30 PM, which contains displays and information about the area and its natural history. An excellent map of the area is also available. Wildflower lovers will appreciate the first leg of the hike, which passes near a power line cut. The exposure to the sun allows many species not found in the darker woods to thrive.

How the name Pyramid came to be associated with the mountain is a fairly recent story. The first edition of the *New York Walk Book* (1923) directed hikers toward a "pyramidal shaped mountain." Indeed, the mountain has a triangular shape when viewed (without foliage) from near the present-day visitors center. Later editions of the book simply referred to it as "Pyramid Mountain," and the name stuck. In the 1990s, a conflict erupted over the proper name for the peak, with some local residents contending that its official name should be High Mountain. The matter was handed over to the United States Geological Survey for a decision, and it determined that Pyramid Mountain is the official name.

As of December 2013, some of the trails at Pyramid Mountain are closed due to construction on the power lines that cross the park. It is anticipated that all trails will reopen by the fall of 2014. For current information on the status of the trails, call the visitors center, 973-334-3130.

Bear Rock   DANIEL CHAZIN

HOW TO GET THERE

If coming from the north, take I-287 South to Exit 47 (Montville/Lincoln Park) and turn left at the bottom of the ramp onto Main Road (US 202). In 0.7 mile, just before reaching a fire station, turn right onto Taylortown Road and continue for 1.8 miles to Boonton Avenue (County Route 511). Turn right and continue for 0.7 mile to the entrance to the Pyramid Mountain Natural Historic Area, on the left, opposite Mars Park.

If coming from the south, take I-287 North to Exit 44 (Main Street, Boonton) and bear right onto Lathrop Avenue. Turn right at the stop sign onto Main Street (County Route 511), proceed along Main Street for 0.3 mile, then turn right onto Boonton Avenue. Continue on Boonton Avenue, still designated County Route 511, for 3.3 miles to the parking area for the Pyramid Mountain Natural Historic Area, on the left (the parking area is opposite Mars Park, about 0.7 mile north of the intersection of Route 511 and Taylortown Road).

THE TRAIL

From the southern end of the parking area, follow the access trail, which starts just north of a large bulletin board and immediately passes a memorial plaque for Stephen Klein Jr. In 150 feet, you'll reach a junction with the blue-blazed Mennen Trail. Continue ahead on the blue-blazed trail, which soon crosses Stony Brook on a wooden footbridge. Just beyond, the Yellow Trail begins on the right, but you should continue ahead on the blue-blazed Mennen Trail, which soon begins a short but steep climb to the shoulder of Pyramid Mountain. The climb continues under a high-voltage tower. A short distance ahead, a large cairn on the left marks the start of the white-blazed Kinnelon-Boonton Trail, but you should proceed ahead, continuing to follow the blue blazes. When you reach the next junction (also marked by a large cairn), turn left and continue on the Red Trail.

After a short uphill stretch, you'll pass a viewpoint to your left over the power line cut. Some interesting glacial erratics are nearby. For the next half mile, the Red Trail heads through a rocky area and then proceeds gradually downhill to a junction with the white-blazed Kinnelon-Boonton Trail. A left here will take you to the Morgan Place—the foundation of an old house near the power line cut, where the notorious Morgans lived in the late nineteenth century. Known as the Tar-Rope Gang, they used to go on raids into nearby Boonton. But to continue with the hike, turn right at this junction and follow the white blazes away from the power lines on an old road, with rock walls on either side, and Bear House Brook on the right.

In about a quarter of a mile, the yellow-blazed Kincaid Trail joins from the left. A short distance beyond, you'll reach the massive Bear Rock. Standing alone in the woods at the edge of a large swamp, Bear Rock has been used as a boundary marker for at least 200 years. Even today, it marks the borders of Kinnelon and Montville boroughs. Although it is difficult and even dangerous to scale, there are some very old surveying markers found near its highest points. Bear Rock is one of the largest glacial erratics in New Jersey, made up of a type of light-colored granite called alaskite. Alaskite does not occur at Pyramid Mountain and was probably transported by the glacier from outcrops southeast of Greenwood Lake. After the encasing glacial ice melted, Bear Rock split along a fracture, and the top third of the boulder toppled over. This fragment, now lying on its side, can be visually refitted back onto the side of the main boulder. The original boulder weighed approximately 600 tons; the main piece today weighs about 450 tons. About 500 feet to the northwest is a waterfall that cascades over bare rock during the spring and after heavy rains.

From Bear Rock turn right, now following white, blue, and yellow blazes, cross a wooden footbridge over the brook, and follow along the edge of Bear Swamp. Along the path are many dwarf ginseng plants, pepperbush, and spicebush. Soon, you'll come to a fork, where the Yellow Trail leaves to the right. Bear left, continuing to follow the blue and white blazes, and begin a steep, rocky climb up to the ridge of Pyramid Mountain. You'll gain only about 150 feet in elevation, but this is the steepest climb of the hike. Lining the trail are clusters of mountain laurel, which create a tunnel effect in places. As you reach the crest of the ridge, the trail arrives at a T-junction. Turn left here, following the white blazes, and in about 500 feet you'll reach Tripod Rock.

Perhaps the most massive perched boulder of its kind in the entire Northeast, Tripod Rock is the focal point of what may be an ancient calendar site. The sheer size and bizarre appearance of it—a 160-ton boulder standing on three medicine-ball-sized rocks—staggers the imagination. If it is simply a chance product of the last Ice Age, as most geologists believe, then it is unique. Others suggest that it was modified by humans. Nearby are two smaller stones partially perched on exposed bedrock. An observer seated on a lip protruding from a piece of bedrock 4 feet high will see, through the gap between these two stones, the summer solstice sunset. The

Tripod Rock

alignment constitutes a simple solar observatory. Whether or not it was used by the early inhabitants of the area is an open question.

From Tripod Rock, retrace your steps to the junction and continue heading south along the ridge, now following the blue blazes of the Mennen Trail. This section of trail is overshadowed by tall rhododendrons and mountain laurel, a beautiful sight in winter. When Little Cat Swamp, where peepers croak in spring, appears on the left, look for a blue-and-white-blazed side trail on the right. Follow this trail, which leads in about 300 feet to Lucy's Overlook, named for Lucy Meyer, who led the long crusade to save this beautiful area from development. The overlook offers views to the south and west over Stony Brook Mountain from rock outcrops.

Return to the main trail and turn right (south), continuing to follow the blue blazes. Soon, the Yellow Trail joins from the right and, in a short distance, leaves to the left.

The blue-blazed Mennen Trail gradually climbs to the highest elevation on the Pyramid Mountain ridge (934 feet). Here, a sign indicates that the trail turns right, but first bear left and head to an east-facing overlook from open rocks, with the New York City skyline visible on the horizon on a clear day.

After taking in the view, return to the blue trail and follow it as it gradually descends the southwest face of the mountain on switchbacks. Continue straight ahead past the junction with the Red Trail, and follow the blue blazes back to the parking area where the hike began.

19

Mount Hope Historical Park

Total distance: 2.7 miles
Hiking time: 2 hours
Vertical rise: 350 feet
Rating: Easy
Maps: USGS Dover; Morris County Park Commission Mount Hope Historical Park map
Trailhead GPS Coordinates: N 40° 55' 17" W 74° 33' 11"

Most of the hikes in this book lead you through forests to natural areas such as ponds, lakes, mountaintops, rock formations, interesting botanical areas, and the ocean itself. On this hike you tour a natural area of a different sort—a human-modified area. What this area looked like 100 years ago is hard to imagine, but whatever was going on there left a powerful imprint. There is nothing quite like the landscape you will traverse on this hike. Some may find it disturbing, others may find it utterly fascinating. Yet there is a wildness to the park that stands in sharp contrast to its obvious human disturbance.

Iron mining in the Dover area of New Jersey has a long history, and towns like Mine Hill and Mount Hope were built around this economic activity. The oldest mines in the region date back to 1710. The Dickerson Mine in Mine Hill is the oldest iron mine in the United States. The Mount Hope Mine, just to the north of this hike, was the largest iron ore producer in New Jersey, with six million tons having been produced since it was first opened. Mount Hope Historical Park itself is a historic site that preserves the remains of one of the more active mining and processing sites in the region. It is composed of three distinct groups of mines: the Allen Mine, the Richard Mine, and the Teabo Mine. Three veins of high-grade magnetite iron ore that ran the length of the park were mined here over the course of about 150 years. Approximately 5.7 million tons of ore were removed from these mines. During the early 20th century the mines were consolidated into one holding, but in 1959 operations

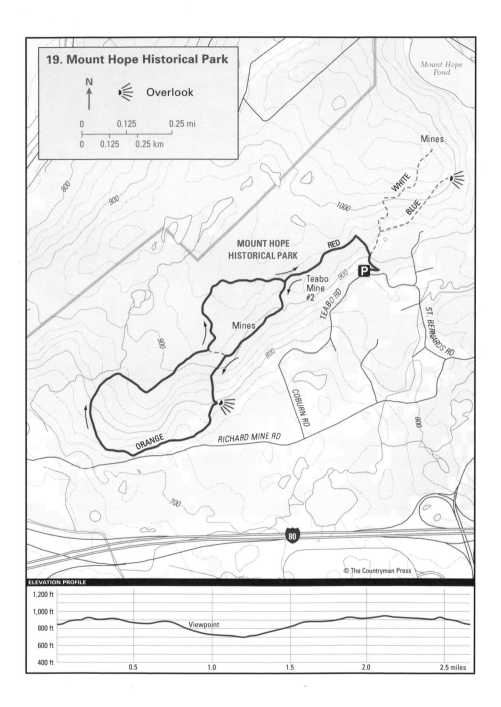

19. Mount Hope Historical Park

N

≤ Overlook

0   0.125   0.25 mi
0   0.125   0.25 km

Mount Hope Pond

Mines

WHITE

BLUE

RED

MOUNT HOPE HISTORICAL PARK

Teabo Mine #2

TEABO RD

P

Mines

ST. BERNARDS RD

COBURN RD

ORANGE

RICHARD MINE RD

80

© The Countryman Press

ELEVATION PROFILE

1,200 ft					
1,000 ft					
800 ft		Viewpoint			
600 ft					
400 ft	0.5	1.0	1.5	2.0	2.5 miles

Iron bars and rock walls from former mining activity   DANIEL CHAZIN

ceased and the property was abandoned. This very recent ending of mining in the park will give you much to think about—especially in regard to nature's power to heal itself.

Mount Hope Historical Park mines are located in the New Jersey Highlands province, a belt of mostly Precambrian (roughly 500 million to 1 billion years old) gneisses that have limited deposits of iron and zinc ore. Veins of iron ore vary from a few inches to over 50 feet in thickness and can be a mile or more wide. These belts follow the fold patterns of the gneiss and trend, as do the Highlands, in a northeast-to-southwest direction. Mining operations would follow a vein as far as was possible as it dipped into the ground. The landscapes at Mount Hope Historical Park are the remnants of collapsed mine shafts that today look like huge craters.

The hike described below is not particularly strenuous, but some special factors should be taken into consideration. First, the mine pits present something of a hazard. Tailings from the mines are not always stable, and hiking with small children will require that you restrain them. Much of the hike is quite rocky, and sturdy boots are recommended.

HOW TO GET THERE

From I-80, take Exit 35 (eastbound) or Exit 35A (westbound) and proceed north on Mount Hope Avenue, passing the Fox Hills condos. In 0.5 mile, turn left onto Richard Mine Road. Signs will direct you through winding roads in a residential area—drive carefully. Follow Richard Mine Road for 0.7 mile and turn right onto Coburn Road. The park entrance is 0.7 mile ahead on the left. The parking area for Mount Hope Historical Park is located is just below the power lines that mark the southern boundary of the park.

THE TRAIL

The trailhead is at the east end of the parking area near a kiosk. A historic plaque for Richard Mine and a picnic table are located here, too. Follow an unmarked trail up a switchback to a trail junction under the power lines. It is here that the trail system of the park actually begins. To the right are two relatively short trails. These are the Blue Trail, which terminates at a viewpoint under the power lines, and the White Trail, which leads to the northernmost mines. For this hike, we turn left onto the Red Loop Trail and enter the woods.

The trail proceeds through a second-growth forest and soon turns left at a junction. By now you will notice that the surroundings are not like most Highlands woods. All around you are piles of rocks, pits, and small rock walls—signs of human activity that has shaped the landscape. After making this left turn, the trail becomes rockier, and soon you will begin to notice that the pits on your left are getting progressively deeper.

After crossing a seasonal stream, the mine pits of Teabo Mine #2 will be on your left. Just beyond, you'll come to a junction. Bear left and continue following the red-blazed trail around a huge pit (a veritable crater) on your left and then past a series of pits on your right. At the next junction, continue straight ahead, leaving the Red Loop Trail (which goes off to the right) and begin following the Orange Loop Trail, which heads downhill. Just before the trail crosses under the power lines, look for unmarked paths that lead up to an overlook just beyond the power lines. The vista includes the Rockaway Town Square Mall, with I-80 in the foreground. Here are also two old, rusted water tanks and the remains of a small reservoir.

Return to the main trail and continue following the Orange Loop Trail as it crosses the power line cut, turns right, then immediately turns left into the woods again. Now following a cinder path, the trail parallels the power line cut, passes under it again, and swings very close to paved Richard Mine Road, which it follows for a short distance before it swings to the right. Next, watch for another junction—keep right here on a gravel road that begins to climb. At the next junction, which faces a vernal pond and lies in a wet area, turn right. After another climb the trail enters a dry oak forest and begins to level off. Just past a mine pit on your left, you will arrive at another junction with the Red Loop Trail. Turn left here.

The trail now climbs to the highest point in the hike and then swings gradually around to the east. The land is very dry here and there are no mines. Just after passing two small boulders on your left, you will reach the junction you came to earlier, where the Red Loop Trail splits. At this junction, make a left. Walk past the pits, keep right at the junction, and reach the power lines. From here, follow the path downhill to the parking area, where the hike began.

If you have a little extra time you could first follow the Blue Trail to the northeast, along the power line cut, to a viewpoint. The Mount Hope Mines may be seen to the north, the New York City skyline is visible to the east, and the town of Dover is to the south. Retrace your steps on the Blue Trail to the junction under the power lines and descend on the path to your car.

20

Mahlon Dickerson Reservation

Total distance: 4.7 miles	
Hiking time: 3 hours	
Vertical rise: 400 feet	
Rating: Easy to moderate	
Maps: USGS Franklin; NYNJTC Jersey Highlands Trails (Central North Region) #126; Morris County Park Commission Mahlon Dickerson Reservation map	
Trailhead GPS Coordinates: N 41° 00' 45" W 74° 33' 52"	

The Morris County Park Commission (P.O. Box 1295, Morristown, NJ 07062; 973-663-0200, www.morrisparks.net), steward of this 3,200-acre reservation, believes that only 10 percent of its parkland should be developed for intensive recreation (picnic sites, ball fields, and playgrounds), while most of it should be left in its natural state. As a result, hikers in Morris County have a number of excellent nearby parks to enjoy. Mahlon Dickerson Reservation, the largest county park, contains tent sites, several Adirondack-type shelters, and trailer camping areas. There is also a ball field, 20 miles of multi-use trails, a picnic area, and Saffin Pond.

The reservation was named for one of Morris County's great achievers, Mahlon Dickerson (1770–1853). Dickerson, who lived near Dover, lived a model life of political service. He never married but was successful in nearly everything he tried. He mastered several languages and attained distinction as a botanist. He owned and operated the Succasunna iron mines, some of the largest in the county. He was a general in the military, served in the state legislature, and was governor of New Jersey for a short period. He served as a member of Congress between 1817 and 1829 and, during the presidency of Andrew Jackson, served as Secretary of the Navy. He was said to have been popular with everyone and very consistent in his political faith.

Many of the marked hiking trails in the reservation are old logging roads and fire lanes. Some are covered in gravel. These woods roads are well suited for cross-

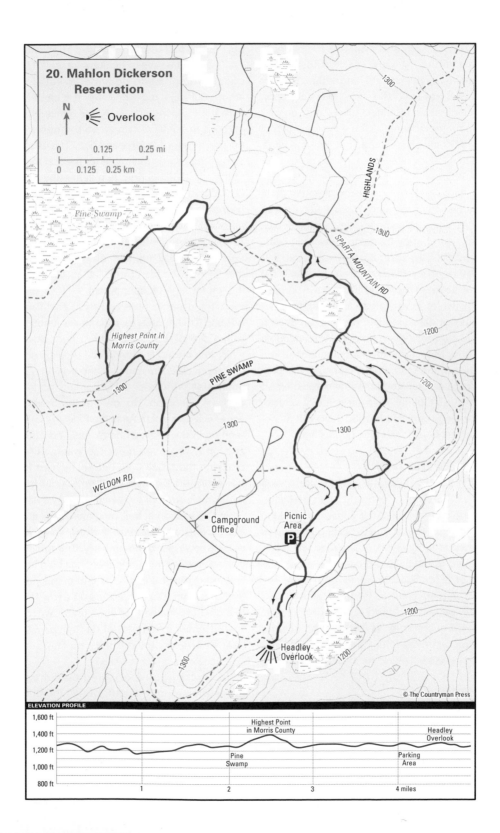

20. Mahlon Dickerson Reservation

N

Overlook

| 0 | 0.125 | 0.25 mi |
| 0 | 0.125 | 0.25 km |

Pine Swamp

HIGHLANDS

1300

1300

SPARTA MOUNTAIN RD

1300

1200

Highest Point in Morris County

PINE SWAMP

1200

1300

1300

1300

WELDON RD

Campground Office

Picnic Area

P

1200

Headley Overlook

1300

1200

ELEVATION PROFILE

1,600 ft					
1,400 ft			Highest Point in Morris County		Headley Overlook
1,200 ft					Parking Area
1,000 ft		Pine Swamp			
800 ft					
	1	2	3	4 miles	

country skiing, and because the average elevation in the park is 1,200 feet, snow remains on the ground longer than in many other areas in north Jersey. Many are open to horses and mountain bikes, and you may encounter them along the way. A section of the 150-mile Highlands Trail (see the Introduction) also passes through the park.

Although this hike does not offer sweeping views of the countryside, the change in woodland environments more than makes up for it. Along the route are deciduous forests, rocky scrub growth, damp hemlock groves, laurel thickets, and remote swampland. The reservation is located on a high plateau in the New Jersey Highlands Province. The bedrock, which is very close to the surface because of glaciation, is Precambrian gneiss, a granitic rock that contains large amounts of iron. There are a few long-abandoned iron mines in the reservation. Because the park is large and located in the most remote part of Morris County, many species of wildlife, including red-tailed hawks, deer, and an occasional bear, make their homes here.

HOW TO GET THERE

From I-80 (Exit 33), take NJ 15 north for 5 miles. Turn right, following signs to Milton and Weldon Road. After 2 miles on Weldon Road, you'll see a sign indicating that you've entered the reservation. The road will swing around to the right and pass the large parking area for Saffin Pond. In roughly another mile, you will come to the reservation's three main entrances, the first two for campers. At 4.3 miles from NJ 15 take the second entrance on the left, which leads to a large parking area, a picnic area, and the trailhead.

THE TRAIL

Walk north on the wide asphalt path past a workout station, a picnic area, and a ball field. The access trail you are following is part of the teal diamond–blazed Highlands Trail, with some white markers as well. The pavement will soon become gravel, and in just 0.1 mile you will arrive at a junction with the Pine Swamp Trail, a 3.5-mile loop marked in white that passes through the northern part of the reservation. The Highlands Trail shares this route for the first third of the hike. Make a right turn at this junction; walk downhill and cross over a small brook. At the next junction, bear left, continuing to follow the white and teal diamond blazes. After a short climb, the trail curves to the right at a grassy intersection (with a bench and a kiosk), heads downhill, then swings to the left through an open forest.

After a short level stretch, the Pine Swamp Trail comes to a triangular junction with a pink-blazed trail and turns right, down a hill, to a brook. This unnamed brook is one of the principal drainages of the swamp that dominates the interior of the northern portion of the reservation. Notice that the brook's water is a dark color. As in the Pinelands, the tannins in the roots of hemlocks and other swamp evergreens color the water. After crossing the brook on a bridge, be alert for a left turn off the main path onto a cut trail through a corner of the swamp.

In this section of trail, mountain laurel and rhododendron dominate, putting on a display of flowers in June and July. The footing is much rockier here, and there can be a few wet areas. As you reach the end of this part of the swamp, the trail climbs up a few feet to higher ground and turns left onto a woods road. Because this part of the trail passes near Sparta Mountain Road, you may hear an occasional motor vehicle.

In another 500 feet, a red-blazed trail proceeds straight ahead, but you should turn right to remain on the white-blazed Pine Swamp Trail. Soon the trail crosses a bridge and gains elevation. At the next

View from the Headley Overlook

DAN BALOGH

intersection, with Sparta Mountain Road just to the right, the Highlands Trail turns right, but you should turn left to continue along the white-blazed Pine Swamp Trail. After a short climb, the trail levels off and gradually descends, entering the area of the Pine Swamp. Just ahead on your left, at the edge of a small cliff, look for an area that overlooks the dense foliage of the swamp. This rocky spot is a pleasant place to stop for a rest or to have a snack or lunch. Below you is not a typical swamp of grasses and water, but a pine swamp with tall spruce, hemlock, rhododendron, and laurel.

Continue farther along on the trail, which now heads downhill to the level of the swamp, and get a closer view of this fascinating area. About 0.2 mile ahead, the trail—a dry woods road—comes closest to the swamp itself. Off to your right you can see how wet the area is and how huge boulders protrude from the ground, providing drier areas in their cracks for plants incapable of growing in water or very wet soil.

You are now in one of the most remote areas of the reservation. On your right, the swamp extends for perhaps a mile into Sussex County. It is virtually inaccessible, and no paths cross it. You get a feeling of wilderness here, broken only by the calls of birds or an occasional aircraft. In fact, some years ago a small private plane crashed in the swamp one May. It wasn't until that November that the wreckage and the bodies were found.

The trail, which follows a high area between two parts of the swamp, continues under tall hemlocks, crosses a small brook, and then begins a climb, leaving the swamp for good. You'll pass junctions with a red-blazed trail on the left and then an orange-blazed trail on the right. Continue climbing gradually on the white-blazed trail to the flat, rounded summit of an unnamed hill that, at 1,395 feet, is the highest point in Morris County. The trail passes just to the northeast of the height of land, but unfortunately there are no views except through the trees during winter. Just beyond, at a curve to the left, a blue-blazed trail begins on the right, but you should bear left to continue on the white-blazed Pine Swamp Trail.

The trail swings to the right as it descends to lower ground. Follow it through a low area and up a gradual climb. You can find a few remnants of 19th-century iron mining—mostly pits and rockpiles—by exploring the woods to your left and uphill. At a three-way junction, the trail turns left (a blue-blazed trail is on the right) and heads northeast on a wide footpath. After about 0.25 mile, keep right at a junction with a pink-blazed trail and continue walking on a wide path, keeping to the left at the next junction, where a blue-blazed trail begins on the right. In another 500 feet, you'll arrive at the trail junction where you began the loop hike, marked by signs. Make a right here and follow the path through the picnic area and back to your car.

If you still have energy and would like to take in a vista, the Headley Overlook is less than 0.25 mile away. Follow the teal diamond blazes of the Highlands Trail as they leave the parking area behind the kiosk, cross Weldon Road and continue to the overlook. The rocky overlook offers a view to the south and west that includes an arm of Lake Hopatcong.

21

Jenny Jump State Forest

Total distance: 5 miles

Hiking time: 3.5 hours

Vertical rise: 950 feet

Rating: Moderate

Maps: USGS Blairstown; DEP Jenny Jump State Forest map

Trailhead GPS Coordinates: N 40° 54' 42" W 74° 55' 17"

Jenny Jump State Forest was named for a young colonial girl. As the tale goes, Jenny was out picking berries with her father. Some hostile Native Americans came across the pair and her father yelled out for her to jump from the cliff—if only to save her chastity. Although Jenny was successful in keeping herself pure, the result was her death . . . or so the tale goes.

In addition to about 12 miles of hiking trails, this state forest has a number of campsites that may be rented by the public. There are also eight shelters (which are actually enclosed cabins) for rent. Each shelter has four bunks and a wood burning stove, with restrooms located nearby. For more information, contact Jenny Jump State Forest, P.O. Box 150, Hope, NJ 07844; 908-459-4366; www.njparksandforests.org.

HOW TO GET THERE

To reach Jenny Jump from Exit 12 of I-80, turn left at the bottom of the ramp (turn right if coming from the west) onto County Route 521 and drive 1.1 miles into the village of Hope. At the blinking light, bear left onto County Route 519 (Johnsonburg Road). In another mile, turn right onto Shiloh Road (this and other intersections are marked with small Jenny Jump State Forest directional signs). In 1.1 miles, turn right onto State Park Road and proceed to the park entrance, 1 mile on the left. After entering the park, stop at the park office for a free map, then drive uphill and park in a small parking area opposite a restroom building.

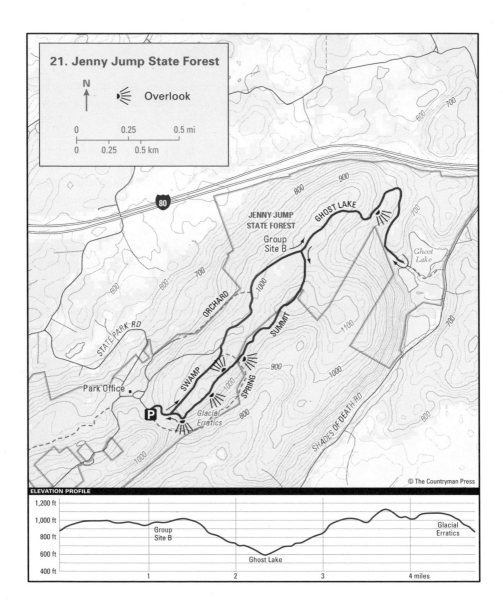

21. Jenny Jump State Forest

N

◁≣ Overlook

| 0 | 0.25 | 0.5 mi |
| 0 | 0.25 | 0.5 km |

JENNY·JUMP
STATE FOREST

Group
Site B

GHOST LAKE

Ghost
Lake

ORCHARD

SUMMIT

STATE PARK RD

SWAMP

SPRING

Park Office

P

Glacial
Erratics

SHADES OF DEATH RD

© The Countryman Press

ELEVATION PROFILE

1,200 ft
1,000 ft
800 ft
600 ft
400 ft

Group
Site B

Ghost Lake

Glacial
Erratics

1   2   3   4 miles

THE TRAIL

You'll begin your hike on the red-blazed Swamp Trail, which is co-aligned with the yellow-blazed Summit Trail for the first few minutes. A sign marks the start of these trails, which head uphill on a woods road and bear right. After passing Campsite #9, the trails bear left. Soon afterward, you'll reach a junction, marked by a signpost, where the two trails split. Bear left to continue on the red-blazed Swamp Trail. (The yellow-blazed Summit Trail will be your return route.)

The wide Swamp Trail climbs gently through a grove of fir trees and then a forest of deciduous trees. The gorge off to the right contains some small, wet areas that probably gave the trail its name; however, the going is generally dry and easy. You'll pass many trees that were felled by Hurricane Sandy in October 2012. Soon, the trail begins to descend. It passes a sign for the Swamp Trail, a sign for Campsite #18, and then a sign for the Summit and Spring Trails. A short distance beyond the signs, the Swamp Trail ends at a paved road opposite a restroom building.

Turn right and follow the paved road past several more campsites. Just beyond another restroom building note the large glacial erratic on the left side of the road—as well as the small tree growing right out of the rock. Continue ahead on the road, passing a sign for the white-blazed Orchard Trail, which

leaves to the left. Just before Group Site B, there is a sign on the right for the Ghost Lake and Summit Trails. Turn right here, following the co-aligned turquoise-blazed Ghost Lake Trail and yellow-blazed Summit Trail, which climb gently on a woods road, then bear left and descend.

At a signpost, the yellow-blazed Summit Trail leaves to the right. Unless you want to significantly shorten the hike (and forgo a 500-foot, up-and-down elevation change), stay on the turquoise-blazed Ghost Lake Trail, which continues straight ahead. It narrows to a footpath and climbs a little, passing some rock outcrops on the right, then continues over undulating terrain.

At a high point, marked by a glacial erratic on the left, the trail begins a steady descent. The first part of the descent is on

Ghost Lake

Sandstone erratic along the Summit Trail

DANIEL CHAZIN

switchbacks, after which the trail descends more steeply, passing through a rocky area. At the base of the steep descent, the trail turns left onto a woods road, which it will follow the rest of the way to the lake. A short distance beyond, a branch road to the right leads to the foundations of a former cabin, with east-facing views over Allamuchy Mountain State Park and the Pequest River valley. (One version of the legend contends that this is the actual site from which Jenny jumped.)

As the trail continues to descend on the woods road, it approaches I-80, which may be heard and seen ahead through the trees. The trail now bends sharply right and begins to head south, away from the noisy highway. It passes several huge rock outcrops on the left, then swings left and parallels a stream in an area covered with ferns. The Ghost

Lake Trail ends just before the grass-covered causeway across Ghost Lake, about 45 minutes to one hour from Group Site B.

There is some debate about how Ghost Lake acquired its name. One story involves a massacre between two warring Native American tribes, the other a mucky, pre-lake swamp where mosquitoes bred and spread sickness and death. The local road leading to the lake is named Shades of Death Road—the subject of a page or two of the Weird New Jersey Web site (www.weirdnj.com /stories/shades-of-death-road).

After spending some time at the lake (which, despite its name, is actually very attractive), retrace your steps, following the Ghost Lake Trail back to the signpost at the junction of the Ghost Lake and Summit Trails, and turn left onto the yellow-blazed

Summit Trail. (If you start seeing both blue and yellow blazes, you've gone too far, and you need to return to the junction.) You'll follow the yellow blazes of the Summit Trail for the rest of the hike.

The Summit Trail climbs steadily to the ridge of Jenny Jump Mountain. When it reaches the top, it begins to descend, following along the crest of the ridge. After a section where the trail runs a little below the crest, it continues along the ridge, following undulating terrain.

About two-thirds of a mile from the junction, the Summit Trail begins a steady climb. At the top, a side trail on the left leads to an east-facing viewpoint from a rock outcrop. A short distance beyond, you'll pass a concrete post on the right marked "NJ 78." This may be a forest boundary marker (the park map shows the Summit Trail crossing outside the forest boundary for a short distance). Next, you'll reach a junction with the blue-blazed Spring Trail. Continue ahead on the yellow-blazed Summit Trail. You're now entering a more heavily used area of the park and will likely encounter a greater number of hikers.

In another 300 feet, you'll reach a west-facing viewpoint over the Delaware Water Gap from a rock outcrop to the right of the trail. A bench has been placed just below the viewpoint. In another five minutes, you'll come to two large glacial erratics in an open area. The one on the right is formed of sandstone, while the one on the left is composed of granite gneiss. The bedrock in the area is granite gneiss, not sandstone, so the erratic on the right must have been transported a considerable distance. About 100 feet beyond, a side trail leads left to another southeast-facing viewpoint.

The yellow trail now widens into a woods road. In another five minutes, it turns right and begins a steady descent. Just beyond this turn, a side trail on the left leads 100 feet to a panoramic viewpoint from a rock outcrop amid cedars. The Pinnacle is directly ahead, farmlands are below to the left, and the Kittatinnies are visible to the right (through the trees). Notice, too, the rock surface underfoot. The striations were made by the glaciers during the Ice Age.

After enjoying the view, return to the main trail and turn left, continuing to descend. Soon, the red-blazed Swamp Trail joins from the right. The co-aligned trails pass Campsite #9 and end at the parking area where the hike began.

22

Point Mountain

Total distance: 2.8 miles	
Hiking time: 2.5 hours	
Vertical rise: 535 feet	
Rating: Moderate	
Maps: USGS Washington; Hunterdon County Division of Parks and Recreation Point Mountain Trail Map and Guide	
Trailhead GPS Coordinates: N 40° 45' 59" W 74° 54' 39"	

As you drive along NJ 57 south of Hackettstown you will notice that you are in a very fertile valley, nestled between two long mountain ranges. On your left will be the distinctive Musconetcong mountain range, a long ridge that is the remains of an ancient thrust fault in the Precambrian rock of the New Jersey Highlands. This thrust fault pushed older resistant rock on top of younger and softer rock, resulting in a ridge and an accompanying valley through which the Musconetcong River flows. The Musconetcong Mountain ridge and Musconetcong River are located in the northern portion of Hunterdon County. The highest point on the ridge is Musconetcong Mountain in Bloomsbury, where it reaches an elevation of 955 feet. The vertical relief from river valley to the nearby summit ridge is substantial—from 400 to 500 feet. Point Mountain, named for its sharp profile when seen from the south, is an outstanding feature of the Musconetcong mountain range and attains an elevation of 935 feet.

The 1,140-acre Point Mountain Reservation is managed by the Hunterdon County Division of Parks and Recreation (P.O. Box 2900, Flemington, NJ 08822; 908-782-1158; www.co.hunterdon.nj.us/depts/parks/parks.htm). Located in the northernmost portion of the county, this mostly undeveloped area (no facilities other than parking) is open to fishing, hiking, horseback riding, cross-country skiing, and mountain biking. There are two main access points to the trail system on Point Mountain. One is located on Penwell Road, from where you pass a

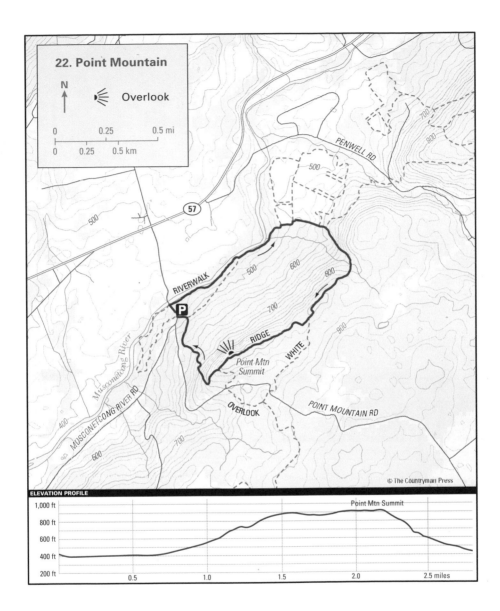

22. Point Mountain

N

Overlook

| 0 | 0.25 | 0.5 mi |
| 0 | 0.25 | 0.5 km |

PENWELL RD

500

57

500

RIVERWALK

500

600

800

P

700

RIDGE

WHITE

900

Point Mtn
Summit

OVERLOOK

POINT MOUNTAIN RD

400

MUSCONETCONG RIVER RD

600

700

Musconetcong River

700

800

© The Countryman Press

ELEVATION PROFILE

1,000 ft				Point Mtn Summit	
800 ft					
600 ft					
400 ft					
200 ft	0.5	1.0	1.5	2.0	2.5 miles

series of fields before entering the forested mountain ridge. The Penwell Mill, named for a descendant of the Penn family in Pennsylvania, as well as an 1830 farmhouse and barn (now a private residence), are located near the Penwell Road trailhead. The other access point, the one used for this hike, is on Point Mountain Road, just below the summit of Point Mountain.

The hike described below first leads alongside the Musconetcong River and past open fields. It then climbs the ridge of Point Mountain to arrive at the spectacular viewpoint near the summit. A short but steep

Musconetcong River

descent from this viewpoint brings you back to your car. Those with less time to spare may wish to walk directly from the parking area to the viewpoint—a short but very steep hike.

HOW TO GET THERE

From Exit 26 on I-80 (Budd Lake/Hacketts-town) proceed west on US 46 for 7.4 miles to Hackettstown. Turn left onto NJ 182 and follow it for 1 mile, then turn right onto NJ 57, following signs to Washington and Phillipsburg. Follow NJ 57 for 6.5 miles and turn left onto Point Mountain Road. The parking area is 0.5 mile ahead on the left, just past the bridge over the Musconetcong River. From I-78, take NJ 31 north for 8 miles and turn right onto County Route 632 (Asbury–Anderson Road). Drive 4 miles to NJ 57, follow NJ 57 to Point Mountain Road, turn right and continue across the bridge over the Musconetcong River to the parking area on the left.

THE TRAIL

From the parking area (trail maps may be available at a kiosk), walk back down Point Mountain Road toward the Musconetcong River. Just before reaching the bridge, turn right onto the blue-blazed Riverwalk Trail and follow it alongside the river in a northeasterly direction. You'll pass rock outcrops and boulder fields composed of Precambrian Highlands gneiss on your right. At a small clearing, the trail jogs right and then turns left onto a more established path. At the next fork, keep left, continuing along the river. Not far ahead, the trail leaves the river, crosses a tributary stream, and climbs to an open field. The trail follows the edge of the woods along the right side of the field.

At the end of the field, the trail turns left, briefly follows the eastern edge of the field, and soon reaches a junction with the orange-blazed Ridge Trail. Turn right onto it, passing an owl box on a tree in a patch of woods. The trail continues alongside the south edge of the field as it rises up the hill. At the end of the field, the trail enters the forest and soon reaches a junction with the White Trail, which begins on the left. Continue ahead on the orange-blazed Ridge Trail, which begins a steady climb up the ridge of Point Mountain on a woods road.

After crossing a stream, the trail turns right, leaving the road, and continues on a footpath. It climbs some more and soon reaches the crest of Point Mountain. In another quarter mile, the trail turns sharply left and descends to an old stone wall. It turns right and parallels the wall, soon reaching a junction with another branch of the White Trail, which begins on the left. Continue on the orange-blazed Ridge Trail, which now turns right, climbs a little to regain the ridge, and heads southwest along the ridge.

As the trail climbs ever higher, views over the Musconetcong Valley begin to appear

View from Point Mountain   DANIEL CHAZIN

to your right. The trail becomes increasingly rugged as it works its way past boulders and rock outcrops. Huge boulders jut out from the ridgetop, and you may need to use your hands in places. After descending to a junction with the yellow-blazed Overlook Trail, the Ridge Trail climbs to reach a panoramic viewpoint over the Musconetcong River valley from a rock outcrop just to the right of the trail at the summit of Point Mountain.

After taking in the view, continue ahead on the orange-blazed Ridge Trail, which heads steeply downhill on a rocky footpath. Be aware that poison ivy may be found here, especially during the first part of the descent. With a private home visible ahead, the trail curves to the right and continues to descend. Trail builders have made a few stone steps in places that offer some relief from the steady downhill walking—and you will thank them for their efforts. After the steepest part of the descent, the trail levels off and reaches a junction. Here, the Ridge Trail ends at a junction with the blue-blazed Riverwalk Trail. Continue straight ahead (do not turn right), and follow the blue blazes down to the parking area where you left your car.

23

Schooley's Mountain County Park

Total distance: 2.2 miles

Hiking time: 1.5 hours

Vertical rise: 500 feet

Rating: Easy to moderate

Maps: USGS Hackettstown; Morris County Park Commission Schooley's Mountain County Park map (available online at www.morrisparks.net)

Trailhead GPS Coordinates: N 40° 48' 08" W 74° 47' 00"

Schooley's Mountain County Park is a relatively small park of less than 800 acres, but it has much to offer outdoors enthusiasts. The hiking trails are mostly easy, except along the first part of this hike, where the footing on the Falling Waters Trail is quite rocky. However, the gorge and falls made by the Electric Brook are well worth the trip. Electric Brook takes its name from the old electric generating plant once installed here, which used the brook for power. There is only one viewpoint, but the shade trees make for a very pleasant outing on a hot summer day. Benches have been placed at various locations along the trails.

The park is administered by the Morris County Park Commission (P.O. Box 1295, Morristown, NJ 07962-1295; 973-326-7600; www.morrisparks.net). Restrooms, a picnic shelter, a playground, and a lodge are located near the main parking area (the lodge may be rented for functions such as weddings and parties). Paddleboats and rowboats may be rented for use on Lake George (fishing is permitted, but swimming is not allowed).

The park is named for the Schooley family, who owned much land in this locality in the 1700s. Originally a large part of the park was used for a Morristown YMCA camp called Camp Washington, but it was purchased by the Morris County Park Commission in October 1968 and opened to the public in May 1974.

HOW TO GET THERE
Take I-80 to Exit 27A, proceed south on US 206 for 4.4 miles, and turn right onto

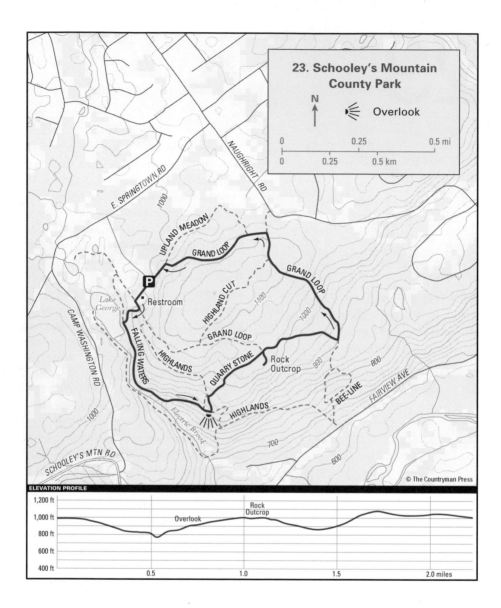

23. Schooley's Mountain County Park

N

Overlook

| 0 | 0.25 | 0.5 mi |
| 0 | 0.25 | 0.5 km |

ELEVATION PROFILE

Flanders-Bartley Road (County Route 612). In 1 mile, bear right just before a railroad crossing to continue on Bartley Road. Proceed another 2.5 miles and turn right onto Naughright Road. In 2.2 miles, turn left onto East Springtown Road. Follow East Springtown Road for 0.5 mile to the park entrance, on the left. Parking is available at the end of the park entrance road.

THE TRAIL

Begin your trek by walking uphill on the grassy area toward the restroom building. To the right of the building, you'll notice a trail

South-facing view from overlook

junction. Do not take the Grand Loop Trail straight ahead; rather, head downhill on a gravel road toward Lake George, bearing right at the fork (the path on the left leads to an overlook above the lake). Turn left at the base of the short descent and follow along the lake. Just past the dam at the south end of the lake, you'll notice a triple-blue blaze on a tree that marks the start of the Falling Waters Trail.

The Falling Waters Trail descends steadily along the pools and cascades of Electric Brook. The path is rocky, and care needs to be taken, particularly after rain, when the footpath may be slippery. Be sure to stop and look around to admire the unspoiled scenery. The two attractive waterfalls are reached within 0.3 mile; this is a good spot for a break.

A short distance beyond, at a PRIVATE PROPERTY sign, the Falling Waters Trail turns left, leaving the brook, and begins a steady climb. At the top of the climb, a huge jumble of large boulders remaining from a rock quarry is on your right. Here, a triple-blue blaze marks the end of the Falling Waters Trail. Turn right and follow the joint Patriots' Path (white blazes) and Highlands Trail (teal diamond blazes) for only about 50 feet. Where the trail makes a sharp left turn, continue ahead to a rock outcrop with a south-facing overlook. Rest awhile and enjoy the view over a serene, beautiful valley, then retrace your steps to the junction with the Falling Waters Trail. Proceed ahead another 50 feet, but when the Patriots' Path/Highlands Trail turns left, continue ahead on a wide gravel woods road, designated on the park map as the Quarry Stone Path. The road is unblazed, but it is wide and easy to follow.

In about 15 minutes, you'll reach a junction (marked by a sign) with the yellow-blazed Grand Loop Trail. Just before this junction, a short unmarked trail on the right leads to an interesting rock outcrop. This is

Waterfall in Electric Brook

Highlands

a worthwhile detour (there are limited views through the trees from the outcrop during leaf-off season).

After taking a short break here, return to the junction. To the left, the Grand Loop Trail leads directly back to the parking lot, but you should turn right, following the arrow that points to the Bee-Line Trail. The Grand Loop Trail descends on a narrower footpath to another junction, where the Bee-Line Trail heads right towards Fairview Avenue and the Columbia Trail. You, however, should turn left to continue along the yellow-blazed Grand Loop Trail. The trail now heads steadily uphill for about 15 minutes until the height of land is reached. Here there is a cairn, a signpost, and a triple-red blaze that marks the start of the Highland Cut, which heads southwest across the mountain.

Do not take the Highland Cut, but continue ahead on the Grand Loop Trail, which now descends gently. Be alert for a sharp left turn, where the trail leaves the wide woods road it has been following and continues on a narrower path through ferns. Stay on the yellow-blazed Grand Loop Trail when the Upland Meadow Trail goes off to the right. After walking through an attractive forest, you'll reach the end of the Grand Loop Trail (there is a triple-yellow blaze here facing the other direction). Turn left, passing a bench and a signpost, and you'll emerge at the parking lot where the hike began.

24

Black River Trails

Total distance: 6.6 miles

Hiking time: 4 hours

Vertical rise: 800 feet

Rating: Moderate to strenuous

Maps: USGS Chester; Morris County Park Commission Black River Trails (available online at www.morrisparks .net)

Trailhead GPS Coordinates: N 40° 46' 43" W 74° 43' 13"

This linear hike, which runs from north to south in Chester Township, requires a short car shuttle. If you don't have two cars, a one-car option is provided at the end of this hike description. This walk has much to recommend it. In addition to the hike itself, there are interesting historical features to visit at both ends, if time permits. The terrain used by the hike is varied. After following an old railroad grade, the trail parallels the Black River as the water rushes through its rocky gorge, then climbs through cool and dense deciduous and pine forests to finish with a meander through several meadows.

Cooper Mill, at the northern end, is a gristmill dating from 1826. Both the visitors center and the mill are closed during the winter, and opening times vary from May through October. The Bamboo Brook Outdoor Education Center is at the southern end of the hike, and the Willowwood Arboretum is also close by. The hike uses the Black River, the Conifer Pass, and the Bamboo Brook Trails, and crosses two paved roads—Pottersville Road and Longview Road. The Patriots' Path is co-aligned with these trails, and occasionally you will notice its distinctive path-and-tree logo.

HOW TO GET THERE

Drive both cars to the Bamboo Brook Outdoor Education Center parking lot. Head south on I-287 to Exit 22 (Bedminster /Pluckemin) and continue north on US 206 for 4 miles to Pottersville Road (County Route 512). Turn left and continue on Pottersville Road for 0.5 mile, then turn right

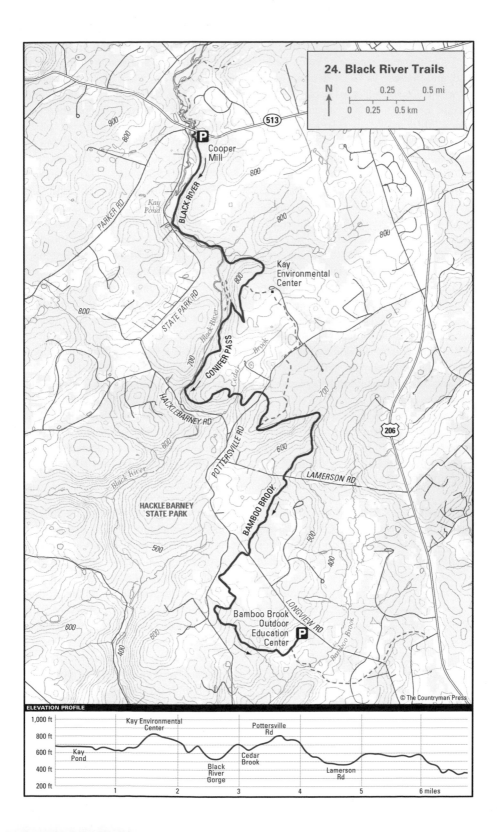

24. Black River Trails

N

| 0 | 0.25 | 0.5 mi |
| 0 | 0.25 | 0.5 km |

513

P
Cooper
Mill

BLACK RIVER

Kay
Pond

PARKER RD

Kay
Environmental
Center

STATE PARK RD

Black River

CONIFER PASS

Cedar Brook

700

800

800

800

800

900

700

HACKLEBARNEY RD

800

POTTERSVILLE RD

600

LAMERSON RD

206

BAMBOO BROOK

HACKLEBARNEY
STATE PARK

Black River

500

500

400

400

600

800

400

600

Bamboo Brook
Outdoor
Education
Center

LONGVIEW RD

P

Bamboo Brook

ELEVATION PROFILE

1,000 ft		Kay Environmental Center			Pottersville Rd			
800 ft								
600 ft	Kay Pond				Cedar Brook			
400 ft				Black River Gorge		Lamerson Rd		
200 ft								
	1	2		3	4	5		6 miles

onto Lisk Hill Road. Continue for 0.1 mile to a T-junction, turn right onto Union Grove Road, and proceed for 0.3 mile to a Y-junction, where you turn left onto Longview Road. Proceed for about 1 mile until you reach the parking lot for the Bamboo Brook Outdoor Education Center, on the left.

Leave one car at the Bamboo Brook parking lot, and drive north to the Cooper Mill and visitors center. Turn left out of the parking lot onto Longview Road and continue for 0.8 mile to a T-junction with Pottersville Road. Turn right onto Pottersville Road, and in 0.7 mile turn left onto the unsigned Hacklebarney Road. Infrequent brown signs for Cooper Mill will confirm your route. Continue on this narrow, partly gravel road for 0.7 mile and turn right onto State Park Road. Proceed for another 2 miles, passing the old Kay Pond ice house, and turn right onto County Route 513. Almost immediately, turn right into the parking lot for the Cooper Mill and visitors center.

If you drive back to the Cooper Mill at the end of your hike, a right turn onto County Route 513 leads to US 206, where a left turn (north) accesses I-80, and a right turn (south) takes you to I-287.

THE TRAIL

Walk to the northwest corner of the parking lot toward the Cooper Mill County Park sign, and continue to the kiosk in the direction of the mill. When the demand for local grains declined in 1913, this last operating mill in Chester was closed. Descend the small flight of wooden stairs by the side of the mill and begin the hike on the Black River Trail, marked with blue paint blazes. The Black River (aka the Lamington River) is now on your right, but the trail soon leaves its banks. The area is lush, with some large trees, and the dirt footpath, which crosses several small plank bridges, is crisscrossed by tree roots.

About 0.3 mile from the start, the trail turns left onto the abandoned route of the Hacklebarney Branch of the Central Railroad of New Jersey, built in 1873 to transport ore from the Hacklebarney Mine, and abandoned in 1900. The now wider trail soon passes through a cut with piles of rocks to the side and blasting grooves in the rock wall.

After about 20 minutes, lily pad–covered Kay Pond can be seen on the right. Great blue herons and other wildlife can often be seen around the pond, which is man-made. The pond takes its name from Alfred and Elizabeth Kay, who moved from Pittsburgh in 1924 and built their summer home, called Hidden River Farm, nearby. During the 1930s, Mrs. Kay grew herbs that she sold by mail, and she also opened a local tearoom called the Herb Farm. The Kays donated much of their property to the Morris County Park Commission, and in 1994 Hidden River Farm was dedicated as the Elizabeth D. Kay Environmental Center. The building is now an office for The Nature Conservancy. A few steps to the right of the trail, the dam makes a pleasant place to take a quick break. One of the remaining ice houses still stands on the other side of the dam.

A short distance beyond, the trail passes the old Hacklebarney Mine on the left. This mine was closed in 1896 and is now protected by fencing. Hacklebarney was Chester's oldest and most productive iron mine. At first limited to surface mining, Hacklebarney was developed into an underground mine after large iron deposits were found. This mine recorded more accidents than any other in Chester.

Almost immediately, the trail crosses a tributary on a substantial bridge with a handrail and, on the right, approaches a barricaded paved road. The blue blazes indicate that the trail turns left. Soon, the railroad grade ends and the trail continues on a

Black River gorge

DANIEL CHAZIN

Kay Pond

slightly rougher footpath parallel to the river. About 1.2 miles from the start, the trail bears left and begins to head uphill. Here, to the right of the trail, a short herd path leads to abandoned concrete abutments in the river.

The trail bears left at the next fork and soon begins to parallel a tributary stream. The trail now curves right and continues to climb, passing a stone wall to the right and continuing through former fields, now overgrown with dense vegetation.

Soon, the trail reaches a junction in a clearing, marked by a signpost. Turn right and begin to follow the red-blazed Conifer Pass Trail, which follows switchbacks on sidehills on its way down to the Black River.

The river, with its waterfalls, can be glimpsed through the trees on the right, but when the trail begins to descend more steeply, the river becomes more visible as it tumbles through its deep and narrow gorge. The trail parallels the Black River for a short distance before climbing on switchbacks away from this wild and scenic spot. Take care to follow the red trail blazes, as the trail is sometimes a little indistinct here, and notice the indications of some test mining.

After descending to cross Cedar Brook, the trail begins to climb, passing through a stand of evergreens to reach paved Pottersville Road. The trail crosses the road and continues to climb. After leveling off, the trail bears left and reaches a wooden signpost that marks the end of the Conifer Pass Trail. (One-car option: Turn left at the signpost to reach the Kay Environmental Center in 2.2 miles and the Cooper Mill in 3.6 miles.)

Our hike continues by turning right and following the Bamboo Brook Trail. After about ten minutes of walking downhill, the trail reaches the brook itself and turns left to parallel it. On the left is an old stone wall that the trail crosses several times before reaching Lamerson Road.

Cross the road and continue ahead on a woods road. In this section, there are several intersecting woods roads, so be sure to follow the blue blazes. After several turns, the trail becomes more open and receives more sunshine. In about a half mile, the trail reaches an old rock wall and turns right.

Follow the wall for about 50 feet, then turn right and continue to Longview Road.

Cross Longview Road and follow the Bamboo Brook Trail, which heads through the woods and then emerges onto an open field. Here, the trail turns right and continues along the side of the field. After turning left and following another side of the field, the trail heads to a second field, which it skirts on the left. It then reenters the woods.

After passing through a pine plantation, the trail descends and begins to parallel a tributary of Bamboo Brook, to the left. Soon, the trail crosses the stream and climbs to skirt a field. It reenters the woods and then skirts a second field. Finally, the trail emerges onto yet another field, with the Bamboo Brook parking lot visible down to the right. Walk around the sides of this last field and head down to your car.

25

Merrill Creek Reservoir

Total distance: 7.5 miles	
Hiking time: 4 hours	
Vertical rise: 400 feet	
Rating: Easy	
Maps: USGS Bloomsbury; Merrill Creek Reservoir trail map	
Trailhead GPS Coordinates: N 40° 44' 25" W 75° 05' 33"	

Merrill Creek Reservoir, located in Harmony Township, Warren County, was built to augment the supply of water from the Delaware River when its water levels are low. The present reservoir replaced a smaller one built in 1903 by Ingersoll-Rand to supply water to its plant in nearby Phillipsburg. Ground was broken for the new reservoir in September 1985 and, because of the workers' long hours—sometimes as many as 20 a day—the reservoir was completed in April 1988. Seven electric utility companies combined efforts on this project.

The 650-acre reservoir is stocked with a variety of game fish. It has a maximum depth of 225 feet and more than 5 miles of shoreline. The reservoir stores 16 billion gallons of water for release to the Delaware River during low-water periods to augment the river water used by its generating stations. A 3-mile pipeline, 57 inches in diameter and about 6 feet below ground, links the reservoir to the Delaware. Water is pumped up the mountain from the river by three 8,000-horsepower pumps and returned through the same pipeline when needed. The inlet/outlet tower controls water flow. Ports are provided along the tower to permit water to be released from whatever depth in the reservoir best matches the river's temperature.

A 290-acre wildlife preserve juts into the reservoir, and a total of 2,000 acres of open space surround it. Nesting bald eagles have been observed at Merrill Creek Reservoir since 1997. In June 2011, two eagle chicks born at the reservoir were fitted with satellite transmitters that will allow scientists to

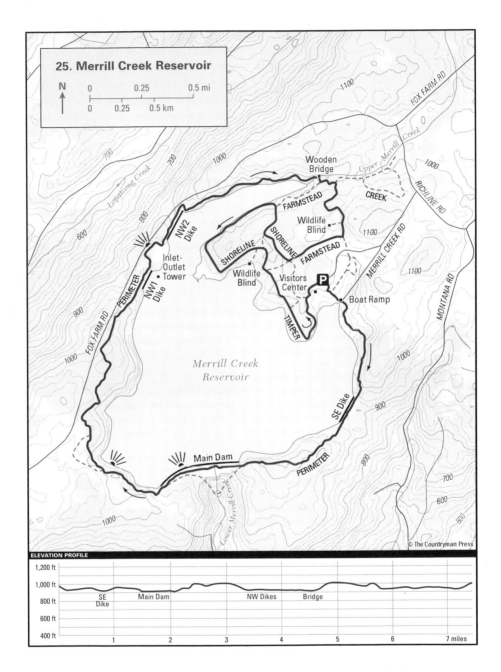

25. Merrill Creek Reservoir

N

| 0 | 0.25 | | 0.5 mi |
| 0 | 0.25 | 0.5 km | |

monitor the birds for up to three years as they move away from their nest and begin to establish their own territories. This was the first instance of a long-term eagle research project being conducted in New Jersey.

The visitors center contains an exhibit that shows the methods used to move the water. Another exhibit uses a unique method to illustrate in sand the tracks left by wild animals. A large collection of animal skulls is displayed in a glass case, and stuffed birds are suspended from the ceiling. The visitors center is open daily (except on certain holidays), and the hiking trails are open daily from dawn to dusk. For more information, contact Merrill Creek Reservoir, 34 Merrill Creek Road, Washington, NJ 07882; 908-454-1213; www.merrillcreek.com.

This hike is easy walking, largely on flat, wide trails, but with a few rocky sections. The trails used are the Perimeter Trail (black), which circles the reservoir, as well as parts of the Farmstead (yellow), Timber (red), and Shoreline (blue) trails. The trails are for hiking only and are blazed with metal markers with the MCR logo.

HOW TO GET THERE

From I-78 take Exit 4 (Warren Glen/Stewartsville). Turn right at the bottom of the exit ramp and continue for 1.8 miles to a blinking stoplight in Stewartsville. Turn right onto County Route 638 (Washington Street, then New Village Road) and continue 2.3 miles to NJ 57 (along the way, you will see a sign that instructs you to turn left to reach NJ 57; ignore this sign and continue straight ahead). Turn right onto NJ 57, then immediately turn left onto Montana Road. In 2 miles, bear left at a fork onto Richline Road, and in another 0.3 mile, turn left onto Merrill Creek Road. Bear right at the next fork and continue to the main parking lot for the Merrill Creek Reservoir. Park here and walk to the visitors center, where you can obtain a trail map and view the interesting exhibits (if the visitors center is closed, a trail map may be obtained from a kiosk in the parking lot).

THE TRAIL

With your back to the front door of the visitors center (the reservoir is to your right), proceed ahead (away from the visitors center) and bear right when you reach a paved road. You will soon notice a black MCR blaze, marking the start of the Perimeter Trail, which will be your route for the first part of the hike. Turn right, downhill, and enter the woods. Just ahead, you'll reach a junction. Bear right and continue to descend on the black-blazed trail to the boat ramp and boaters' parking area. Continue straight ahead across the parking area (keeping the boat ramp and the reservoir on your right), but before you reach the second parking area, bear right, go around a metal gate, and proceed uphill along a wide gravel dirt road, following the black blazes. You'll soon cross a beautiful meadow. Bluebirds, a common sight at Merrill Creek Reservoir, like to nest in the open, and nesting boxes have been erected in many locations (including this area). Two of the dams crossed by the Perimeter Trail are visible. A gentle upgrade, followed by an equally gentle downgrade, brings the first dam of the reservoir (shown on the map as SE Dike) into view. Continue straight ahead across the dam. At the end of the dam, the trail heads slightly uphill and continues through the woods.

About half an hour from the start of the hike, you'll reach the main dam of the reservoir. An alternate route leads to the left, but to avoid a steep descent and ascent, continue ahead through a stile and cross the dam. The dam provides excellent views of the reservoir, as well as a south-facing vista over the hills of Warren County. On the left, you'll pass the end of a wooden instrument-access staircase, which is closed to the public. A pipe under the rocks is used to release water from the reservoir into Lower Merrill Creek.

When you reach the west end of the half-mile-long main dam, go through the stile and bear right. The trail now proceeds through

Merrill Creek Reservoir

DAN BALOGH

a stand of red pine trees. You'll notice a number of fallen trees, uprooted by Hurricane Sandy in October 2012. After passing a viewpoint over the reservoir on the right, you'll continue through a section of the pine forest that was devastated by the hurricane, which toppled most of the trees in this area. Bear right at the next junction to continue on the black-blazed Perimeter Trail. Soon, a flat expanse to the right of the trail, with some brickwork, a large white pine, forsythia, daffodils, daylilies, and periwinkle, denotes the site of an old homestead. The trail is a little rockier here, and it climbs slightly until it reaches a bench, which overlooks a narrow slice of the reservoir. You have now covered nearly 2.5 miles.

Just beyond, you'll come to an intersection. Turn right to continue on the Perimeter Trail, but bear left at the following intersection. The trail to the right leads down to an observation point along the shore of the reservoir (an optional side trip, but you've already been afforded many panoramic views of the reservoir from the Perimeter Trail). Continue ahead, gently downhill, passing through another area devastated by Hurricane Sandy.

Soon, you'll reach a third crushed-rock dam (shown on the map as "NW 1 Dike"). Cross the dam, with the Inlet-Outlet Tower, which controls the flow of water between the Delaware River and the reservoir, to the right. Go around the gate at the end of the dam and cross a paved road. Here there is a bulletin board and a portable toilet screened by a wooden fence.

Follow the arrow on the sign and turn left, now proceeding along a gravel road that soon bears right. To the left, the view across the valley includes two gaps (the more northerly one is the Delaware Water

Gap). Through the tunnel under this valley, the water makes its way back and forth between the reservoir and the Delaware River. From this vantage point you also look down on paved Fox Farm Road.

After bearing right and then left again, you'll reach the southern end of another crushed-rock dam (shown on the map as "NW 2 Dike"). Cross the dam and, when you reach the northern end, turn sharply right and follow a footpath back into the woods. Almost immediately, you'll join a woods road, but you'll soon turn right, leaving the road, and continue on a footpath that parallels the shore of an arm of the reservoir. You will notice many dead and submerged trees in this arm of the reservoir. Also look for tulip trees with their long straight trunks, a spruce fir stand, and at the top of a short rise, a large tulip poplar to the right of the trail with a bulbous base and bark that grows in interesting patterns. Naturalists cannot account for the way this tree has grown.

After closely following the arm of the reservoir for about a mile, the trail turns right and crosses a wooden footbridge over Upper Merrill Creek. You now have walked approximately 5 miles. Almost immediately after crossing the bridge, you'll come to a T-junction. Here, the yellow-blazed Farmstead Trail joins from the right. Turn right, now following both black and yellow blazes. The trail follows a wide woods road, climbing gently. At the next intersection, the orange-blazed Creek Trail begins on the left, but you should turn right, continuing to follow both black and yellow blazes along a footpath. In about 15 minutes, the trail emerges onto a gravel road, with a side trail on the right leading to a wildlife blind overlooking a grassy area. Turn right to visit the blind, then backtrack, and turn right onto the black-and-yellow-blazed trail, which soon passes the ruins of the Upper Beers Farm (#5 on the park map).

Here, you have two options. If you wish to cut the hike short at this point, bear left and follow the black and yellow blazes to the entrance road, then continue to follow green and black blazes. At the next intersection, turn right and head uphill to the visitors center. If you wish to follow a longer route, turn right behind the ruined building, now following only the yellow blazes of the Farmstead Trail. After crossing a field, the trail reenters the woods.

At the next intersection, reached in about a half mile, turn right onto the blue-blazed Shoreline Trail. Soon, the yellow-blazed Farmstead Trail joins from the left. At the following intersection, the yellow blazes proceed straight ahead, but you should turn left, continuing to follow the blue-blazed Shoreline Trail. The Shoreline Trail now follows a rocky footpath along an arm of the reservoir, with the route of the Perimeter Trail, which you followed earlier in the hike, visible across the water. Many dead trees, killed when the reservoir was filled with water, can be seen at the edge of the reservoir.

Before reaching the tip of a peninsula that juts out into the reservoir, the trail turns left and heads gradually uphill to reach an open area, with views of the Inlet/Outlet Tower across the reservoir. You can often see geese and other waterfowl from here. A wooden bench provides an enjoyable resting place, and the tall post with the nesting platform is intended to attract ospreys.

Now proceed downhill until, almost at the water's edge, the blue markers direct you left onto a wide woods road. Soon a side trail to the right leads to another wildlife observation blind, this one on the water's edge. From this point, the visitors center is approximately 1 mile away.

Just before reaching the next intersection, on the right you'll notice the ruins of a lime kiln (#4 on the park map). Lime kilns

Stone ruins along the trail

DANIEL CHAZIN

were built on high ground where timber was plentiful and where the elevation caused an updraft, rather than close to the source of the raw materials needed for making lime. The kilns resembled huge stone fireplaces and sometimes served more than one farmstead. A wagon path was built to the top. The kiln was loaded with alternating layers of fuel—usually wood—and limestone chunks. When the fire was lit, temperatures frequently reached 2,000 degrees Fahrenheit, sometimes breaking up the stone with an explosive bang. The burnt lime filtered down and was used on the fields as a fertilizer.

Turn right at this intersection, now following both blue and yellow blazes. The yellow blazes leave to the left at the next intersection, with the Cathers-Shafer Farm site (#3 on the park map) on the right and the ruins of the Spring House (#2 on the park map)

on the left. Continue straight ahead, now following just blue blazes. A little farther down the trail, the ruins of the Cathers House (#1 on the park map) are on the left.

At the next intersection, you can return to the visitors center by turning left, following both blue and red blazes. But if you want to take in the final loop, continue ahead, now following the red-blazed Timber Trail. You soon reach the shore of the reservoir, with a bench at the water's edge. The red-blazed trail continues along the reservoir for a short distance and heads inland. When you reach the top of a rise, the blue trail joins in, and the visitors center can be seen immediately ahead.

At the back of the visitors center is a small garden whose plants were chosen to attract butterflies, bees, hummingbirds, and beneficial insects—a pleasant place to unwind after the hike.

26

Jockey Hollow

Total distance: 5.6 miles

Hiking time: 3 hours (allow additional time for a visit to the Wick House)

Vertical rise: 670 feet

Rating: Easy to moderate

Maps: USGS Mendham; NPS Jockey Hollow Area trail map

Trailhead GPS Coordinates: N 40° 45' 43" W 74° 32' 33"

At just under 1,000 acres, Jockey Hollow is the largest section of the Morristown National Historical Park (Morristown, NJ 07960; 973-539-2085; www.nps.gov/morr), about 3 miles south of the city of Morristown. The site, a unit of the National Park Service, is open year-round, but the visitors center and Wick House are closed on Thanksgiving, Christmas, and New Year's Day.

The visitors center offers a book nook, an orientation film, and a "talking" display of a soldier's hut. At this writing, due to budget cuts, trail maps are not available at the visitors center, but you can download a map from the park's website before you arrive. For cartographic fans, a very detailed orienteering map is available for $3.95.

You should allow time, before or after the hike, to visit the Wick House, just behind the visitors center. Henry Wick built his house around 1750 and made his living from farming and from his large woodlot. While better off than most, the family was by no means wealthy. During the winter encampment of 1779–80, the farm served as both the Wicks' home and as the headquarters of Major General Arthur St. Clair. The main building has been restored, and there is usually a ranger in attendance in period dress to explain the fascinating history.

The hike is suitable for cross-country skiing (conditions permitting) as well as hiking. There are signposts at almost every trail junction, which each include a trail map and corresponding location number. These location numbers are indicated in the text (usually within parentheses).

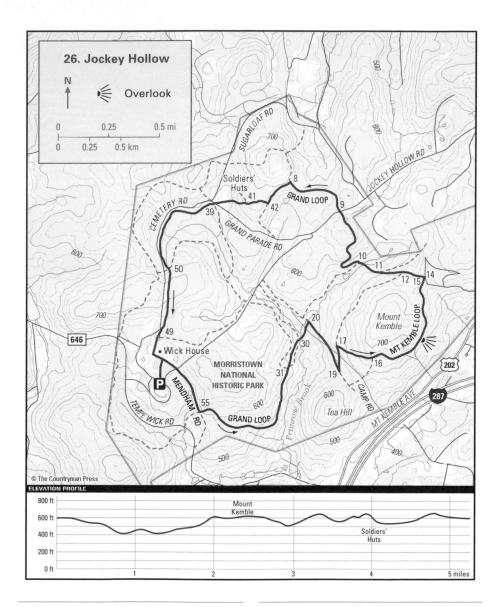

HOW TO GET THERE

Take I-287 to Exit 30B. Turn right at the traffic light onto US 202 north and follow it for 1.8 miles to Tempe Wick Road. Turn left onto Tempe Wick Road and continue for 1.3 miles to the park entrance, on the right. Drive uphill to the parking area behind the visitors center.

THE TRAIL

After stopping at the visitors center, leave by the rear door and continue along a paved path for about 250 feet. When the paved path curves left (just before an interpretive sign for the Wick Farm), you should turn right, leaving the paved path, and continue along a grassy road (shown on the park map

Soldiers' Huts

as Mendham Road). You parallel a split-rail fence on the left, with the Wick Farm orchard beyond. After crossing a paved park road, you'll pass an interpretive sign for Hand's Brigade. Continue straight ahead on the grass-covered woods road, descending slightly.

After about five minutes, you will reach a junction, marked by signpost 55. Turn left and proceed into the woods on the joint Patriots' Path/Grand Loop Trail, marked with the distinct Patriots' Path logo blaze (a tree with a path underneath on a white background) as well as white paint blazes for the Grand Loop Trail. This multi-use trail (no bikes are allowed in the park, but horses can use the trails) is a partially completed linear park, running generally alongside the Whippany River from Mendham to East Hanover.

The trail follows a wide woods road, and the walking is easy. Take time to note the surrounding forest. The huge tulip trees are not typical of New Jersey. Since the National Park Service began managing the area in the 1930s (and probably for some time before

that), there has been only inconsequential cutting of timber. The result is an unusually mature forest with a lush understory. Unfortunately the lushness is mostly the invasive Japanese barberry, a big problem in this area. For 15 to 20 minutes, the route ambles through this forest, passing many huge trees felled by Hurricane Sandy in October 2012.

After descending steadily, the trail begins to run along the side of a hill, and it becomes narrower. The trail climbs a little and descends to reach a junction (31) with the red-blazed Primrose Brook Trail, a loop trail that you will cross again in a short distance. Continue ahead, crossing two streams flowing under wide wooden bridges, the first one with a railing and the second without. Just beyond the second bridge is signpost 30 and the second crossing of the Primrose Brook Trail. Continue ahead on the joint Patriots' Path/Grand Loop Trail, which bears left.

At the next signpost (20), the Patriots' Path/Grand Loop Trail turns left, but you should turn right onto a blue-blazed trail, which heads uphill. In about ten minutes, you'll come to the next signpost (19). Ahead is a National Park Service (NPS) ranger residence, but your route turns sharply left toward the Mount Kemble Loop. A few minutes later you reach another signpost (17). Going straight ahead would shorten the hike a little by avoiding the loop, but, unless you're tired, make a right as the trail, still marked with blue blazes, now starts to circle Mount Kemble. Soon, you'll see a yellow house through the woods on the right—the same NPS ranger residence you already saw. The sounds you now hear are from I-287—the eastern boundary of the park is close by.

When you reach the next signpost (16), continue ahead on the blue-blazed trail. Just ahead, off the trail on the right, is a fenced-in exclosure. This and four others in the park were erected in the late 1980s to keep the deer out of these small areas and to study the effect their browsing has on the local vegetation.

You will shortly reach an opening in the woods with a view to the east. If you are lucky enough to have a clear day, the tall building in the distance is the top of the Empire State Building. The rest of New York City is hidden from view by the Watchung Mountains. This area was the camping grounds of Stark's Brigade—New Hampshire frontiersmen who fought at Bunker Hill, Trenton, and Princeton. Take a few moments to read the signs. This is a good spot for a break or lunch. The Watchung Mountains are the reason George Washington chose this tract for his winter encampment. Some 30 miles from New York City, and Howe's British troops, they provided a fine natural defense. Lookouts posted on ridgetops could easily spot enemy troop movements toward Morristown or across the plains toward the "capital" of Philadelphia.

In another five minutes, after passing more huge trees taken down by Hurricane Sandy, you reach a metal gate and signpost (15). A woods road leads left to a grassy area, but you should continue ahead on the blue-blazed trail, passing a private home on the right. In another minute, you'll reach signpost 14. Here, you should turn left, continuing to follow the blue blazes. You pass another metal gate and proceed slightly downhill.

When you reach the next signpost (12), which is where you would rejoin the hike if you had shortened it, take the right fork and continue to follow the blue blazes, heading slightly downhill. Bear left at signpost 11 and soon cross a small stream running through a culvert. Just beyond the culvert, you reach signpost 10. Here, the blue-blazed trail branches off to the left, but you should bear right and begin to follow the white-blazed Grand Loop Trail, which winds uphill. The trail runs close to the northeastern boundary of the park, where you can see more private residences to your right.

Cross paved Jockey Hollow Road (9), with metal gates on both sides. After descending gently, the trail begins to climb—first gradually, then more steeply. This section is the only one on which most novice skiers may have to walk.

The climb is short, and soon you reach signpost 8 at a T-intersection. The white-blazed Grand Loop Trail turns right, but you should turn left onto an unmarked trail. This trail follows undulating terrain for about five minutes until it reaches signpost 42. Here, you turn right on the yellow-blazed Soldiers Hut Trail, which heads over the hill, toward the soldiers' huts. Bear left at signpost 41, and soon you'll reach the soldiers' huts.

The NPS has reconstructed five huts as typical examples of those built by Continental troops. The one you come to first was for officers; the ones with 12 beds were for

Wick House

the troops. Some 200 huts lined this hillside during the winter of 1779–80, while perhaps as many as a thousand stood in all of Jockey Hollow. Washington ordered all of them to be constructed alike, in neat lines, with officers' huts in the rear. The majority were finished by Christmas, and those for the officers in January and February.

Proceed down and across the open field. At the base of the descent, there are several interpretive signs which explain the conditions that the soldiers endured during the harsh winter they spent here. Cross the road and proceed ahead through a grassy field with some mature cedar trees. After passing a boulder with a plaque commemorating the war dead buried here, you'll come to signpost 39 at the edge of the woods. Continue ahead along the yellow-blazed Soldiers Hut Trail, which heads gently uphill, roughly paralleling Cemetery Road.

After about 10 minutes, observe a narrower path parallel to you on the left. Look down. The stone structure with the slate top is a springhouse. The trail circles above it and soon reaches signpost 50. Turn right, following the sign for the Wick House, and proceed uphill on a yellow-blazed gravel path, passing by a number of tall trees. After descending and going through an area with much barberry and many fallen trees, the trail ends on a paved road at signpost 49, just below the Wick House barn. Turn left and follow the paved road past the barn to the Wick House. If you didn't visit the house at the start of the hike, now is a good time to do so. Follow the paved path from the Wick House back to the visitors center and your car.

You may wish to combine the hike with a visit to Washington's Headquarters and Fort Nonsense in Morristown, also part of the Morristown National Historical Park. You also might want to visit the nearby Scherman-Hoffman Wildlife Sanctuary (Hike 27).

27

Scherman–Hoffman Wildlife Sanctuary

Total distance: 1.5 miles

Hiking time: 1 hour

Vertical rise: 300 feet

Rating: Easy

Maps: USGS Mendham/Bernardsville; Scherman–Hoffman Wildlife Sanctuary park map

Trailhead GPS Coordinates: N 40° 44' 29" W 74° 33' 12.5"

The sanctuary is named for Mr. and Mrs. Harry Scherman, who donated the first 125 acres of land to the New Jersey Audubon Society in 1965, and for G. F. Hoffman, who donated adjacent parcels in 1973 and 1975 and bequeathed his home and the adjacent grounds to the society upon his death in 1981. The two-story Hoffman house, built in 1929, is now the center of sanctuary operations, housing offices, a museum, a bookstore, and rooms for programs. The sanctuary covers almost 300 acres of open space and supports more than 60 species of nesting birds. No dogs are permitted in the sanctuary.

The hike begins near the New Jersey Audubon Society facility in Bernardsville (11 Hardscrabble Road, P.O. Box 693, Bernardsville, NJ 07924; 908-766-5787; www.njaudubon.org). The Morristown National Historical Park at Jockey Hollow and the Cross Estate property are adjacent. The Hoffman Building, which houses the visitors center, should not be missed. It includes a well-stocked book and gift store, and an observation window overlooking a bird-feeding area. Stop here to obtain the park map. The Hoffman Building is closed on Mondays, although the parking lot is open daily until 5:00 PM.

HOW TO GET THERE

Take I-287 to Exit 30B and bear right at the end of the ramp onto North Maple Avenue. At the traffic light by the Olde Mill Inn, go straight across US 202 onto Childs Road; in a short distance, bear right at the fork onto Hardscrabble Road. Proceed on

Hardscrabble Road for 0.9 mile to the entrance to the New Jersey Audubon Society's Scherman-Hoffman Sanctuary, on the right. Continue up the driveway to the Hoffman Building.

THE TRAIL

To begin the hike, leave the Hoffman Building and drive back down the entrance road. Turn right onto Hardscrabble Road and take the first right into the Scherman parking lot (51 Hardscrabble Road). Walk to the kiosk at the eastern end of the parking area. Just beyond the kiosk, the footpath splits, and the Dogwood Trail is signed for both directions. The trail ahead is the one on which you will return at the end of the hike, but for now turn left and head uphill. The trail is marked by red paint blazes and by New Jersey Audubon logo blazes. There are also Patriots' Path logo blazes (a tree with a path underneath on a white background).

The trail climbs on switchbacks, steeply in places. In 0.2 mile, you'll reach a junction, marked by a signpost. Here, the Patriots' Path leaves to the left, but you should bear right to stay on the Dogwood Trail, which continues to ascend. The invasive, nonnative species of barberry has a real hold on these woods. Seeds of these plants are spread by birds and animals, and the bushes are difficult to eradicate.

River Trail along the Passaic River

DANIEL CHAZIN

Highlands

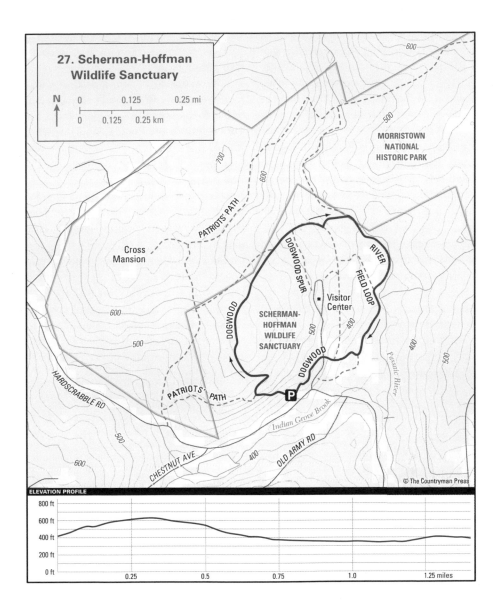

As the trail approaches the crest of the rise, the grade moderates. There are some interesting boulders to the right of the trail at the very top. The trail now begins to descend, soon passing a tree wedged at a 45-degree angle between two trunks of another tree. Interestingly, both trees are still alive, and the tree on the angle now has a trunk that is growing straight up!

A short distance beyond, a white-blazed connecting trail from the Cross Estate comes in from the left. You should bear right, continuing along the Dogwood Trail, which now descends a little more steeply.

To your right is a fenced-in deer exclosure. Soon, you'll reach a sign that indicates that the Dogwood Spur to the Hoffman Center goes off to the right, but you should continue ahead on the main Dogwood Trail. Just beyond, you'll pass several huge fallen trees below on the left.

At the next junction, bear left, following the sign for the River Trail. Follow this yellow-blazed trail (also marked with New Jersey Audubon Society logo markers) down to the Passaic River. Here, the river is an uncontaminated brook funneled between two hills, tumbling over rocks toward the Great Swamp and to Paterson and Newark beyond. Those familiar with the Passaic River farther downstream, where it is polluted and runs through industrial areas, will be surprised to find it in such pristine condition here.

The trail continues along the river for about 0.25 mile, passing several huge trees along the way—including a tulip tree that is four feet in diameter. This is the most beautiful part of the hike, and it's a good spot to take a short break.

After crossing a footbridge over a tributary stream, the River Trail ends at a junction with the green-blazed Field Loop Trail. Turn left onto the Field Loop Trail, which follows a wide woods road along the river, then bears right, away from the river. The trail crosses several wet areas on raised boardwalks and soon reaches an intersection with a signpost. Turn right, following the sign for the Field Loop Trail, which begins to ascend.

Soon, you'll emerge onto a paved road. Follow the road uphill, cross the entrance road to the sanctuary, and reenter the woods, now following the red-blazed Dogwood Trail. Continue along the Dogwood Trail for about 750 feet until you reach the parking area on Hardscrabble Road where the hike began.

Piedmont

28

Palisades

Total distance: 5.75 miles
Hiking time: 3.5 hours
Vertical rise: 600 feet
Rating: Moderate
Maps: USGS Central Park (NY/NJ); NYNJTC Hudson Palisades Trails #108 & #109; Palisades Interstate Park Commission map
Trailhead GPS Coordinates: N 40° 57' 11" W 73° 55' 14"

The Palisades Interstate Park Commission was established in 1900, mainly to curb the opening of quarries that supplied traprock for the concrete used in building roads and skyscrapers. Most of the 2,472-acre Palisades State Park is in New Jersey. The average width of the parkland between the Hudson River and the clifftop is less than 0.2 mile. Apart from the talus at their bases, the cliffs are well wooded with a variety of trees and shrubs, some of them remaining from former estate gardens. The highest elevation along the Palisades cliffs in this hike is 520 feet.

The Long Path runs along the top of the Palisades, and the Shore Trail runs along the Hudson River, following the base of the Palisades. These trails are linked by several connecting trails. This hike uses the Closter Dock Trail (orange) to descend to the Shore Trail (white), ascends on the Forest View Trail (blue/white), and returns using a section of the Long Path (aqua).

Enjoyment of the Shore Trail is enhanced by the sound of lapping water, and both the Shore Trail and the Long Path afford many superb views of the river and the Westchester County communities on the opposite shore. Hikers should beware of the ubiquitous poison ivy, especially on the Shore Trail.

HOW TO GET THERE

The hike begins at the Administration Building of the New Jersey Section of the Palisades Interstate Park (Alpine, NJ 07620; 201-768-1360; www.njpalisades.org). Access is from Exit 2 of the Palisades Interstate Parkway, approximately 7 miles north of the

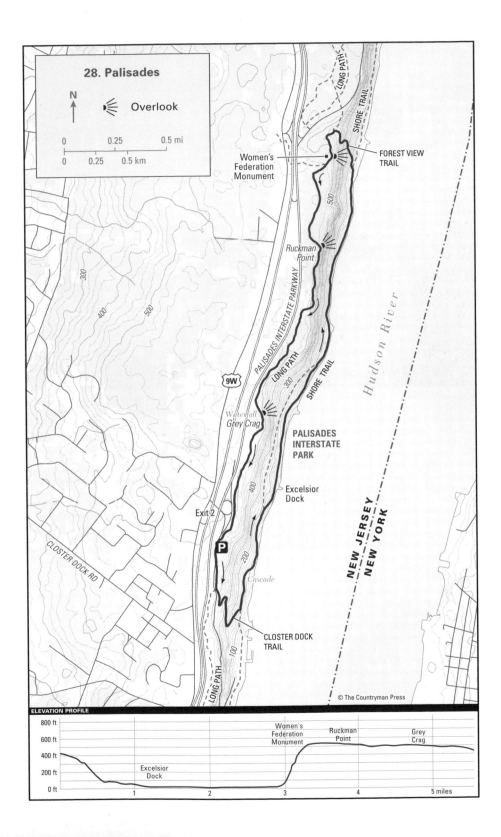

28. Palisades

N ≡ⅇ Overlook

| 0 | | 0.25 | | 0.5 mi |
| 0 | 0.25 | | 0.5 km | |

FOREST VIEW TRAIL

LONG PATH

SHORE TRAIL

Women's Federation Monument

Ruckman Point

PALISADES INTERSTATE PARKWAY

LONG PATH

9W

Waterfall
Grey Crag

SHORE TRAIL

Hudson River

PALISADES INTERSTATE PARK

Excelsior Dock

Exit 2

P

CLOSTER DOCK RD

Cascade

NEW JERSEY
NEW YORK

CLOSTER DOCK TRAIL

LONG PATH

300
400
500

300

400

200

100

© The Countryman Press

ELEVATION PROFILE

			Women's Federation Monument	Ruckman Point		Grey Crag	
800 ft							
600 ft							
400 ft							
200 ft		Excelsior Dock					
0 ft							
	1	2	3		4		5 miles

View from Ruckman Point

George Washington Bridge. From the exit, follow signs to "Police Headquarters" and park in the parking lot for the Administration Building.

The hike can also be accessed by public transportation. Take the Rockland Coaches (Coach USA) #9 or #9A bus from the George Washington Bridge Bus Terminal at 179th Street and Broadway in New York City (or the #9T or #9AT bus from the Port Authority Bus Terminal at 42nd Street and Eighth Avenue in New York City) to Closter Dock Road and US 9W in Alpine, NJ. Walk north along US 9W for about 500 feet and turn right onto the orange-blazed Closter Dock Trail, which heads east and proceeds through a tunnel under the Palisades Interstate Parkway. After going through the underpass, turn left and follow the joint Closter Dock Trail and Long Path north for 0.2 mile to a tunnel under the Alpine Approach Road. At the end of the tunnel, turn right and follow the description below.

Before starting the hike, you may wish to obtain a copy of the park map at the Administration Building (the map is also available online at www.njpalisades.org).

THE TRAIL

From the wooden sign that reads NEW JERSEY HEADQUARTERS, PALISADES INTERSTATE PARK COMMISSION (at the southern end of the parking lot) proceed ahead (south) on the Alpine Approach Road. After a very short roadwalk, you'll notice a path diverging on the left, marked by a sign that reads PATH TO RIVER and has a "no bikes" logo. Bear left and follow this path, marked by the aqua blazes of the Long Path. After passing a seasonal stream on the left, you'll come to a stone tunnel. Here, the Long Path turns right and goes through the tunnel, but you should continue straight ahead, now following the orange-blazed Closter Dock Trail, which descends on switchbacks, along a stone-lined road. The descent is about 350 feet over the course of 0.5 mile. At the base of the descent, the Closter Dock Trail ends at a junction with the white-blazed Shore Trail.

If time permits, you might want to take the opportunity, before continuing on the hike, to visit the Kearney House, just 0.1 mile down the trail to the right from this junction. Part of the house probably dates to the 1760s, and it was formerly known as Cornwallis's Headquarters. The Kearney House suffered significant damage during Hurricane Sandy in October 2012, but it is expected to be restored by the summer of 2014. The house is usually open from May through October between noon and 5 PM, but check at the Administration Building for current hours if you wish to visit the house.

If you don't visit the Kearney House, turn left at the junction and head north on the Shore Trail, which follows a wide, level path. Soon, you'll notice stone steps climbing the hillside on the left. These steps lead past a gate in a ruined fence to a stone bunker that was once used by the park to store dynamite. A short distance beyond, you'll pass a waterfall, with a circular stone wall, on the left. Then, a little farther along the Shore Trail, a side trail on the right leads downhill to a small, rocky beach with views of Yonkers, directly across the river.

About a half mile north of the Closter Dock Trail, you'll come to a fork in the trail. Here, a fallen stone marker indicates that the path to the left is known as the Upper Trail. You should bear right and continue to follow the white-blazed Shore Trail, which

descends to the river on a stone-lined road. As you approach the river, you'll pass cascades on the left and a stone jetty on the right. This jetty is all that remains of the former Excelsior Dock.

The trail continues along the river on a rocky path, with panoramic views across the river. You can see both Amtrak and Metro-North trains traveling along the east bank of the river. In half a mile, you'll pass another cascade on the left and then a stone jetty on the right. This is the site of Twombly's Landing, believed to have been a Native American campsite because of the layers of oyster shells found here. Note the quaint stone picnic tables in this area. A short distance beyond, you'll pass on the left the northern end of the Upper Trail and continue ahead on a level dirt path, soon passing more old stone picnic tables.

A little farther north on the trail, you'll reach the first unobstructed views of the Palisades cliffs. Above, you can see Ruckman Point, and it is interesting to note that in a little while you will be looking down at the river from this point on the cliffs. A short distance beyond, you get a good view of Indian Head, farther north along the river, and you can see the Tappan Zee Bridge in the distance.

After passing through an area with many tangled vines, you'll reach a junction with the blue/white-blazed Forest View Trail, marked by a sign and a triple blaze. The Shore Trail continues ahead to the Giant Stairs, a difficult rock scramble, but you should turn left onto the Forest View Trail, which begins a steady climb on switchbacks and rock steps. You'll be climbing about 400 vertical feet in only 0.3 mile.

At the top of a long flight of rock steps, you'll come to a trail junction. Directly ahead, the trail crosses a stream on a wooden footbridge, but you should turn left to continue on the blue/white-blazed Forest View Trail,

Women's Federation Monument

DANIEL CHAZIN

which is now joined by the aqua-blazed Long Path. After climbing another 100 vertical feet, you'll reach a stone "castle," known as the Women's Federation Monument. This "castle" was built by the New Jersey Federation of Women's Clubs in 1929 to commemorate their efforts in the late 19th century to preserve the Palisades from quarrying. This spot affords a panoramic view over the Hudson River, and you'll want to stop here and take a break.

When you're ready to continue, proceed ahead on the joint Forest View Trail/Long Path. In a short distance, the Forest View Trail turns right onto a woods road leading to a footbridge over the Parkway, but you should cross the woods road and continue ahead. In about 500 feet, follow the aqua-blazed Long Path as it turns left onto another woods road. You'll pass through an area where many trees were felled by Hurricane Sandy in October 2012. Soon, the road curves to the left and crosses a concrete bridge over a stream. Just ahead is a concrete-block wall at the cliff edge. To its right is Ruckman Point, a rock outcrop with carved graffiti, some of which is more than a century old! This outcrop, which stands 520 feet above the river, offers panoramic views up and down the Hudson, with a particularly dramatic section of the cliffs visible just to the north. In the river, just beyond these cliffs,

you may notice some pilings jutting out of the water. These are the remains of the former Forest View marina, abandoned after World War II.

The Long Path now heads south, parallel to the cliffs. At one point, it bears right, crosses a stream on rocks, then turns left and runs closer to the Parkway. In the next mile, you'll cross two wooden bridges over streams. Just beyond the second bridge, look for a short trail on the left that heads toward the cliff edge. The trail leads to a viewpoint over a seasonal waterfall pouring through a cleft in the cliff, with panoramic views of the Hudson River below. Be sure to take care when you approach the cliff edge, as there is no protective fencing at this location. In the spring, drifts of snowdrops bloom here.

Only a short distance farther down the main trail, watch for another footpath to the left, leading over a bridge to a secluded lookout called Gray Crag. Here, a section of rock has separated from the cliff. The bridge has no railings, so use caution if you choose to cross it.

A short distance beyond, you'll cross another stream on a wide wooden bridge. Soon, the trail approaches the ramps of Exit 2 of the Parkway, and it finally emerges onto the parking lot by the Administration Building, where you left your car.

29

Rockleigh Woods Sanctuary and Lamont Reserve

Total distance: 2.4 miles

Hiking time: 1.5 hours

Vertical rise: 400 feet

Rating: Easy to moderate

Maps: Maps: USGS Central Park (NY/NJ); NYNJTC Hudson Palisades Trails #109; NYNJTC Rockleigh Woods/Lamont Reserve trail map

Trailhead GPS Coordinates: N 41° 00' 14.5" W 73° 55' 32.5"

The land traversed by this hike, on the western slope of the Palisades, was formerly owned by the Lamont family, which donated it to the Boy Scouts of America, Greater New York Councils. For many years, it was part of the Boy Scouts' Alpine Scout Camp. In 1975, the Borough of Rockleigh (one of the smallest municipalities in New Jersey, with a population of only about 500) purchased more than 81 acres of the Lamont tract from the Boy Scouts and established the Rockleigh Woods Sanctuary.

Then, in the early 1990s, the Scouts decided to put the remainder of the Lamont tract—which was not extensively used as part of the camp—up for sale. The most likely use was going to be residential development. Residents of the boroughs of Rockleigh and Alpine, in which the tract was located, did not wish to see houses built on the slope of Palisades overlooking their communities. Working with Bergen County and the Green Acres program of the State of New Jersey, they raised the necessary funds to acquire the 134-acre Lamont Reserve and preserve it as open space.

Soon after the Lamont tract was acquired in 1996, a network of trails was established on the property and on the adjacent Rockleigh Woods Sanctuary. The trails, however, were not maintained and became difficult to follow. In 2005, the New York–New Jersey Trail Conference assumed maintenance of the trail system in the area, and the trails have been improved and expanded under the leadership of dedicated volunteers.

This delightful hike loops around the

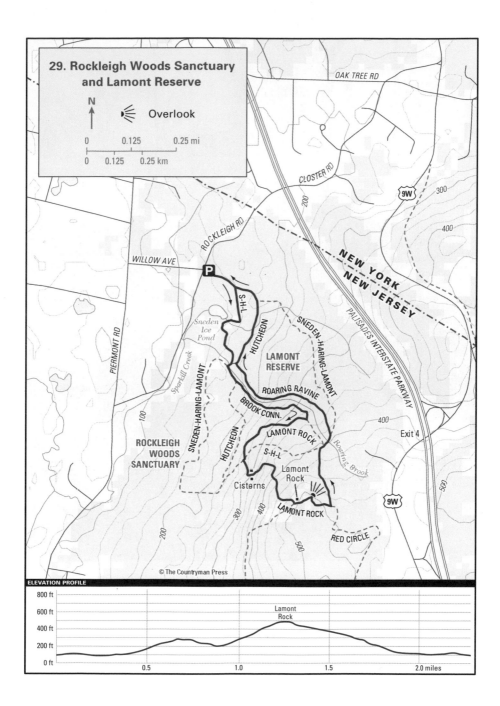

29. Rockleigh Woods Sanctuary and Lamont Reserve

N

Overlook

0   0.125   0.25 mi

0   0.125   0.25 km

OAK TREE RD

CLOSTER RD

ROCKLEIGH RD

WILLOW AVE

P

NEW YORK
NEW JERSEY

9W

300

400

200

Sneden
Ice
Pond

S-H-L

HUTCHEON

SNEDEN-HARING-LAMONT

PALISADES INTERSTATE PARKWAY

LAMONT
RESERVE

ROARING RAVINE

BROOK CONN.

Sparkill Creek

SNEDEN-HARING-LAMONT

HUTCHEON

LAMONT ROCK

S-H-L

ROCKLEIGH
WOODS
SANCTUARY

Cisterns

Lamont
Rock

LAMONT ROCK

Roaring Brook

400

Exit 4

9W

500

100

300

400

200

500

RED CIRCLE

© The Countryman Press

ELEVATION PROFILE

800 ft				
600 ft		Lamont Rock		
400 ft				
200 ft				
0 ft	0.5	1.0	1.5	2.0 miles

Lamont Rock

reserve and sanctuary, climbing a scenic ravine along the cascading Roaring Brook and
passing several features of historical interest. The trailhead is at the rear of Rockleigh
Borough Hall, where parking is available. For
more information, contact the Borough of
Rockleigh, 26 Rockleigh Road, Rockleigh,
NJ 07647, 201-768-4217; www.rockleigh

.org. A free trail map (without contours) is
available online at www.nynjtc.org.

HOW TO GET THERE

Take the Palisades Interstate Parkway to Exit
4. Turn left at the bottom of the ramp onto
US 9W (if coming from the north, turn right
onto US 9W) and proceed for 1.1 miles,

entering New York. At the next traffic light, turn left onto Oak Tree Road and, in 0.2 mile, turn left onto Closter Road. In 0.5 mile, after crossing under the Parkway, you reenter New Jersey, and the road becomes Rockleigh Road. Continue for another 0.2 mile to the Rockleigh Municipal Building (26 Rockleigh Road) and turn left into the driveway. Park behind the building.

THE TRAIL

From the parking area, follow a handicapped-accessible path to a playground, where a triple blue blaze on a tree to the right marks the start of the Hutcheon Trail. Follow this blue-blazed trail past a GREEN ACRES sign into the woods.

In a short distance, you'll notice a triple yellow blaze on a tree to the right. Turn right and follow the yellow-blazed Sneden-Haring-Lamont Trail, which heads south, closely paralleling the sanctuary boundary. Continue to follow this trail as it turns right and crosses a brook on a culvert. To the right is the Sneden Ice Pond. In the 19th century, ice was cut from this pond in the winter and sold locally to those having their own ice houses. When snow covered the ground, the ice was transported in horse-drawn wooden sleds. Just beyond, the trail turns left at a signpost and crosses the inlet stream of the pond.

As the trail approaches the wide Roaring Brook, the blue-blazed Hutcheon Trail joins from the left, and both trails cross the brook on rocks. This crossing can be difficult when the water is high, and there are plans to improve it. On the other side, turn left and follow the blue blazes, which parallel the brook. Soon, you'll notice a triple-orange blaze, which marks the start of the Brook

Sneden's Ice Pond

DANIEL CHAZIN

Connector Trail, on a tree to the left. Turn left and follow this trail—the newest trail in the sanctuary, blazed by volunteers in early 2013—which continues to parallel the scenic Roaring Brook.

In a quarter mile, the Brook Connector Trail ends at a junction with the white-blazed Lamont Rock Trail. Turn right onto this trail, which descends briefly, then bears left, crosses an old, eroded woods road, and passes an area with many trees toppled by Hurricane Sandy in October 2012. The Lamont Rock Trail briefly joins the yellow-blazed Sneden-Haring-Lamont Trail, but when the two trails diverge, turn left and continue to follow the white blazes.

The Lamont Rock Trail now climbs steadily, soon passing two old stone cisterns, part of a system that once supplied water to homes in the area. It continues to climb to Lamont Rock (a huge boulder), on the left. Note the rectangular depression on one side of the boulder, where a plaque was once affixed. Just beyond, the white trail turns left and is joined by the Red Circle Trail that leads into Boy Scout Camp Alpine.

Follow the joint white and red trails as they climb on a footpath to the highest point in the preserve (440 feet). The view from this spot is largely obscured by foliage, but you can catch a glimpse of the Hudson River through the trees when they're bare.

The joint trails now turn right and begin to descend. Soon, the Red Circle Trail leaves to the right, but you should turn left and continue along the white-blazed Lamont Rock Trail. In about 0.2 mile, the yellow-blazed Sneden-Haring-Lamont Trail joins from the left, and the Lamont Rock Trail ends just beyond.

Bear left and follow the yellow trail along a wide woods road, crossing Roaring Brook on rocks. A short distance beyond, turn left onto the red-blazed Roaring Brook Trail and follow it as it descends along the north side of the brook. You followed the other side of this brook on the way up. At the base of the descent, the Roaring Brook Trail ends at a junction with the blue-blazed Hutcheon Trail. Turn right onto the blue-blazed trail, which descends gradually, crossing an old stone bridge over a brook, and follow it back to the parking area where the hike began.

30

High Mountain

Total distance: 4 miles	
Hiking time: 2.5 hours	
Vertical rise: 400 feet	
Rating: Moderate	
Maps: Maps: USGS Paterson; NYNJTC Jersey Highlands Trails (Central North Region) Map #125; Wayne Township High Mountain trails map	
Trailhead GPS Coordinates: N 40° 57' 07" W 74° 12' 01"	

This loop hike traverses the 1,154-acre High Mountain Park Preserve. In August 1993, Wayne Township, the State of New Jersey, and The Nature Conservancy acquired the lands that compose this preserve from Urban Farms, Inc., a subsidiary of McBride Enterprises of Franklin Lakes, NJ. The preserve is managed jointly by the three owners. It is situated along the Preakness Range, a northern continuation of the Second Watchung Ridge. The hike climbs to the summit of High Mountain, the highest mountain on the East Coast south of Maine with a view of the ocean, which offers a spectacular view of the New York City skyline.

A free trail map is available online at www.waynetownship.com/maps/mountain park.pdf

HOW TO GET THERE

Take NJ 208 west to the second Goffle Road exit (towards Hawthorne/Paterson) and turn right at the end of the ramp. At the next light, just beyond the intersection with Goffle Hill Road, turn right onto North Watchung Drive. At a stop sign at the top of the hill, turn sharply right onto Rea Avenue, which becomes North Haledon Avenue and then Linda Vista Avenue. At a T-intersection with Terrace Avenue, turn right, then bear left to continue on Linda Vista Avenue, which leads into William Paterson University (Entry 6). At the next stop sign, turn right and continue for 0.4 mile to a small parking area on the right, with a sign reading HIGH MOUNTAIN PARK.

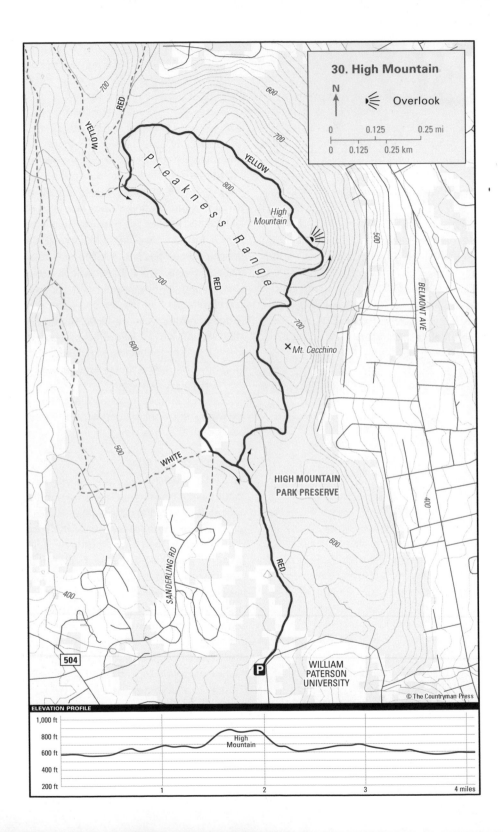

30. High Mountain

N

Overlook

| 0 | 0.125 | 0.25 mi |
| 0 | 0.125 | 0.25 km |

RED

YELLOW

Preakness Range

700

800

600

700

YELLOW

High Mountain

500

RED

700

× Mt. Cecchino

BELMONT AVE

700

600

500

WHITE

400

HIGH MOUNTAIN
PARK PRESERVE

SANDERLING RD

400

600

RED

504

P

WILLIAM
PATERSON
UNIVERSITY

© The Countryman Press

ELEVATION PROFILE

1,000 ft			
800 ft	High Mountain		
600 ft			
400 ft			
200 ft			
1	2	3	4 miles

THE TRAIL

From the kiosk near the entrance to the parking lot, follow a gravel path across an open area that heads northeast, parallel to College Road. A double-red blaze at the edge of the woods marks the start of the Red Trail, which you should follow into the woods. After passing a huge boulder on the left, the Red Trail turns left onto a footpath. It soon reaches a T-intersection, where it again turns left, this time onto an eroded woods road.

In another half mile, you'll reach a high point on the trail where a triple-yellow blaze on a small rock marks the start of the Yellow Trail. Turn right onto this trail, which descends to cross a small stream in a wet area. It then curves north, passing just west of the low ridge known as Mt. Cecchino. Three-quarters of a mile along the yellow trail, you'll cross a small stream. From here,

the trail begins a steady climb to the summit of High Mountain. Near the top, the trail bears left, bypassing an eroded section of the road, but it soon rejoins the road.

Just before arriving at the summit, you'll reach a panoramic east-facing viewpoint. On the horizon, beyond the suburban sprawl of northeastern New Jersey, you can see the New York City skyline, the Verrazano-Narrows Bridge and even a corner of the Atlantic Ocean. Continue up to the summit, which resembles a grassy southern bald, with a few large exposures of the basaltic bedrock. From the summit, both the New York City skyline to the east and the ridge of the Watchung Mountains to the south are visible.

Head northwest across the broad summit, following the yellow blazes on rocks, and continue downhill on the Yellow Trail. Take care to follow the yellow blazes, as

East-facing view from the summit of High Mountain DANIEL CHAZIN

Summit of High Mountain

several paths and woods roads lead down the mountain. The Yellow Trail crosses a secondary summit, levels off, and then descends steeply on an eroded woods road.

Near the base of the descent, be alert for a sharp left turn where the yellow blazes leave the woods road and enter the woods on a footpath. This section of the trail is a refreshing change from the worn woods roads that you have been following. Continue along the Yellow Trail, which descends to a stream, parallels it, and then crosses it. About 250 feet beyond the stream crossing, you'll reach a woods road.

The Yellow Trail turns right here, but you should turn left onto the road, marked with

the red blazes of the Red Trail. Head south on this trail, passing through an area which is often wet. After a woods road branches off to the left, the trail becomes drier.

Further down the road, the trail passes several clusters of cedar trees, and it descends over slabs of exposed basalt. After you hike about a mile on the Red Trail, the White Trail begins to the right, but you should continue following the Red Trail. Then, in another 500 feet, you'll reach the junction with the Yellow Trail that you encountered earlier in the hike. Proceed ahead on the Red Trail (now retracing your steps) and follow it back to the parking lot where the hike began.

31

South Mountain Reservation

Total distance: 8.7 miles (short hike
is approximately 5 miles)

Hiking time: 6 hours (short hike is
approximately 4 hours)

Vertical rise: 750 feet

Rating: Moderate

Maps: USGS Caldwell/Roselle;
Essex County Park Commission
South Mountain Reservation map

Trailhead GPS Coordinates:
N 40° 43' 39" W 74° 18' 14"

South Mountain Reservation has much to offer in the midst of a built-up area. The 2,048-acre tract contains a substantial river, many streams and cascades, a 25-foot waterfall, and 19 miles of trails through gentle woodland. At least for the first part of the hike, the trails are mostly free from traffic noise. The first and second of the three Watchung ridges form the eastern and western boundaries of the reservation. The name "Watchung" is a legacy from the Lenape Native Americans, to whom the ridges were the "high hills." The Watchung ridges are intrusions (or extrusions) of lava similar to those of the Palisades. As these layers rose from west to east and were glaciated, the top layer of the Watchungs cooled more quickly than the lower layers that formed the Palisades. Because the layers in South Mountain Reservation cooled more quickly, the hexagonal columns that formed are considerably smaller than those on the Palisades. These ridges were heavily lumbered before the Revolutionary War to supply firewood for New York City and again in the late 19th century to provide wood for the nearby paper mills. A number of very large trees remain in the reservation, some of them twisted into deformed shapes.

This figure-eight hike follows the yellow-blazed Lenape Trail, the orange-blazed Turtle Back Trail, and the white-blazed Rahway Trail. The Lenape Trail honors the state's original inhabitants and preeminent foot travelers; the Turtle Back Trail was named for the rocks in the reservation that show erosion markings similar to the markings on a

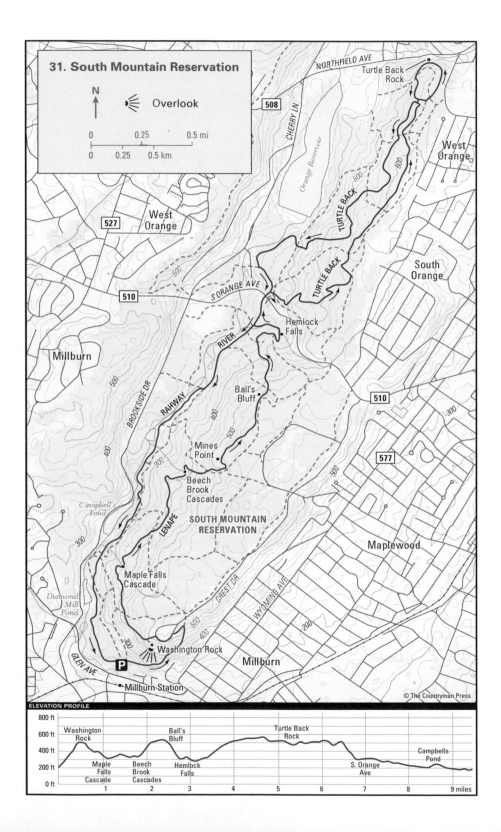

31. South Mountain Reservation

N

≋ Overlook

| 0 | 0.25 | 0.5 mi |
| 0 | 0.25 | 0.5 km |

NORTHFIELD AVE

Turtle Back Rock

508

CHERRY LN

Orange Reservoir

TURTLE BACK

West Orange

500

600

West Orange

527

South Orange

S ORANGE AVE

510

Hemlock Falls

TURTLE BACK

RIVER

500

Millburn

RAHWAY

Ball's Bluff

510

300

BROOKSIDE DR

400

Mines Point

500

577

Campbell's Pond

Beech Brook Cascades

300

LENAPE

SOUTH MOUNTAIN RESERVATION

Maplewood

400

Diamond Mill Pond

Maple Falls Cascade

CREST DR

500

WYOMING AVE

400

200

300

GLEN AVE

300

P

≋ Washington Rock

Millburn

Millburn Station

© The Countryman Press

ELEVATION PROFILE

800 ft								
600 ft	Washington Rock		Ball's Bluff		Turtle Back Rock			
400 ft								Campbells Pond
200 ft	Maple Falls Cascade	Beech Brook Cascades	Hemlock Falls				S. Orange Ave	
0 ft	1	2	3	4	5	6	7	8	9 miles

turtle's back; and the Rahway Trail takes its name from the river it parallels. Turtle-back rocks were formed when the volcanic basalt rock characteristic of the Watchungs, known as "traprock," fractured into small hexagonal blocks. The cracks filled with minerals, and, when erosion wore away the traprock faster than the minerals, the result was a patterned rock similar to the markings on the back of a turtle. There are several examples of this type of rock throughout South Mountain Reservation, and one at the northeastern corner of the park, along the route of this hike, is actually called Turtle Back Rock. It is believed that the word "traprock" is derived from the Scandinavian word, "trappa," meaning "stair step." When the traprock layers erode, the resulting rock formation often resembles steps.

The Essex Park Commission was established in 1895 and, drawing on the ideas of famed landscape architect Frederick Law Olmsted, and in consultation with his firm, created 23 parks and three reservations within the county. Olmsted also designed New York City's Central Park. Although the concept of South Mountain Reservation was Olmsted's, many of the features of the reservation, such as bridges, trails, and steps, were built by the Civilian Conservation Corps in 1934.

The distance covered in this hike is nearly 9 miles, although a shorter 5-mile option, which leaves out the northern loop, is also possible. Except at the very start, there are no long climbs, so the hike is useful for developing a good walking pace and increasing hiking stamina. The woods and rhododendron groves make the trail an excellent spring hike, although the area near the Rahway River is sometimes wet. The groves of rhododendron, wild azalea, and mountain laurel were planted, together with white pine and hemlock, when the land was acquired by the Essex County Park Commission at the beginning of the 20th century in an effort to eradicate the previous damage done by logging and paper mills.

Although maps are not available at the reservation, a black-and-white trail map for South Mountain Reservation can be found online at www.essex-countynj.org/p/SMR-Trail-Map_letter.pdf.

HOW TO GET THERE

Driving from the east, take I-78 to Exit 50B (Maplewood, Millburn) and continue north on Vaux Hall Road for 0.7 mile. Turn left onto Millburn Avenue, and in 0.5 mile, bear right onto Essex Street, where a one-way traffic system begins. Just past the Millburn railroad station, turn right onto Lackawanna Place. Turn right at the next intersection (Glen Avenue) and make an immediate left turn into the Locust Grove parking area.

Approaching on I-78 from the west, you will need to make a U-turn at Exit 54.

The trailhead is readily accessible by public transportation, as the Millburn station on the Morristown Line of NJ Transit is directly opposite the Locust Grove parking area. From the western end of the platform at the Millburn station, walk down the stairway to Lackawanna Place, turn right, and cross Glen Avenue to enter the park at the Locust Grove parking area.

THE TRAIL

From the kiosk at the northeast corner of the parking area, follow the yellow-blazed Lenape Trail, which bears right onto a gravel road leading to a picnic area. The trail continues through the picnic area, where there is a year-round spring on the left protected by a small brick structure. Past the rain shelter and picnic tables, the trail begins climbing the First Watchung Mountain on a wide path. It bears right at a fork, then turns right at a T-intersection (marked by a chain-link fence) onto a woods road, continuing to climb. As you climb, you will pass below a large concrete structure, part of the old waterworks system used to supply East Orange with water, and circle it.

At the top of the rise, follow the yellow blazes as they turn left, leaving the road, and continue on a footpath to the paved Crest Drive (closed to vehicular traffic), where the Lenape Trail turns left and begins to follow the road. Here, the first large rhododendrons may be seen. As the road curves to the right, the New York City skyline may be seen to the left on a clear day if there are no leaves on the trees, with the towers of the Verrazano-Narrows Bridge visible in the distance to the right. Just ahead, you'll notice a plaque on a boulder, known as Washington Rock.

Dedicated in 1992, the plaque describes the events of 1780, which George Washington watched from this point. It details the efforts of the British to destroy the American supply base at Morristown, the burning of Connecticut Farms (now called Union), and other military events. The plaque notes that, after the British efforts failed, they were forced to retire and "quit New Jersey soil forever." History tells us that, at the time of the Revolution, nearly all the trees in New Jersey suitable for shipbuilding and housing had been chopped down, providing enough visibility to observe the movements of the British in the valley. A sentry was posted at Washington Rock, and as soon as he became aware of troop movements in the valley below, a bonfire was lit to alert the soldiers at Jockey Hollow. Another stone marker commemorates Paul R. Jackson, a friend of the park.

Continue along the yellow-blazed Lenape Trail, which turns left, leaving the road, and descends to an observation platform with stone pillars. The view from here is to the southwest, with Millburn and the NJ Transit railroad tracks visible below (partially obscured by the trees), and I-78 and the Watchung Reservation—the continuation of the Watchung range beyond the Millburn-Springfield gap—ahead in the distance.

When you're ready to continue, turn left and follow the Lenape Trail, which descends on a footpath. Soon, you'll notice an unmarked side trail to the left that leads to a fenced overlook. An abandoned quarry is directly below, with Millburn and the Watchung range in the distance. A short distance beyond, the Lenape Trail crosses a bridle path designated on the park map as the Sunset Trail. After a short descent, it crosses a small stream, with the Maple Falls Cascade—where the stream plunges down a 25-foot sluiceway of exposed basalt—to the left, downstream. This is a good spot for a short break.

After climbing away from the brook, the trail follows a relatively level footpath, crossing another bridle path (this one named the Pingry Trail). It turns sharply right at Lilliput Knob (an example of a turtle-back rock) and reaches Beech Brook Cascades—where two brooks converge—about 1.8 miles from the start. Beyond the cascade, the trail begins a gradual climb, paralleling a brook in a shallow ravine to the right. After bearing left and crossing a bridle path called the Overlook Trail, the trail climbs to reach Mines Point—named for exploratory pits dug by copper prospectors around 1800. Here, the trail bears right and heads north, first climbing gently through a relatively open area, then descending to reach Ball's Bluff, where old stone pillars are remnants of a picnic shelter built in 1908.

The Lenape Trail continues to descend, crossing a bridle path (the Ball's Bluff Trail) on the way. Toward the base of the descent, it begins to parallel a stream flowing

Hemlock Falls

South Mountain Reservation

through a ravine to the right. After crossing the stream and turning left, the trail reaches an eroded road, turns right, and climbs to the top of a rise. The trail bears left, leaving the road, descends along a switchback, then turns sharply left. Just beyond, it reaches the base of Hemlock Falls, a scenic waterfall, and crosses a footbridge over the stream. A red-blazed trail climbs stone steps to the top of the waterfall, and benches afford an opportunity to rest and enjoy the beautiful setting. You are now about 3 miles into the hike, and the falls are a wonderful place to take a break.

Cross the stone bridge, leaving the falls on the right, and at the end of the bridge turn left. At first, the trail is on a wide path, but soon after passing another pretty falls on the right and another substantial stone bridge on the left (which now leads nowhere), the footpath becomes narrower and reaches a signpost and a T-intersection with a bridle path. (If you wish to shorten your hike to approximately 5 miles, turn left on the bridle path and pick up the description below).

The River Trail, a bridle path to the left, will be the route for your return journey, and the white-blazed Rahway Trail is straight ahead. Turn right, following the yellow blazes of the Lenape Trail uphill on a wide woods road to the top of the rise, then turn left at an enormous deformed oak tree, just before a metal gate and a small parking lot on South Orange Avenue.

Soon, the trail crosses over South Orange Avenue on a footbridge. Just beyond, you'll

Turtle Back Rock

reach a junction, where the yellow-blazed Lenape Trail turns left. Turn right, leaving the Lenape Trail, and follow the orange-blazed Turtle Back Trail, which curves right, then left, and passes a huge tree. After crossing a bridle path at a culvert, you'll reach a signpost for the Turtle Back Trail. Follow the orange blazes uphill, and at a double blaze continue along the Turtle Back Trail as it turns left onto a footpath and climbs on switchbacks. The trail follows along the side of a hill, overlooking the valley below, then winds around more switchbacks and begins to parallel a ravine, below on the right.

After climbing yet another switchback, you'll reach a four-way junction, where an orange/white-blazed trail begins on the left. You should turn right to continue on the orange-blazed Turtle Back Trail. A short distance beyond, the orange trail approaches a bridle path (the Longwood Trail) but turns left and continues on a footpath. Follow the trail, which now heads north, roughly parallel to the bridle path.

The orange-blazed trail proceeds along a relatively level footpath, passing many trees felled by Hurricane Sandy in October 2012. After crossing three more bridle paths in the next mile, the trail reaches a T-intersection. Here, the orange blazes turn left. You'll be returning on the orange-blazed trail, but you'll first want to see the interesting Turtle Back Rock. To reach this feature, turn right onto an orange/white-blazed trail. Just ahead, follow the orange/white blazes as they turn left onto a bridle path, but when the bridle path curves left, continue straight on a footpath.

The orange/white-blazed trail soon curves to the left and begins to run above the busy Northfield Avenue. After a turn to the right, you'll reach the Turtle Back Rock, named for the patterns on the surface of the rock. An interpretive sign explains how this unusual rock was formed. The best examples of the

turtle-back patterns can be seen on the back of the large rock, as well on smaller adjacent rocks.

Continue ahead, crossing another bridle path (the North Trail), and you'll soon reach a four-way junction. The orange/white-blazed trail turns left here, but you should continue straight ahead, now once again following the orange-blazed Turtle Back Trail. Over the next mile, the trail crosses two bridle paths and begins to descend. You may be able to glimpse the southern end of the Orange Reservoir through the trees when they are bare.

Be alert for a sharp right turn where the orange-blazed trail descends to cross another bridle path (the Reservoir Trail), then bears left and continues to descend on a woods road. Before reaching a stream, the orange-blazed trail turns left onto a footpath and continues parallel to the stream. After climbing a little and passing a cascade in the stream, the trail proceeds through a pine grove. It soon reaches a junction with the yellow-blazed Lenape Trail, where you should turn left and proceed uphill on a wide path, now following both yellow and orange blazes. After passing through a pine grove, you'll reach the junction where you began the loop on the Turtle Back Trail. Turn right, rejoining the yellow-blazed Lenape Trail, and recross the footbridge over South Orange Avenue. Turn right at the familiar distorted old tree on your left and walk down to the signpost. (If you have shortened the hike, pick up the description at this point.)

Head south, straight ahead, on the bridle path (the River Trail) and in about a half mile, turn right toward a bridge over the Rahway River. Just before the bridge, look for white blazes on a tree to the left. Turn left and head south on the white-blazed Rahway Trail, which you will follow to the end of the hike. The trail makes a few detours up to the River Trail to utilize the bridges over streams, crosses another woods road, and enters a prolific rhododendron grove just as Campbell's Pond comes into view.

Shortly thereafter, the trail passes Diamond Hill Pond, and until its end is sandwiched between the bridle path on its left and the beautiful Rahway River on its right. It is interesting to look at the dams across the Rahway River. Some are derelict, with water seeping through the structures, and one in particular is unprotected from the trail side but gated on the other side. The trail passes close to an old building that once served as a steam-driven pumping station. The large boilers housed in this building formerly provided steam for pumping water to a reservoir on the hills, using water from Campbell's Pond. Campbell's Pond is very shallow, probably not more than a foot in depth. Traffic noise from Brookside Drive is encountered along this section of the trail.

The trail goes along the side of a small hill, just before the library and the parking lot for Millburn station become visible to the right. Just beyond, you arrive at the Locust Grove parking area and your car.

32

Watchung Reservation

Total distance: 6.5 miles	
Hiking time: 4 hours	
Vertical rise: 500 feet	
Rating: Moderate	
Maps: USGS Chatham/Roselle; Union County Department of Parks and Recreation park map	
Trailhead GPS Coordinates: N 40° 40' 59" W 74° 22' 27"	

Watchung Reservation is a 2,000-acre patch of wooded land straddling the first and second Watchung ridges in central New Jersey. Although it sits in the middle of sub-urbia, the reservation is large enough for a good workout and also contains a number of interesting features, most of which you will see on this hike.

The name Watchung is derived from the Lenape word for "high hills," *Wachunk*. Along with South Mountain Reservation and Eagle Rock Reservation to the north, Watchung Reservation has preserved as wilderness a portion of the long mountain that overlooks the flat plains leading toward New York City and the Atlantic Ocean. General George Washington used the long Watchung ridge as a natural fortification against the British during the Revolutionary War. He planted a number of lookouts along the ridge and kept his troops safely to the west, in Loantaka and Jockey Hollow. At the end of the previous Ice Age, the Watchung ridge formed the eastern rim of the basin that contained glacial Lake Passaic, a 30-by-10-mile lake, of which the Great Swamp is but a remnant.

Watchung Reservation is laced with wide lanes and horse trails. Several shorter marked trails are found in the vicinity of the Trailside Museum. The longest trail is the white-blazed Sierra Trail. It is 10 miles long, has many ups and downs, and passes near just about every interesting feature the reservation has to offer. It is not a simple path, but one that links many trails in the reservation, making it necessary to watch for double

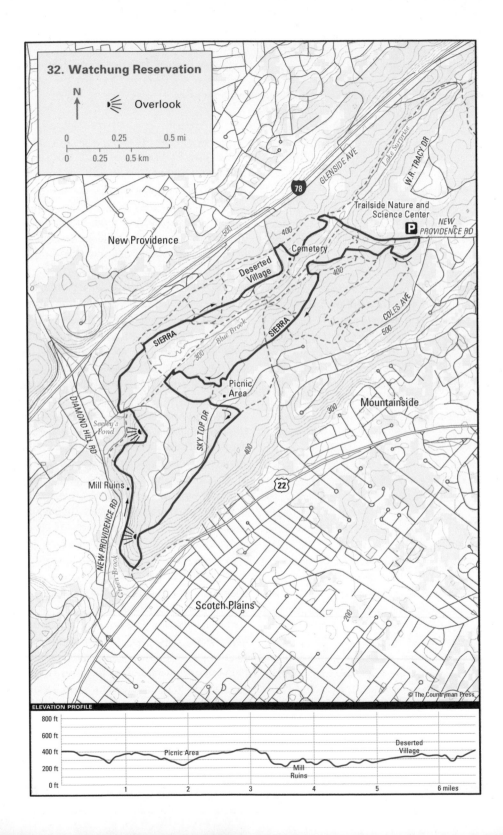

32. Watchung Reservation

N

⤙ Overlook

| 0 | 0.25 | 0.5 mi |
| 0 | 0.25 | 0.5 km |

GLENSIDE AVE

Lake Surprise

W.R. TRACY DR

78

400

500

Trailside Nature and
Science Center

New Providence

NEW
PROVIDENCE RD

P

Cemetery

400

Deserted
Village

COLES AVE

500

SIERRA

SIERRA

Blue Brook

300

Picnic
Area

Mountainside

DIAMOND HILL RD

Seeley's
Pond

300

SKY TOP DR

400

300

Mill Ruins

22

NEW PROVIDENCE RD

Green Brook

Scotch Plains

200

© The Countryman Press

ELEVATION PROFILE

800 ft						
600 ft						
400 ft		Picnic Area				Deserted Village
200 ft				Mill Ruins		
0 ft	1	2	3	4	5	6 miles

blazes that signal turns. You will use a large portion of this trail for your hike.

Unfortunately, I-78 runs along the northern boundary of the reservation, and the noise from this busy highway's traffic can be heard for part of the hike. During the late 1970s and early 1980s, many conservation-minded people tried to prevent the construction of this major interstate highway, which planners wanted to route through the northern section of the reservation. The issue was finally settled by replacing the land used for the highway, which totaled about 70 acres, with land from an adjacent rock quarry. When the deal was struck, $3.6 million was appropriated for the upkeep and development of the reservation. The highway was built low in the ground and is flanked by walls that muffle the sound somewhat. In one place, a cut-and-cover structure—a 220-foot-wide bridge with soil and plants— allows animals to cross the highway safely.

An excellent map of the reservation, published by the Union County Department of Parks and Recreation, is available at the Trailside Nature and Science Center or online at http://ucnj.org/community /watchung-reservation.

HOW TO GET THERE
Take I-78 West to Exit 43 (New Providence /Berkeley Heights). At the first traffic light, turn right onto McMane Avenue. When you reach the T-intersection with Glenside Avenue in 0.7 mile, turn left. Then, in 1.2 miles, turn right onto W.R. Tracy Drive (County Route 645) and enter the reservation. You will pass Surprise Lake and some picnic areas. When you reach the traffic circle in 1.3 miles, take the first right onto Summit Lane, then bear right onto New Providence Road. The parking area is to the right, where the road makes a sharp left turn.

If coming from the west on I-78, take

Exit 44 and turn left at the traffic light onto Glenside Avenue. Turn right onto W.R Tracy Drive (County Route 645) and follow the directions above.

THE TRAIL
From the Trailside Nature and Science Center, adjacent to the parking area, proceed west (downhill) on the extension of New Providence Road, marked with the white blazes of the Sierra Trail. Opposite a DO NOT ENTER sign, turn left, following the white-blazed Sierra Trail, now joined by the Green Trail and the pink-blazed History Trail, and cross a bridge over a brook. As you cross the bridge, note the exposure of bedrock in the streambed. These rocks are basalt, or traprock, which has been quarried extensively throughout the Watchung Mountains.

The trail continues through the woods and, after crossing wooden bridges over two streams, reaches a junction with the Yellow Trail. Turn right, now following both white and yellow blazes, and descend to reach the same brook that you crossed previously. Turn left (do not cross the brook), joining the Orange Trail. Continue ahead at the next junction, where the Orange Trail leaves to the right and the Yellow Trail begins, but at the following junction, turn right, and follow only white blazes.

The Sierra Trail now takes you along the rim of a small glen, quite beautiful in any season. On the left, the brook is eroding the red shales that overlay the basalt. You will soon encounter exposed basaltic bedrock, and— as the glen widens—hemlocks. Along the way, the Blue Trail joins, and the path begins to descend through the hemlocks.

At the end of the gorge, the Blue Trail leaves to the right, but you should turn left, continuing to follow the white-blazed Sierra Trail, which parallels Blue Brook. The trail soon bears left and climbs away from the

Deserted Village of Feltsville

DANIEL CHAZIN

brook, bears left again at the next intersection, then turns right at the next junction. In another quarter mile, the trail crosses a small brook. Be careful to proceed straight ahead here and then bear left, uphill.

After passing several houses to the left, the trail crosses a dirt road and soon begins a gradual descent. There are no hemlocks here, and the ground is higher and drier. Notice on the descent that where the trail has been deeply eroded there are some exposures of shale and sandstone, hardened mud, and silt deposited during the Triassic period. Later, volcanic magma intruded into these shales, forming the erosion-resistant, basaltic Watchung Mountains.

About 2 miles from the start, follow the white-blazed Sierra Trail as it turns left onto a dirt road. Tall cedars line the west side of this road, which was once a driveway. The trail follows the dirt road for a short distance and then turns left, leaving the road and continuing on a footpath. It ascends through a beautiful pine forest, planted by the Civilian Conservation Corps in the 1930s. Soon, you'll reach an open grassy area, with a picnic pavilion ahead. Bear right here and follow a gravel service road out to the paved Sky Top Drive. The trail crosses the road and re-enters the woods, then makes a sharp right turn onto a wide woods road parallel to Sky Top Drive (which often may be seen to the right). About three-quarters of a mile after it crossed the paved road, the trail begins to descend. As the trail bends to the left, a short path to the right leads to an overlook above an abandoned quarry, with I-78 visible in the distance.

After descending more steeply, the trail makes a sharp right turn when it is in sight of US 22 and follows an eroded gully down to the Green Brook. It now runs along the brook, with New Providence Road on the other side of it. Green Brook is a stocked trout stream and attracts many anglers. As the trail heads north along the bank of the brook, it becomes rockier. The trail, the brook, and the road all pass together through a gap in the long wall of the Watchungs. Above on the right, you will see outcrops of basalt rock. If you look closely at the rock, you will note that it has formed hexagonal columns—much like the Palisades of the Hudson, only on a smaller scale.

In about a third of a mile, you will reach the site of an old mill, with many brick and concrete ruins still visible. The mill used the water power from the brook to make paper; later it held a 10,000-gallon still operated by bootleggers, whose product is said to have been world renowned. Here the brook drops quite a few feet in a short distance. After passing the ruins of the dam that was used to divert water to the mill, the trail bears right and climbs steeply to a viewpoint from a rock outcrop, then descends on a woods road and once more reaches Sky Top Drive. You've now hiked about 4.5 miles.

The Sierra Trail turns left and follows the road, crossing Blue Brook on the highway bridge, with Seeley's Pond to the left. This point is at the edge of the reservation, and suburbia is just across the street. After crossing the bridge, the trail immediately turns right, goes through a grassy area, and reenters the woods. It follows a footpath through some fairly dense vegetation and crosses several small brooks on a long wooden boardwalk. In places, the trail is bordered by wild roses; you will find violets and spring beauties where an occasional spring keeps the ground moist. Watch for poison ivy in this section, both as a vine on trees and as a bush.

Just beyond the long boardwalk, the pink-blazed History Trail joins from the right, and both trails climb wooden steps, passing a historical marker for the Drake Farm. About three-quarters of a mile from the crossing of Blue Brook, the Sierra Trail turns left onto a wide dirt road and the History Trail turns right on the road.

At a right turn just before the trail passes a hemlock grove on the right, you will find a partially exposed boulder formed of Shawangunk Conglomerate. This stone is not native to the area—it was dragged south by the glacier for a distance of more than 20 miles.

Suddenly you will see a large building facing you—you've entered the Deserted Village of Feltsville. From 1845 to 1860, David Felt, a New York City businessman, owned and operated a paper mill on Blue Brook. Feltsville was a factory town then, but when the mill closed, it became Glenside Park, a Victorian retreat with lawn tennis and pure water. Some say there are a salt brook and a magnesium spring in the vicinity, which may have been why the area was made a mini-resort between 1882 and 1916. In 1991, a New Jersey Historic Trust grant was awarded for the preservation of Feltsville as a unique resource.

The Sierra Trail follows the paved road through the village for 0.4 mile. After the road curves left and passes the church /store building and an adjacent residence, the Sierra Trail turns right on a bridle path. In 200 feet, it turns right again onto another dirt road and soon passes a small cemetery, which contains the graves of the Willcocks and Badgley families, who first settled the area about 1736. William Willcox, a judge and advocate of the Revolutionary War, died in 1800. Joseph Badgley was a private in the First New Jersey Regiment and died in

Willcocks and Badgley Cemetery

1785. John Willcocks, Sr., a member of the Light Horse Company of the New Jersey militia, died on November 22, 1776.

The road bears left, just beyond the cemetery, and soon narrows to a footpath that meanders through the woods. About a third of a mile from the cemetery, the white-blazed trail turns right and descends on a dirt road. In 400 feet, the white blazes bear left, leaving the road, but you should continue ahead on the dirt road, now unblazed, and cross a bridge over Blue Brook. Just beyond, bear right, then continue ahead on a wide path as the Blue Trail joins from the right. The trail parallels a tributary stream and continues uphill on wide wooden steps. Soon, the blue blazes are replaced by orange blazes. After a few more minutes, you will reach a paved road. Bear right here and walk uphill. The parking area will be on your left.

33

Washington Valley Park

Total distance: 5.7 miles	
Hiking time: 3 hours	
Vertical rise: 550 feet	
Rating: Moderate	
Maps: USGS Bound Brook; Somerset County Park Commission Washington Valley Park brochure and trail map	
Trailhead GPS Coordinates: N 40° 35' 45" W 74° 34' 25.5"	

Long ago, George Washington defended the fledgling United States by positioning his troops between the first and second Watchung Mountains. The mountains served as a natural fortification, and from the heights he kept an eye on British movements. Prominent rock faces such as "Washington Rock" and "Chimney Rock" were important lookouts for the general, places from which intelligence on the British was gathered. A few of these strategic vistas remain. Washington Rock is located within a small county park near the town of Watchung.

Chimney Rock, another strategic vista, was for many years on private land that was unofficially used by the public. Indeed, it was mentioned as a hiking destination in the first edition of the *New York Walk Book*, published in 1923 (pp. 121–22). Along with over 700 acres of surrounding forest and slope, Chimney Rock and its surrounding woods and ravines now comprise Somerset County's Washington Valley Park. This park, located in the midst of the densely populated suburbs of central New Jersey, offers a wide variety of trails for both hikers and mountain bikers. The park is heavily used by local residents, who come to fish, bird watch, bike, hike, or just "hang out." While this is no wilderness—residences can be seen from the trail and the motor traffic rumble is never escaped—wildlife abounds and hikers will find the trails interesting and challenging.

Some of the trails used by this hike are marked, but others are not. The trail system is rather complex, with many trail junctions, and it is a good idea to bring along a trail

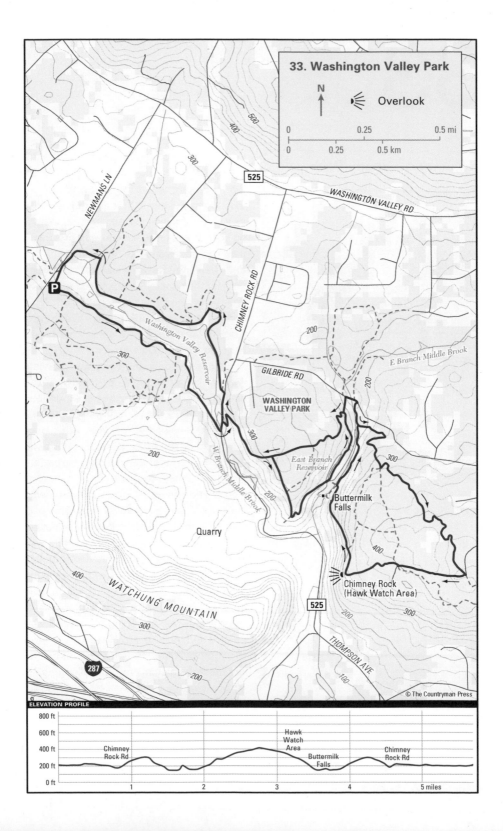

33. Washington Valley Park

N

✺ Overlook

| 0 | 0.25 | 0.5 mi |
| 0 | 0.25 | 0.5 km |

NEWMANS LN

500

400

300

525

WASHINGTON VALLEY RD

P

Washington Valley Reservoir

300

CHIMNEY ROCK RD

200

GILBRIDE RD

E Branch Middle Brook

200

WASHINGTON
VALLEY PARK

300

W. Branch Middle Brook

200

East Branch
Reservoir

300

200

Buttermilk
Falls

Quarry

400

WATCHUNG MOUNTAIN

300

400

Chimney Rock
(Hawk Watch Area)

300

525

200

THOMPSON AVE

100

287

200

© The Countryman Press

ELEVATION PROFILE

800 ft					
600 ft			Hawk		
			Watch		
400 ft	Chimney		Area		Chimney
	Rock Rd			Buttermilk	Rock Rd
200 ft				Falls	
0 ft					
	1	2	3	4	5 miles

map. As of this writing, maps are not provided at the trailhead kiosk, but you can download a map from the Web site of the Somerset County Park Commission, www .somersetcountyparks.org.

The geology of the park is simple. You will be walking on the first Watchung Mountain, a long basalt ridge that is part of an ancient rift valley (see Introduction). At a weak point in the ridge, a drainage developed, and millions of years of erosion have carved out two gorges, each quite interesting. The larger one is that of the West Branch of Middle Brook, the route that Chimney Rock Road follows as it climbs from the Piedmont Plain to the valley between the first and second Watchung ranges. The route along the gorge is unfortunately not accessible to pedestrians, though you can see it from your car. The second gorge is hidden from the road and located just below Chimney Rock. This narrower gorge, formed by the East Branch of Middle Brook, has been dammed between spectacular basalt formations.

HOW TO GET THERE

Take I-78 to Exit 33 and head south on County Route 525 (Martinsville Road). Continue for about 3.2 miles until the road ends at a T-intersection (along the way, the road changes its name to Liberty Corner Road and then Mt. Horeb Road). Turn right at the T-intersection onto Washington Valley Road (County Route 620) and proceed for 0.2 mile to Newmans Lane. Turn left onto Newmans Lane and continue for 0.7 mile to a parking area for Washington Valley Park, on the left side of the road.

THE TRAIL

Begin your hike on the trail that leads out of the rear (east) end of the parking area, near a large chemical toilet. The trail is blazed with both red square and red circle blazes. As you proceed along this rocky trail, you are in the valley between the first and second Watchung Mountains, a valley into which the hills drain, creating the West Branch of Middle Brook. This brook is to your left and is the water supply for the reservoir, which you will pass shortly. You'll pass many outcrops of the distinctive basalt rock of which the Watchung Mountains are formed.

The trail soon reaches the northwestern end of the reservoir. After making a bend away from the reservoir, the trail goes through a stand of tall white pines. Continue heading east, following an informal trail close to the shoreline of the reservoir, though not right up to its edge. Keep your eyes open for the several rocky points along the way that offer a better look at this peaceful body of water. Soon, you'll bear left on a better defined trail that leads right down to the water level and skirts a wet area. At the end of the wet area, bear left at a fork, climb to an opening in a chain-link fence, and turn left onto a dirt road. Follow the road past the dam and down to Chimney Rock Road.

Turn left onto Chimney Rock Road and cross the bridge over the West Branch of Middle Brook. In 150 feet, at the end of the guardrail, cross the road and turn sharply right onto an unmarked trail that climbs steeply on switchbacks. Toward the height of land, the trail widens and comes to a fork. Turn right here and begin to follow along the level ridgetop, through a mostly deciduous forest, on a trail blazed with orange squares. Soon you'll come to another junction, where you should bear right and head downhill, continuing to follow the orange square blazes.

At the following junction, bear left and continue along the orange-blazed trail as it begins to head north. Soon, the trail turns sharply right and heads downhill. Be alert for a sharp left turn and continue to follow the orange-blazed trail along the hillside (this section of the trail is poorly blazed as of this writing, but continue ahead and avoid an unmarked trail that goes off to the right). The trail eventually descends to a rock causeway, made of huge slabs of basalt attached to each other with steel rods, that extends across the small East Branch Reservoir. It is sometimes possible to cross here, but this is not always the case and it is not recommended. Stay on the northwest side of the reservoir and follow a footpath along the edge of a wetland (formerly part of the reservoir), with a talus slope on your left.

At the end of the wetland, the trail bears left, leaving the little valley, and steeply climbs to the crest of the rise. It then descends to paved Gilbride Road. Turn right onto Gilbride Road and follow it for about 200 feet, crossing a bridge over the brook. At the end of the guardrail, turn right onto a trail that leads back into the woods, now following the east side of the East Branch of Middle Brook.

Soon, you'll come to a yellow square–blazed trail. Turn left and follow this trail uphill along a tributary of the brook. The trail soon makes a wide switchback and continues climbing through an open oak and maple forest, with many large trees (some of which were felled by Hurricane Sandy in October 2012). Just past the height of land (elevation about 400 feet), the trail descends briefly and reaches a paved road. Turn right and follow the road for about a quarter mile, to a fork. Bear right at the fork, walk past a parking area, and continue through the opening in the fence. You now proceed downhill on a paved path, blazed with yellow squares and yellow circles, which leads to a viewpoint designated on the park map as "Hawk Watch Area."

Most viewpoints along hiking trails offer an opportunity to contemplate a pristine, natural environment. Even if some civilization intrudes, the primary focus of the view is usually the beauty of nature. This viewpoint is completely different. Staring in your face at the opposite side of the valley is a huge, ugly quarry, with large storage buildings in the foreground and massive machinery to extract the rock from the hills in the background. On the left, you see industrial buildings, with suburbia spreading beyond. Only on the right is there a more natural view—a glimpse into the gentle folds of the Watchung range.

Just ahead, beyond the fence, you'll notice a strange-looking rock, covered with red, white, and blue graffiti. This is Chimney Rock—used by George Washington and the Continental Army to scout for British troops during the Revolutionary War. A beautiful sketch of this historic feature, in its natural condition, appears on page 120 of the 1923 edition of the *New York Walk Book*. (Interestingly, the quarry was there even then; on page 122 the 1923 *Walk Book* states that "the other side of the clove is the scene of elaborate quarrying operations.") But since then, vandals have defaced this historic feature with graffiti, and today it is more of a distraction than a historic feature to be admired. Indeed, it seems that the management of the park is so embarrassed by the present condition of this landmark that it does not even mention Chimney Rock in the official park brochure, referring to the lookout only as a hawk watch site. It certainly is a great spot from which to watch hawks; on a recent visit to the park, we saw hawks swooping by this overlook. But from the point of view of scenery and history, the view from this spot is quite disappointing.

After you've taken in this interesting yet bizarre vista, bear left onto a wide woods road, blazed with yellow squares and circles, that heads downhill. Soon, the yellow circle

Chimney Rock

blazes leave to the right, but you should continue downhill on the woods road, now following only yellow square blazes. Near the base of the descent, you'll notice a waterfall and dam to the left. A side trail leads steeply down to the top of the dam; if you choose to follow it, use caution, as the footing can be treacherous. At this waterfall, known as Buttermilk Falls, the East Branch of Middle Brook cascades over the rough basalt rock. The pristine beauty of the area has been spoiled, however, by the rather ugly concrete dam built on top of the falls.

Just ahead, the trail reaches the level of the East Branch Reservoir at the stone causeway you passed earlier. Under exceptional conditions you might be able to cross here, but most of the time you will need to continue ahead, following the footpath along the east side of the reservoir. At first, the trail (still blazed with yellow squares) is wide and level, but it soon becomes narrow and very rocky. Indeed, it can be dangerous in icy or slippery conditions. (If you encounter problems crossing this rocky stretch of trail, return to the Chimney Rock viewpoint and retrace your steps on the trail you came up on.) Soon, you can see Gilbride Road ahead, and the route becomes easier to navigate. When the yellow square blazes bear right

Washington Valley Reservoir

at the trail junction you encountered earlier, leave the yellow trail and continue straight ahead along the brook to Gilbride Road.

Turn left at Gilbride Road, and follow the road across the brook. Enter the woods on the left and bear right onto the orange square–blazed trail, which switchbacks up to the height of land. At the next fork, bear right and follow the trail past a stand of cedars, a favorite hiding place for deer. Soon you'll arrive at another junction, which you passed earlier. Turn right, leaving the orange-blazed trail, and continue on the unmarked trail, which switchbacks down the hill to Chimney Rock Road.

Cross Chimney Rock Road, turn right, and follow the road for about 750 feet to a small parking turnout on the left, adjacent to the dam of the reservoir. There is an opening in the fence here. Continue ahead through the opening and proceed along the east side of the reservoir, following a pleasant woods road. Just beyond the end

of an arm of the reservoir, turn left onto a footpath and descend to cross a wetland on puncheons. On the other side, bear left at a fork, proceeding through an area devastated by Hurricane Sandy. Soon, you'll approach the shore of the reservoir. Bear right and follow the wide, level trail, lined with attractive cedars and marked occasionally with white square blazes, parallel to the reservoir. This pleasant footpath is a welcome contrast to the rocky trail you followed at the start of the hike, on the opposite side of the reservoir. You'll probably see some fishermen along the shore of the reservoir.

As you approach the western end of the reservoir, the trail curves to the right, away from the reservoir. You'll soon reach a junction, where you should turn left and immediately cross a stream on rocks. The trail parallels Newmans Lane (on the right), crosses the West Branch of Middle Brook on a substantial bridge, and reaches the parking area where the hike began.

34

Sourland Mountain Preserve

Total distance: 4.7 miles	
Hiking time: 3 hours	
Vertical rise: 500 feet	
Rating: Easy to moderate	
Maps: USGS Rocky Hill; Somerset County Park Commission Sourland Mountain Preserve trail map	
Trailhead GPS Coordinates: N 40° 28' 27" W 74° 41' 38.5"	

Sourland Mountain is really a 10-by-4-mile sheet of Triassic traprock, similar to the Palisades, Watchungs, and Cushetunk Mountain (see Introduction). Here a portion of a buried igneous intrusion was tilted, with its eastern edge leaning up, then uplifted. Erosion left the harder igneous rock exposed, and it now overlooks the surrounding plain. The highest elevation on the mountain is 586 feet. Contrast this with the 120-foot elevation of the eastern plain, and you have one of the steepest gradients in central New Jersey. It is on this eastern edge that the hiking trails are located. The western portion of the mountain slopes off into the plain more gradually.

Two factors have allowed Sourland Mountain to remain mostly undeveloped. The first is the fact that the land has never been of much agricultural or commercial worth—something that seems to be reflected in the name. Sourland may have stemmed from the German term sauerland, meaning land that is not sweet. The soil is rocky and acidic and there is little groundwater. The name may also refer to the reddish-brown ("sorrel-land") color of the soil found on the plains beneath the mountain. In some old records, the name is given as "Sowerland."

The second factor that explains why Sourland Mountain has not been developed is that it is far from any major thoroughfare. It has served as a retreat for many, including Charles Lindbergh, whose child was kidnapped there in 1932. The broad, flat top of the mountain is quite rocky, is mostly wooded, and includes about 400 acres of

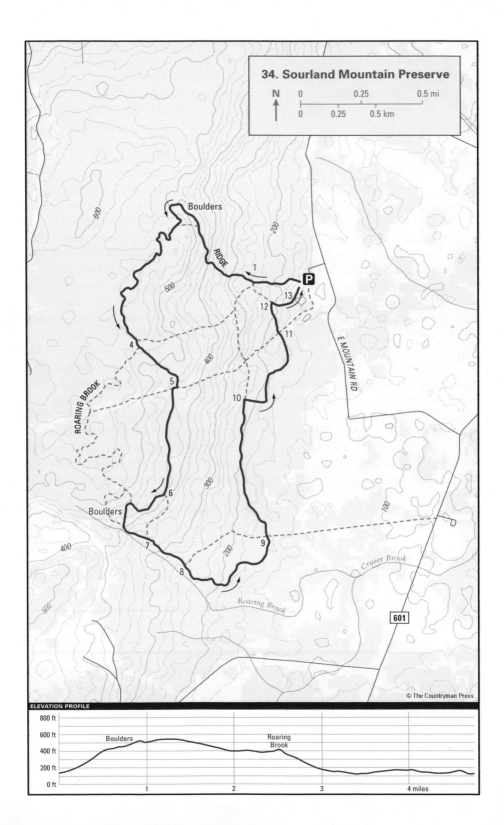

34. Sourland Mountain Preserve

N

| 0 | | 0.25 | | 0.5 mi |

| 0 | 0.25 | | 0.5 km |

Boulders

200

RIDGE

1

P

13

12

11

4

500

400

5

10

E MOUNTAIN RD

ROARING BROOK

300

6

Boulders

100

7

400

8

9

200

Cruser Brook

500

Roaring Brook

601

© The Countryman Press

ELEVATION PROFILE

800 ft				
600 ft	Boulders		Roaring	
400 ft			Brook	
200 ft				
0 ft				
	1	2	3	4 miles

old growth. Many historic buildings still stand along the several quiet country roads that cross over it. But developmental pressure in New Jersey is relentless, and many have become concerned. One such voice is the Sourland Planning Council, which has pushed for preservation of the area since 1986. The matter is complicated by the fact that portions of the mountain fall in Mercer, Hunterdon, and Somerset Counties. To date, only Somerset and Hunterdon Counties have preserved sections of the mountain. The section of the mountain in Mercer County has not yet been protected. The 4,000-acre Sourland Mountain Preserve, the location of this hike, is administered by the Somerset County Park Commission (P.O. Box 5327, North Branch, NJ 08876; 908-722-1200; www.somersetcountyparks.org).

HOW TO GET THERE

Take I-287 to Exit 17 and continue south on US 206 for about 7.6 miles. Turn right onto Amwell Road (County Route 514), being careful not to turn right at New Amwell Road, and proceed for 2.8 miles to East Mountain Road. Turn left onto East Mountain Road and follow it for 1.9 miles to the entrance to Sourland Mountain Preserve, on the right. If you are using a GPS device, enter this address: 425 East Mountain Road, Hillsborough, NJ 08844.

THE TRAIL

From the kiosk at the edge of the parking area (trail maps of the preserve are usually available here), head west across a grassy field. At the edge of the woods, you will notice a wooden post with three blazes: white triangle, white circle, and white square. This marks the start of the three loop trails in the preserve, which head uphill into the woods, paralleling a brook to the left.

Follow the joint trails for about five minutes

until you reach post #1 (all intersections are marked with white-on-green reflective numbers on wooden posts). Here the white-triangle and white-circle trails turn left, crossing the stream on a footbridge, but you should continue ahead on the white square–blazed Ridge Trail, which proceeds steadily uphill through a heavily wooded area.

After about 15 minutes of steady climbing, the trail levels off. Soon, after another short climb, you'll come to an area of huge boulders. This is the most interesting part of the hike, so take your time to enjoy the unusual boulders. At one point, the trail goes through a narrow passage between two huge boulders. Toward the end of the boulder field, you'll notice a large tree that has grown out of a horizontal crack in a boulder. The trail continues through a forest that features many tall, straight tulip trees. In some cases, several tulip tree trunks grow out of the same set of roots.

Finally, after about an hour of hiking, you'll reach post #4. To the left, a connector trail (marked by "C" blazes) leads back toward the parking area, but you should bear right to continue along the white-square-blazed trail. At the next junction, bear left, as the red circle–blazed Roaring Brook Trail begins on the right. Proceed ahead on the white square–blazed trail, which descends, crosses a bridge over a stream, and reaches the right-of-way of the Texas Eastern Gas Transmission Corporation pipeline at post #5. The trail jogs to the right along the right-of-way, then turns left and reenters the woods. Continue following the white square–blazed trail, which crosses several wet areas on a series of boardwalks.

When you reach post #6, at a break in a fence, bear right to continue along the white square–blazed trail (a connector trail, marked by "C" blazes, begins on the left). The white square–blazed trail now begins

The trail passes between these two huge boulders

Piedmont

Tree growing out of a horizontal crack in a boulder

to descend. Bear left at a junction with another connector trail and continue down to Roaring Brook, passing some more large boulders on the way.

In about five minutes, you'll go through a gap in another chain-link fence. Just beyond, you'll notice post #8. A connector trail goes off to the left, but you should bear right to continue on the white square–blazed Ridge Trail. Soon, the trail bears left and heads away from Roaring Brook.

In another 15 minutes, you'll cross a boardwalk over a stream and pass an old stone-and-concrete wall (possibly built as a dam) on the left. Just beyond, you'll reach a four-way intersection marked by post #9, where you should continue straight ahead.

The next stretch of trail is nearly level, with a long boardwalk and many short stretches of boardwalk. In another 20 minutes or so, you'll reach post #10. Here, you should turn right and follow both white-square and white-triangle blazes, soon crossing another long section of boardwalk.

A short distance beyond, at post #11, you'll again cross the Texas Eastern gas pipeline. Continue straight ahead, and you'll soon reach post #12. Turn right and begin to follow three coaligned trails, which are blazed with white triangles, white circles, and white squares. Soon, you'll emerge onto a grassy area and descend toward a small pond. Bear left around the pond, pass post #13, and you'll reach the parking area where you left your car.

35

Washington Crossing to Scudder's Falls

Total distance: 6 miles

Hiking time: 3 hours

Vertical rise: 100 feet

Rating: Easy

Maps: USGS Pennington; DEP Washington Crossing State Park map; DEP Delaware & Raritan Canal State Park

Trailhead GPS Coordinates: N 40° 18' 10.5" W 74° 51' 38"

This hike combines an opportunity to learn about a critical battle of the Revolutionary War at Washington Crossing State Park (355 Washington Crossing–Pennington Road, Titusville, NJ 08560-1517; 609-737-0623; www.njparksandforests.org) with a long walk on the towpath of the Delaware & Raritan Canal. On the towpath (the walkway for the mules that pulled the canal boats) you will be exposed to much sun—a blessing or curse depending on the season or the weather. There is plenty to do at this state park. In all, this 3,500-acre park boasts about 15 miles of trails. Other hiking possibilities besides the one described here include several footpaths through a 140-acre natural area with an interpretive center.

The park's Visitor Center Museum (open year-round, seven days a week, except for certain holidays, from 9 AM to 4 PM) contains a large collection of Revolutionary War artifacts, maps, and descriptive brochures. It offers a 27-minute video that will give you a feel for the momentous event that led to the establishment of the park, and full-length historical films are shown at specific times. There is no charge for admission to the museum, but a $1 per person fee is charged for viewing the video.

The importance of what happened here in 1776 cannot be overestimated. This was the site of probably the single most important offensive in George Washington's military career. At the very least, it kept him and the country alive during the early days of the Revolutionary War.

Since independence had been declared,

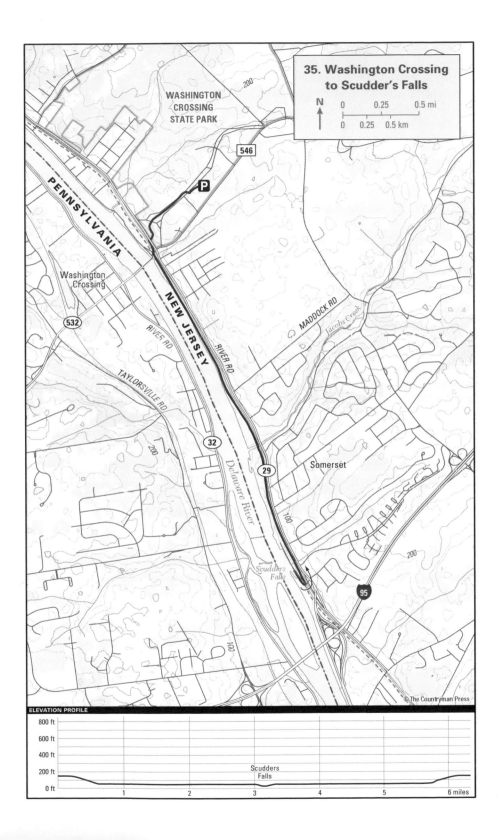

N

| 0 | 0.25 | 0.5 mi |
| 0 | 0.25 | 0.5 km |

WASHINGTON
CROSSING
STATE PARK

546

P

PENNSYLVANIA

NEW JERSEY

Washington
Crossing

532

RIVER RD

RIVER RD

MADDOCK RD

Jacobs Creek

TAYLORSVILLE RD

200

32

29

Somerset

Delaware River

100

200

Scudders
Falls

100

95

© The Countryman Press

ELEVATION PROFILE

800 ft						
600 ft						
400 ft						
200 ft			Scudders			
			Falls			
0 ft	1	2	3	4	5	6 miles

the Continental Army, led by Washington, had not scored a point against the British. Washington and his men had tried to stop the British invasion of Long Island (Brooklyn) but were driven back to Manhattan and then across the Hudson to New Jersey. Denied an adequate number of troops and supplies to meet the threat, Washington had no recourse but to retreat across the middle of New Jersey, cross the Delaware, and hunker down in Pennsylvania. Although the situation appeared to be cause for extreme depression, Washington took a risk and won, and in the process stirred hope for the revolutionary cause.

On the night of December 25, 1776, he ordered three divisions of troops to attack the Hessians (German mercenaries) at Trenton. The plan called for each division to cross the Delaware at a different location and then converge on the enemy. Washington and his 2,400 men crossed the river in ferryboats to reach the site of the present-day state park. After a difficult crossing of the ice-choked river, he and his men marched south to Trenton, caught the Hessians by surprise, and took possession of Trenton. The other two divisions never made the crossing that night because they couldn't navigate their boats through the icy river. Washington immediately followed up the victory with a successful attack on the British at Princeton. Having pushed back the enemy halfway to New York, he took shelter for the remainder of the winter behind the long, curving natural wall of the Watchungs, in central New Jersey. These two battles marked a major turning point in the war, and they kept Washington in place as commander in chief.

HOW TO GET THERE

You will see signs for Washington Crossing State Park as you approach it from any direction. From I-95, take Exit 1 north (the last exit in New Jersey) to NJ 29 north. About 3 miles from the exit, make a right turn onto County Route 546; you will find the main entrance to the park on your right in about a half mile. Alternatively, take Exit 3 and follow signs to the park entrance. Between Memorial Day and Labor Day there is an entrance fee on weekends only. Pass the toll gate, follow signs to the Visitor Center Museum, and park in the large lot just to the north of the center. Parking is free just north of the Nelson House near the river—if there is room. You may wish to park here and walk back to the visitors center to see the museum's collection of artifacts or simply walk south along the towpath as described below. Limited parking is also free at an area located at the intersection of County Route 579 and County Route 546, just off County Route 579. If you park here, you will be able to walk along the historic Continental Lane to the Visitor Center Museum, a mile away. Parking here will add an extra 2 miles to your hike. Another option is to spot cars at each end of the hike. A parking area for boaters is found 3 miles south of the park on NJ 29 near Scudder's Falls.

THE TRAIL

From the Visitor Center Museum, walk over to Continental Lane, the grassy walking path about 100 yards due west (in front) of the center. This path is marked with a red dot. You'll find it between a long line of trees and other plantings just across the paved road. Turn left onto the lane and head toward the Delaware River. Continental Lane is a pleasant, tree-lined walkway between two paved park service roads. Ashes, oaks, white pines, and cedars line the path on either side. After a few minutes, you'll come to a few colonial buildings. To your right is an old barn that now houses restrooms and a flag museum. In front of you is the Johnson Ferry House,

Along the Delaware and Raritan Canal

fronted with an herb garden. You may wish to explore these buildings now, or perhaps on your return. At the terminus of Continental Lane, bear left for just a few feet on the paved road and turn right onto a path marked with a green dot heading south. This path will lead you past a walled-in overlook (overlooking NJ 29 and the Delaware River) and out to a pedestrian bridge over the highway. This area is part of the memorial arboretum, and the varied plant life here may be of interest. Take the pedestrian bridge over NJ 29 and make a left, crossing the road leading to the bridge. A restaurant is located near here. Now head south (through the gate) on the canal feeder towpath. En route you'll pass two stone markers commemorating the crossing.

The towpath, which was used for a time as a bed for the Belvidere-Delaware Railroad, is flat and is surfaced with very fine, though loose, gravel. It gets much use from joggers and bikers as well as walkers. To the right and quite a drop below is the Delaware River. To the left is the feeder canal and, beyond that, NJ 29. It is unfortunate that the highway is so close, but that is an unavoidable reality. This section of towpath is exposed to sunlight and, during hot summer days, it may be advisable to hike in the late afternoon, when the shade from the taller trees on the west bank covers the entire path.

As you walk along the towpath, you'll see vegetation very different from that of the highland mountains or the Pinelands. The plants—weeds actually—are more typical of highways, urban vacant lots, and other places that receive much sunlight. Don't be

Nelson House

put off by this; some of the most valuable medicinal herbs are found in such environments. For example, you'll see thistle, with its prickly leaves and round flower heads, which is used for fevers (it produces sweating). The common mullein—the tall, spikelike plant commonly seen along the roadside—is also found here; a tea made from its leaves and flowers is used for lung complaints and asthma. As for flowers, you'll find purple gentians, black-eyed Susans, goldenrod, and wild carrot (better known as Queen Anne's lace). Poison ivy is in abundance here as well, though it doesn't encroach upon the path. Pokeweed, edible as a young shoot but poisonous when fully matured, is found

here also. You'll find the staghorn sumac with its red berry clusters that, when soaked in cold water, make a lemonade-like drink. At the edge of the dense woods that separates the towpath from the river are flowering dogwoods and even a few catalpa trees with their large heart-shaped leaves and long, beanlike pods.

Where the canal curves slightly to the east, notice the outcroppings of red Brunswick shale, also known as brownstone, on the opposite bank. This rock is the primary bedrock throughout all of central New Jersey, except for the igneous intrusions that make up the Watchungs, Cushetunk Mountain, Sourland Mountain, and Rocky Hill.

Piedmont

A little farther ahead, Jacob's Creek passes under the canal and empties into the Delaware. There's a nice view of this wild and rocky confluence from the towpath, which stands 50 feet above it. Blue herons may be wading in the shallows, where they are safe from intruders. Don't be surprised if you see deer hoof prints on the towpath; they've got a dense woods to hide in during the day.

After passing a flood-control structure, which allows the canal to drain into the river if necessary, you'll see a bridge across the canal ahead of you. Bear right here and head downhill on the paved road. Take one of the pathways to your left down to the river, and you'll come out near Scudder's Falls, a Class II set of rapids on the Delaware.

Scudder's Falls is named for the Scudder family, whose 18th-century farmstead and mill were once located in the area. One well-known member of the family was Amos Scudder, one of Washington's scouts at the Battle of Trenton. John Hart, one of the signers of the Declaration of Independence from New Jersey, was married to a Scudder. Unfortunately, nothing is left of the original house.

Notice the huge sections of concrete on the island just across from the falls. A structure located here once utilized the immense power of the water, which drops several feet in a short distance. These falls, more like a channel or chute between shoreline and island, are popular with kayakers. If you are here during high water and on a weekend, you will no doubt be treated to a display of paddling skills. The area, also heavily used by anglers and partygoers, is quite pleasant and very interesting, making it a good spot for lunch. You can sit on some of the big rocks near the river's edge, listen to the roar of the rapids, and gaze out toward Pennsylvania, far off on the other side.

After watching the rapids, return to the towpath (or follow the road along the river to a gas line and then scramble back up to the towpath) and begin the long walk back to Washington Crossing State Park. The benches placed about every quarter mile can provide a welcome rest, should you need one. Before taking the pedestrian walkway over NJ 29, you may wish to take a look at the Nelson House, just below it, toward the river. There is a portion of the original tavern here at the ferry dock. The building contains a large collection of period pieces, a flag collection, and, adjacent to the building, a reconstruction of one of the original ferryboats that took Washington and his men across the frozen river on that cold December night.

From the Nelson House, take the pedestrian bridge across the highway and bear left through the walled overlook. Continue retracing your steps toward the Johnson Ferry House and flag museum to find Continental Lane that, in 0.3 mile, will bring you to the Visitor Center Museum and parking area—unless, of course, you parked elsewhere.

36

D & R Canal, Bull's Island to Prallsville

Total distance: 3 miles (or 6 miles using one car)

Hiking time: 2 hours (or 3.5 hours)

Vertical rise: Minimal

Rating: Easy

Map: USGS Lumberville/Stockton; DEP Delaware & Raritan Canal State Park map

Trailhead GPS Coordinates: N 40° 24' 37.5" W 75° 02' 07"

This hike traverses a 3-mile section of the Delaware & Raritan Canal State Park. For its entire length, however, it follows the abandoned railbed of the Belvidere-Delaware Railroad high above the canal, rather than the historic canal towpath. In this section, the towpath, which separates the canal from the river, is largely overgrown and is interrupted in a number of locations.

The hike begins at the Bull's Island Recreation Area and ends at the Prallsville Mill complex. The recreation area is located on a densely wooded floodplain of the Delaware River. There are interesting features to explore at each end of the hike, which is nearly level for its entire length.

Construction of the Delaware & Raritan Canal began in 1832. The main section of the canal extended from Bordentown on the Delaware River to New Brunswick, on the Raritan River. To assure an adequate supply of water to the canal, a 22-mile feeder canal was built along the east side of the Delaware River from Bull's Island south to Trenton. An artificial island created by the construction of the canal, Bull's Island was named after Richard Bull, one of the original owners. By 1834, the wingdam at Bull's Island that diverted water from the river to the canal was completed, and the entire canal opened later that year.

The Belvidere-Delaware Railroad, which paralleled the Delaware River from Trenton to Belvidere, was completed in 1855. It was acquired by the Pennsylvania Railroad in 1872. Interestingly, about the same time, the Pennsylvania Railroad also acquired the Delaware

Prallsville Mill complex

DAN BALOGH

& Raritan Canal, which remained in operation for another 50 years until it was abandoned in 1932. Passenger service was operated on the Belvidere-Delaware Railroad until 1960, with service in the 1950s consisting of a single weekday round-trip from Phillipsburg to Trenton and return. Freight service lasted until 1978. The tracks were removed soon afterwards, and a few years later, the rail line became part of the state park.

HOW TO GET THERE

From its junction with US 202, take NJ 29 north for 6 miles to the Bull's Island Recreation Area of the Delaware & Raritan Canal State Park (2185 Daniel Bray Highway, Stockton, NJ 08559; 609-397-2949; www .dandrcanal.com). If coming from the north, take I-78 West to Exit 15. Turn left at the first traffic light onto County Route 513 and proceed for 4.2 miles to Pittstown. Turn right to continue on County Route 513 and follow it for another 7.5 miles to Frenchtown. Turn left onto NJ 29 in Frenchtown and continue for 8.9 miles to the Bull's Island Recreation Area. Follow the entrance road over a one-lane bridge and park in a large parking area near the visitors center.

THE TRAIL

Begin the hike by heading west towards the Delaware River and crossing the river on a five-span pedestrian suspension bridge. The first bridge built in this location was a covered bridge constructed in 1856. This bridge remained in service until 1944, when it was declared unsafe and closed. In 1947, the Delaware River Joint Toll Bridge

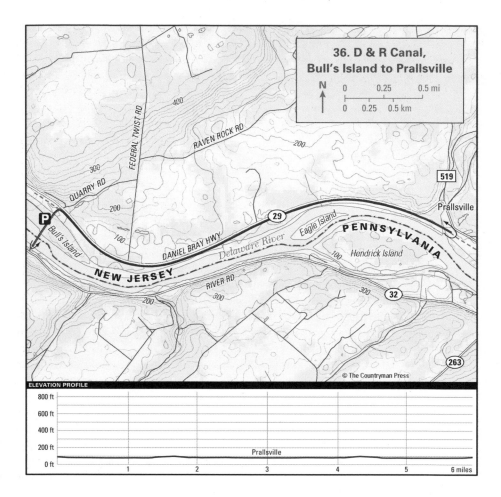

Commission contracted with John A. Roebling's Sons Co. of Trenton (the same firm that built the Brooklyn Bridge about 65 years earlier) to construct a pedestrian suspension bridge on the original stone piers of the 1856 bridge. The cost was $75,000. In 2013, the bridge was extensively rehabilitated at a cost of $3 million. A plaque commemorating the 2013 rehabilitation of the bridge is affixed to its eastern end. Although there is no charge to walk across the bridge, it is maintained by tolls collected at the other bridges operated by the commission.

After exploring this unique bridge, which offers panoramic views up and down the Delaware River, return to New Jersey and head back across the one-lane bridge over the Delaware & Raritan Canal. Just before reaching NJ 29, turn right onto the abandoned right-of-way of the Belvidere-Delaware Railroad, now a multi-use trail suitable for walkers, joggers, and bicycle riders (and, in the winter, cross-country skiers). Go around the gate and begin the 3-mile walk south to the Prallsville Mill complex. For the entire distance, you'll be following a path between NJ 29 on the left and the canal and river on the right (although, for much of the way, the canal and the river are separated from the path by a wide swath of woods).

In a third of a mile, you'll pass milepost 21 on the right. These mileposts were recently installed at half-mile intervals to mark the distance along the path in the Delaware & Raritan Canal State Park. A short distance beyond milepost 20.5, you'll notice an historic concrete milepost with the number 22. This milepost was placed by the railroad to indicate the distance to Trenton. Just before reaching canal milepost 20, you'll cross a high bridge over a stream, with unobstructed views over the canal and river on the right.

Beginning at milepost 19.5, the canal runs closer to the path you are following. In another half mile (just before milepost 19), an interpretive sign on the right provides historical information on a waste gate, used to drain excess water from the canal to the river. There is another unobstructed view over the canal and river here.

A third of a mile beyond, the highway moves away from the path, and a stone retaining wall begins on the left. This stone wall was probably constructed in the 1850s when the railroad was built. The stone used to construct the wall is of the locally quarried Stockton Formation, better known as brownstone. This type of stone has been used in the construction of many historic buildings in New Jersey, including some at Princeton and Rutgers Universities. Just ahead, you'll cross a bridge over the Wickecheoke Creek and reach the Prallsville Mill complex.

Located just north of Stockton, the original mill on the site was constructed by Daniel Howell in 1720. John Prall, after whom the mill is named, bought the property in 1794. He enlarged the original gristmill and sawmill operation by adding a stone building used to mill linseed oil and plaster. In 1874, the original gristmill burned, ignited by a spark from a passing steam engine on the Belvidere-Delaware Railroad, but the mill was rebuilt on the old foundations three years later. After milling came to an end in the late 1940s, the entire complex of seven buildings was acquired by the state and is gradually being restored by the Delaware River Mill Society (P.O. Box 298, Stockton, NJ 08559; 609-397-3586; www.drms-stockton.org), which leases the site. What makes the Prallsville Mill unique is that it is the only historic multiple milling operation remaining in the state.

Today, the displays at the restored mill include an industrial herb garden, an exact-scale model of the mill built by the last mill owner, and a crafts shop, along with the restored buildings themselves. Near the old sawmill is a picnic table, a good place to have lunch or a snack after the walk from Bull's Island.

After visiting the mill, head back to Bull's Island the way you came—or leave from here if you have arranged a car shuttle.

37

D & R Canal, Kingston to Rocky Hill

Total distance: 4 miles

Hiking time: 2 hours

Vertical rise: Minimal

Rating: Easy to moderate

Maps: USGS Monmouth Junction/Rocky Hill/Hightstown; DEP Delaware & Raritan Canal State Park map

Trailhead GPS Coordinates: N 40° 22' 27" W 74° 37' 08"

When it opened in 1834, the Delaware & Raritan Canal served as a major transportation link between Philadelphia and New York. The canal extended a distance of 44 miles, from the northernmost point of navigation on the Delaware River at Bordentown to the head of navigation on the Raritan River at New Brunswick. To assure an adequate water supply for the canal, a 22-mile-long feeder canal was built to divert water from the Delaware River at Raven Rock to the main canal at Trenton. Both main and feeder canals had towpaths (walkways for the mules that pulled the barges along). When the canal was abandoned as a transportation corridor in 1932, the waterway was retained because it supplied water to nearby communities. In 1974, it became a state park. Today, 34 miles of the towpath along the main canal are used by hikers, joggers, canoeists, and nature lovers. The Delaware & Raritan Canal State Park is a green corridor through the center of the nation's most densely populated state, and though it is never far from suburbia, it offers many miles of walking. For more information, contact the D & R State Park, 145 Mapleton Road, Princeton, NJ 08540; 609-924-5705; www.dandrcanal.com.

HOW TO GET THERE

The linear D & R Canal State Park has many access points. For this hike, you will use a large parking area that is located near a canal lock on the south side of NJ 27 in Kingston, where the highway passes over the canal and river. (There is additional parking at the Flemer Preserve across the street.)

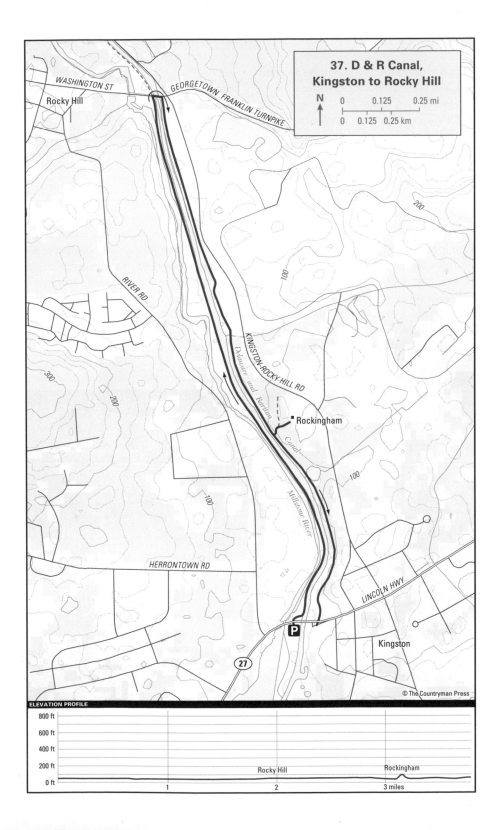

37. D & R Canal, Kingston to Rocky Hill

N

| 0 | 0.125 | 0.25 mi |
| 0 | 0.125 | 0.25 km |

Rocky Hill

WASHINGTON ST

GEORGETOWN FRANKLIN TURNPIKE

200

RIVER RD

KINGSTON-ROCKY HILL RD

Delaware and Raritan Canal

300

200

100

■ Rockingham

Millstone River

100

HERRONTOWN RD

LINCOLN HWY

P

Kingston

27

© The Countryman Press

ELEVATION PROFILE

800 ft			
600 ft			
400 ft			
200 ft		Rocky Hill	Rockingham
0 ft			
	1	2	3 miles

THE TRAIL

Begin the hike by taking a look at the Kingston Lock and the adjacent lock tender's house, both located just south of NJ 27. Locks on the Delaware & Raritan Canal, which measure 220 by 24 feet, allowed boats to move from one section of the canal to another with a different water level. Though seven locks were necessary in the 6-mile stretch of canal from Bordentown to Trenton, only seven more were needed for the remaining 38 miles—a low route that follows the valleys of the Millstone and Raritan rivers. The house behind the lock is one of the old lock tenders' houses found near every lock.

The passage of a boat through a lock was a social event. Exchanges of news would take place between the lock tender and the boatmen. Telegraph connections were in place, and information, such as the arrival of boats, could be sent on to other locations. The lock tender and his family would often trade with the canal boatmen who, like many of today's truckers, owned their own vehicles.

After viewing these interesting remnants of the canal, head under the highway via a corrugated metal tunnel. On the other side, a trail heads to the right and soon reaches the canal towpath. Turn left and head north along the towpath, which runs between the Millstone River (on the left) and the canal (on the right). Although the towpath is wide enough for a vehicle, motorized vehicles are not allowed on the towpath, which is reserved for use by hikers, joggers, bicyclists, horseback riders, and anglers. The densely vegetated strip of land between the river and the canal is part of the river's floodplain.

Lock along the canal

Spillway along the Delaware & Raritan Canal

At one point, a paved road runs relatively close to the towpath, but it soon moves away from the canal, and the sounds of traffic fade away. You will get a feeling of isolation through this stretch. All kinds of wildflowers grow along the towpath here, including yarrow, wild carrot, pokeweed, and lobelia, as well as clusters of arrowroot in the water, a favorite food of Native Americans. The trees that line the towpath are mostly oak and maple, with some horse chestnut, ash, and sumac. The great blue heron is also frequently seen along the canal. A word of caution: poison ivy abounds along the towpath. This toxic plant is frequently found along the towpath as a tree-climbing vine. Although the walkway is wide enough to avoid any contact with the plant, when leaving the towpath and approaching either the canal or the river more closely, be sure you know how to identify it.

In about a mile, you'll come to a section of the towpath that is about a foot lower than the level of the towpath on either side. This area is a spillway, which allows excess water in the canal to spill out into the floodplain of the adjacent Millstone River. An interpretive sign explains how this and other, more sophisticated flood-control devices are used to regulate the water level in the canal. Then, about five minutes later, you'll notice a square concrete pillar with a tapered top, on the left side of the towpath. This is a canal milepost (actually a replacement for one of the original stone markers). Notice that the number 21 is facing south and that on the other side, facing north, is the number 23. These figures indicate the number of miles from Trenton and New Brunswick, respectively. Adding the two gives the total mileage between these points: 44 miles.

Around this point, you will notice several

large buildings on the other side of the canal. These buildings are part of a traprock quarry that is located just east of the canal. One of the largest and oldest quarries in the area, it supplies traprock, or crushed basalt, to road builders. The rock is quarried from what was once a large igneous intrusion, similar to and the same age as Sourland Mountain, the Watchungs, and the Palisades. If you are hiking during the week, your solitude may be spoiled by the activities of this large operation. Thanks to an exchange of land between the quarry and the state, the property formerly owned by the quarry adjacent to the canal has been transferred to the state, and it is quickly reverting to its natural state. About 45 minutes into the hike, just before you reach the bridge over the canal at Rocky Hill, an inviting rock outcrop extends into the Millstone River, on your left. When you reach the paved road, turn right and cross the canal on a wooden vehicular bridge. On the other side, turn right again and pass the reconstructed stone foundations of the bridge keeper's house. Continue south along the east bank of the canal.

You're now following the right-of-way of the Rocky Hill Branch of the Pennsylvania Railroad, built in 1864 and abandoned in 1983. The line was primarily used to ship rock quarried near Rocky Hill (today, the rock is shipped by truck). The first mile of this rail-trail has a dirt surface and is often somewhat muddy in wet weather.

A little over a mile from Rocky Hill, a bench and a sign along the trail mark the start of a short side trail that leads uphill to the historic house known as Rockingham. The oldest part of the house dates back to 1710. In 1783, George Washington lived in the house for over two and one-half months. It was during his stay here that Washington composed his "Farewell Orders to the Armies of the United States" on November 2, 1783, which marked the conclusion of the Revolutionary War. During his residence at the house, Washington did much official entertaining—for a few months, this area was the social capital of the new nation. The house has been relocated several times and was moved to its present location in 2001. Guided tours of the house are offered hourly. For more information, go to www.rockingham.net.

For the last part of the hike, a gas pipeline (marked by yellow posts) parallels the trail. After curving sharply to the right, the trail emerges onto a grassy area, with a parking area for the Flemer Preserve on the left. Continue ahead, cross NJ 27 (use extreme care when crossing this busy highway), and turn right to return to your car.

38

D & R Canal, Weston to East Millstone

Total distance: 4.2 miles

Hiking time: 2 hours

Vertical rise: Minimal

Rating: Easy

Map: USGS Bound Brook; DEP Delaware & Raritan Canal State Park

Trailhead GPS Coordinates: N 40° 31' 43.5" W 74° 34' 52.5"

A century ago, the Delaware & Raritan Canal was the scene of intense commercial activity. Hard coal was the most important item shipped on the canal, accounting for 80 percent of its total tonnage. Many of the canal boats used on the canal were of the hinge-boat variety; they measured about 90 by 10 feet and drew about 5 feet of water. Long strings of these canal boats loaded with coal were pulled by steam tugs, while other canal boats were towed by mules. Towing charges varied according to the service used. At one point steam tugs were charged a flat rate of $22.22, plus an extra $11.11 per barge, for the trip to New York City. Mules and horses were available from barns at Bordentown, Griggstown, and New Brunswick. The open season on the canal was about 250 days a year, from early April to mid-December. Canal hours were from 6:00 AM to 6:00 PM, and the speed limit for canal boats was 4 miles per hour. When steam tugs began to be used on the canal, the wash began to undermine the banks in places. A stone lining called riprap was installed and can still be seen today in many places.

When the canal closed in 1932, the State of New Jersey took it over and rehabilitated it to serve as a water supply system—a purpose it still serves today. In 1973, the canal and its remaining structures were entered on the National Register of Historic Places, and the following year it became a state park. Today, the Delaware & Raritan Canal State Park is one of central New Jersey's most popular recreational corridors for jogging, hiking, bicycling, fishing, and canoeing. For more

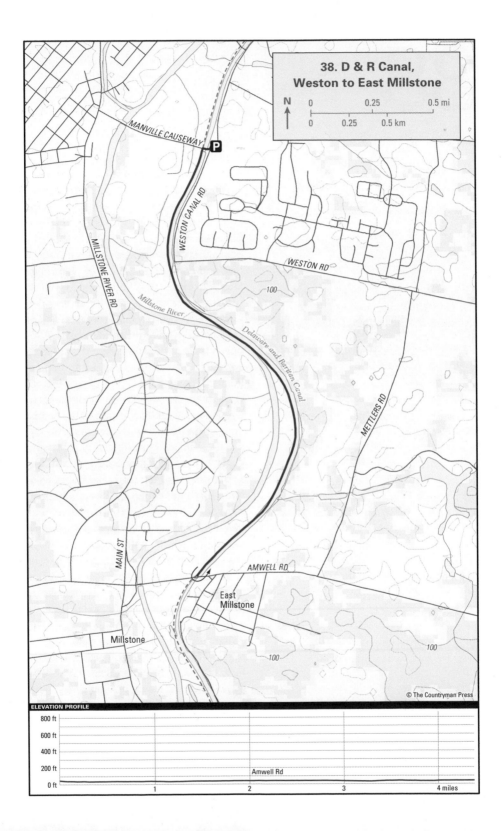

38. D & R Canal, Weston to East Millstone

N

| 0 | | 0.25 | | 0.5 mi |
| 0 | 0.25 | | 0.5 km | |

MANVILLE CAUSEWAY

P

WESTON CANAL RD

WESTON RD

MILLSTONE RIVER RD

Millstone River

Delaware and Raritan Canal

METTLERS RD

100

MAIN ST

AMWELL RD

East
Millstone

Millstone

100

100

© The Countryman Press

ELEVATION PROFILE

| 800 ft |
| 600 ft |
| 400 ft |
| 200 ft |
| 0 ft |

Amwell Rd

| 1 | 2 | 3 | 4 miles |

Along the Delaware & Raritan Canal

information, contact the D & R State Park, 145 Mapleton Road, Princeton, NJ 08540; 609-924-5705; www.dandrcanal.com.

HOW TO GET THERE

To reach this section of the Delaware & Raritan Canal State Park from I-287, take Exit 12 (Weston Canal Road). At the end of the ramp, turn left (south) onto Weston Canal Road, following signs to Manville. In 1.7 miles, pass Ten Mile Lock and the lock tender's house on the right and, after that, the community of Zarepath. In 3 miles, the road will swing around and cross the canal. The parking area, created from a remnant of older pavement, is located on the right, just before the road crosses the canal.

THE TRAIL

Cross over the bridge and turn left onto the towpath, heading south. On the other side of the canal (the east bank) is the old bridge tender's house, built circa 1831. Originally, a swing bridge spanned the canal here. If you are hiking in summer or early fall, notice the duckweed, the miniature lily pad-like plant that floats in clusters on the water. This plant tends to accumulate, sometimes covering the entire canal surface for the final 10 to 15 miles of the waterway, before its terminus in New Brunswick. The trees, mostly oak and maple, form an intermittent canopy over the towpath. On the other side of the canal is Weston Canal Road, a country road with light traffic. On your right is the large Millstone River floodplain.

In a few minutes, you'll notice on the right a wooden post, which indicates that you are at milepost 25 of the canal. These mile markers were installed as an Eagle Scout project in 2010, and the mileages do not correspond with the historic mileages of the canal. After another half mile, you'll notice that the Millstone floodplain, undoubtedly

Milepost 31 along the canal DANIEL CHAZIN

turtles startled by your intrusion fill the void left by the absence of sounds of traffic. If you are lucky, a great blue heron may wing its way down the canal. The only evidence of civilization is the boat dock for a day camp on the opposite bank of the canal.

After passing milepost 24, you'll come to a stone-faced spillway. On the right, as you reach the spillway, you'll notice a concrete milepost with the numbers 31/13. This original canal artifact tells you that you are 13 miles from New Brunswick and 31 miles from Trenton. About five minutes later, you'll reach a footbridge which spans the canal and leads to Colonial Park. Just beyond milepost 23.5, the canal goes over a culvert through which Spooky Brook runs, on its way to the Millstone River. This is an example of one of the many streams that were channeled underneath the canal in order to keep its water level stable.

All too soon, you'll begin to hear the sounds of traffic, and the quiet and privacy of this section of towpath come to an end. In another half mile, you'll reach Amwell Road in East Millstone, with a parking area and a bridge over the canal. If you're interested, cross over the canal on Amwell Road and take a short walk into East Millstone, a small town that has changed very little over the years. On the left, you'll pass a bridge tender's house and then the historic Franklin Inn, built in 1734. The first road on the right leads to a small grocery store and deli (closed on Sundays). On the way, you'll pass the headquarters of the Millstone First Aid Squad and, behind it, East Millstone Park, a filled-in area which once served as a basin for boats on the canal. Today, it features a basketball court and recreational equipment for children.

After your visit to East Millstone, return to the towpath and retrace your steps to your car.

very fertile, is being used as a field. At about the point where the cornfield ends, Weston Canal Road turns away from the canal, and the towpath enters one of its very few sections not paralleled by a road. For the next 1.5 miles, the walking through this quiet and somewhat wild area—rare in densely populated central New Jersey—becomes very pleasant.

As the sounds of civilization fade out, the towpath takes on a wilder look. The Millstone River itself swings close to the canal, but 20 feet below it. The sounds of insects, fish jumping, and the hurried scrambling of

Coastal Plain

39

Cheesequake State Park

Total distance: 3.3 miles

Hiking time: 2 hours

Vertical rise: Approximately 200 feet

Rating: Easy to moderate

Maps: USGS South Amboy; DEP Cheesequake State Park map

Trailhead GPS Coordinates: N 40° 26' 10" W 74° 15' 56"

Located in the transition zone between New Jersey's distinctive northern and southern plant communities, the 1,610-acre Cheesequake State Park (300 Gordon Road, Matawan, NJ 07747; 732-566-2161; www .njparksandforests.org) may be of particular appeal to those interested in botany. There are a variety of habitats throughout the park, including salt- and freshwater marshes, northeastern hardwood forests, pine barrens, and a cedar swamp. Cheesequake is one of the oldest state parks in New Jersey, dating back to 1937, when acquisition of some farms, orchards, and salt marsh began. It was formally opened in 1940. Family camping is available April 1 through October 31.

The area was occupied as early as 5,000 years ago by Native Americans who hunted and fished here. The name Cheesequake was taken from a word in the language of the Lenni-Lenape tribe, which lived in New Jersey when the Dutch and English colonists first arrived. Some say the word means "upland people." During the 18th and 19th centuries, a fine-quality clay used to make stoneware pottery was mined in the area and shipped to pottery-making sites up and down the Atlantic Coast. Red clay was also mined to make bricks that some say were used extensively in the building of New York City. As late as the early 20th century, a steamboat dock existed on Cheesequake Creek, at the end of Old Dock Road; from there, products and produce were sent to markets.

There are several marked trails in the park (mostly footpaths) that are color coded. This hike uses three of the park's four marked

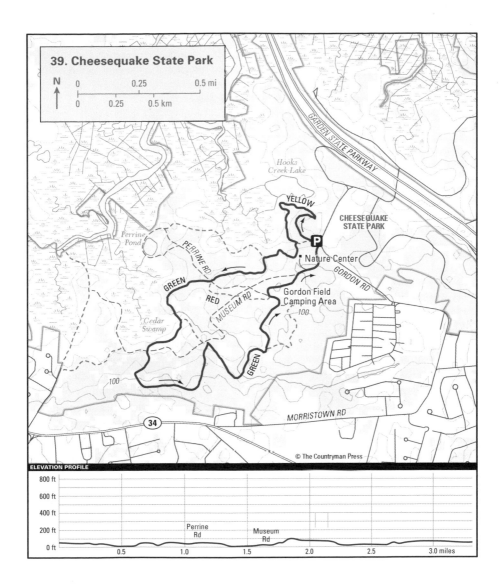

39. Cheesequake State Park

N
0   0.25   0.5 mi
0   0.25   0.5 km

Hooks
Creek Lake

YELLOW

CHEESEQUAKE
STATE PARK

P

Nature Center

Perrine
Pond

PERRINE RD

GORDON RD

GREEN

RED

MUSEUM RD

Gordon Field
Camping Area

100

Cedar
Swamp

GREEN

100

34

MORRISTOWN RD

© The Countryman Press

ELEVATION PROFILE

800 ft					
600 ft					
400 ft					
200 ft		Perrine Rd	Museum Rd		
0 ft	0.5	1.0	1.5	2.0	2.5	3.0 miles

hiking trails. The trails traverse various wet sections on boardwalks and bridges, and there are a number of wooden stairs. Rugged footwear is not required. Mountain bikes are not allowed on the hiking trails (there is a multi-use trail designated for them in another section of the park), but evidence of their trespass is widespread. Because of the proximity to swamps and marshes, it may be best to visit the park during the fall, when both insect and human populations are at their lowest.

HOW TO GET THERE

From the Garden State Parkway, take Exit 120 and turn right (east) at the end of the ramp, following the brown STATE PARK signs. Turn right at the first traffic light onto

Morristown Road. Turn right again at next light onto Gordon Road, which in 1 mile will take you to the park entrance. Pass the park office and drive to the parking area on the left, about 0.2 mile ahead. A kiosk with a map of the trails marks the trailhead. A parking fee of $5 daily, $10 weekends is in effect from Memorial Day through Labor Day. There is no charge during the rest of the year.

THE TRAIL

Begin your hike at the trailhead, just to the left of the kiosk. At the first fork, just a few hundred feet from the trailhead, turn right onto the Yellow Trail and follow it to Hooks Creek Lake. This section of the trail is noted for the many lady's slipper orchids that grow alongside the path. Follow the trail along the south shore of the lake and then descend the wooden stairs from the high area that overlooks the lake. At the base of the stairs, turn left and follow the trail back through an area that borders a freshwater floodplain. The trail then reaches a junction with the Red, Green, and Blue Trails. From this junction, follow the three trails across a small brook on a wooden bridge (the first of many), then climb to the park's Nature Center, which contains exhibits illustrating the natural and cultural history of the park. You'll find a turtle display with live turtles in a tank, a model of a Lenni-Lenape village, both fresh- and saltwater aquariums, and restrooms.

Continue on the Red, Green, and Blue Trails through some sweet pepperbush, perhaps the most common plant along the trail. Pepperbush is related to mountain laurel and blueberry, also common in the park. During the spring, wild honeysuckle is in bloom here and in other sections of the trail. After leveling off, the trail passes a protected wet area on the right that's filled with tall ferns. Ahead is a view through the trees to the salt marsh below. Continue downhill on wooden steps and a boardwalk, then climb a long flight of wooden steps. Just beyond the top of the steps, the Blue Trail leaves to the right, but you should bear left, following the green and red blazes.

The Green and Red Trails now pass through a large stand of lowbush and highbush blueberries among some large pines (more typical of the Pinelands of southern New Jersey) mixed with the usual hardwoods. In this dry section are some large clusters of mountain laurel that bloom in June. After crossing a bridge over a small brook, the trail comes out to a sand road (Perrine Road) near a bench. It is here that the Green Trail splits from the Red Trail. Just beyond the road crossing, bear right to continue on the Green Trail.

Along this level section are many small sassafras trees, as well as some chokecherry, beech, maple, chestnut oak, and white oak. Soon, the trail heads rather steeply downhill. At the base of the descent, the trail passes close to the tall sedges, rushes, and grasses of the saltwater marsh, which forms the western boundary of the park. After a short climb, proceed down a slope to a long boardwalk over a freshwater swamp, heavily overgrown with arrowwood, elderberry, and buttonbush. The end of the boardwalk has been built around several large red maple trees. This quiet area, rich in plant and animal life, is a change from the woods and brush environments traversed so far.

At the end of the swamp, the trail climbs wooden steps and bears right. Soon, it descends to cross another boardwalk, this one over a cedar swamp. Here, the environment is even cooler and darker than that of the freshwater swamp you passed a few minutes ago. The eastern white cedars—which grow out of black clay—dominate, shutting out light for other plants. The extreme moisture and the decomposing leaves make the

A long set of wooden steps along the trail

soil very acidic, preserving any cedar logs that become buried. In some similar areas of New Jersey, old cedar logs in good condition have been mined from the dense acidic soil. Great horned owls are known to frequent this swamp. Beyond the swamp, the trail climbs over a ridge and descends to cross another sand road (Museum Road).

The trail now enters a woods dominated by huge white pines. Because of their height and straightness, these trees were used by shipbuilders during colonial times—particularly during the Revolution—for masts. Overharvesting of the original white pines eventually forced the lumbering industry out of the state. These trees are estimated to be between 100 and 150 years old and are used as nesting sites by owls and hawks.

Boardwalk through the Cedar Swamp

The trail through this section is narrow and crowded in by pepperbush, mountain laurel, and rhododendron.

After climbing another set of wooden steps, you will reach the highest elevation on the hike. The woods are dry here and composed mostly of oak, which provides food for the gypsy moth that has left evidence of its appetite in the form of standing dead trees. On the floor of the forest are large quantities of false Solomon's seal. At a junction, the trail bears left, leading to a stand of pitch pines typical of the Pinelands of South Jersey. Pitch pine grows in dry, sandy soil as well as on rocky outcrops (as it does in northern New Jersey) and can survive with few nutrients.

From this high area, the trail crosses two ravines on wooden bridges and gradually descends. The trail, which skirts the southern boundary of the park (houses visible), is sandy here as it passes through a forest of hardwoods. After coming close to, but not touching, Museum Road, the trail continues along a path through a forest floor with numerous wildflowers, such as the wild lily of the valley and the pink lady's slipper, both of which bloom in the spring. You can find violets, starflowers, and jack-in-the-pulpits here as well. Only plants that can tolerate frequent inundations survive here. Long stretches of boardwalk keep you dry and clean in this section of black mud, clear brooks, and wet swamps. After descending into a ravine and crossing a wooden bridge, the trail climbs to Perrine Road.

Turn left onto the road, following the green blazes past the Gordon Field camping area. Just ahead, the Green Trail, now joined by the Red Trail, turns right and reenters the woods. The trail follows the edge of the cleared area, then bears left and descends to Museum Road. Bear right here and follow the road, which in 0.2 mile leads to the trailhead and your car.

40

Hartshorne Woods Park

Total distance: 2.7 miles
Hiking time: 1.5 hours
Vertical rise: 300 feet
Rating: Easy to moderate
Maps: USGS Sandy Hook; Monmouth County Park System Hartshorne Woods Park trail guide
Trailhead GPS Coordinates: N 40° 24' 3.5" W 74° 00' 46"

The 794-acre Hartshorne Woods Park has the most extensive trail network in the Monmouth County park system, with over 14 miles of trails. The area, portions of which rise 245 feet above the Navesink River Bay, is surprisingly hilly for central New Jersey. It features forests of oak, hickory, beech, and maple, interspersed with mountain laurel and holly. For more information, contact the Monmouth County Park System, 805 Newman Springs Road, Lincroft, NJ 07738; 732-872-0336 or 2670; www.monmouth countyparks.com.

Hartshorne Woods is named for its original owner, Richard Hartshorne, who purchased the tract from Native Americans in the 1670s. The local pronunciation of Hartshorne is "harts horn," or horn of the hart (an old English word for deer).

This hike follows the Laurel Ridge Trail, a loop trail that explores the Buttermilk Valley section of the park. The Laurel Ridge Trail, like nearly all the trails in the park, is a multiuse trail, and it is heavily used by mountain bikes—especially on weekends. Under park rules, bikers are required to yield to hikers, and both bikers and hikers must yield to horses. If you wish to avoid bikes entirely, two very short trails for foot traffic only begin at the main trailhead: the 1.5-mile Candlestick Trail and the 1.1-mile Kings Hollow Trail.

In the late 1980s, Hartshorne Woods, formerly a relatively quiet woods for walkers, became extremely popular with mountain bikers (due in part to the closing of parks in nearby counties to bicycles). Trails in Hartshorne Woods quickly became degraded,

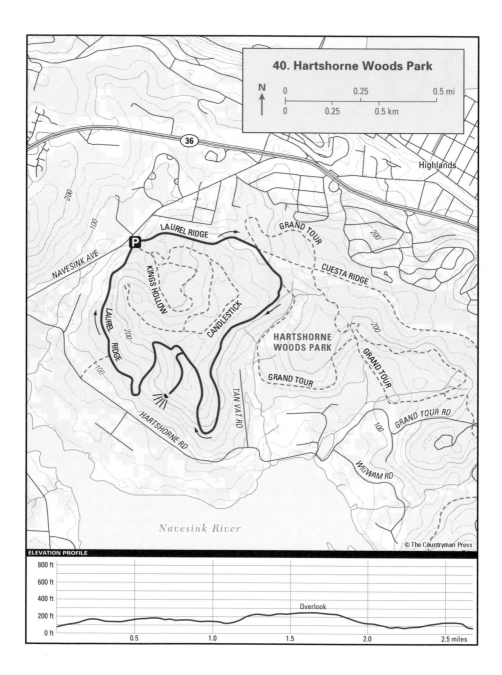

40. Hartshorne Woods Park

N

| 0 | | 0.25 | | 0.5 mi |

| 0 | | 0.25 | | 0.5 km |

Highlands

36

Navesink Ave

LAUREL RIDGE

GRAND TOUR

CUESTA RIDGE

KINGS HOLLOW

LAUREL RIDGE

CANDLESTICK

HARTSHORNE WOODS PARK

GRAND TOUR

GRAND TOUR

GRAND TOUR RD

TAN VAT RD

HARTSHORNE RD

WIGWAM RD

Navesink River

© The Countryman Press

ELEVATION PROFILE

800 ft					
600 ft					
400 ft			Overlook		
200 ft					
0 ft	0.5	1.0	1.5	2.0	2.5 miles

forcing the Monmouth County Park Commission to find a solution to this problem. They launched a major trail rebuilding project and decided to make most of the park's trails multiuse—unlike other county and state agencies, which have chosen to keep bikers and hikers on separate trails where possible.

In 1991, the multiuse trail plan was

Along the Laurel Ridge Trail

devised and implemented with the help of some 40 volunteers. New trails were cut and opened to the public, and worn and abused trails were closed and blocked. Junctions were posted with signs, and trails were color coded and labeled to indicate differing degrees of difficulty.

It should be noted, however, that this rating system (modeled after downhill ski standards) is designed with bikes in mind. For hikers, even the "black diamond" trails are no more than moderately difficult. The color markers appear only at junctions; the trails themselves are not blazed, but they are clearly delineated and easy to follow.

Hartshorne Woods Park is divided into four sections: Buttermilk Valley, Monmouth Hills, Rocky Point, and Claypit Creek. Trails connect the first three sections, and hikers desiring a longer walk may wish to extend the hike by including a loop on the 3.1-mile Grand Tour Trail. The 2.3-mile Rocky Point Trail, which circles the site of former military fortifications, is another attractive option.

HOW TO GET THERE

Take the Garden State Parkway south to Exit 117. Bear left beyond the toll booths and continue on NJ 36 for 11.5 miles. After passing through Atlantic Highlands, turn right at the exit for Red Bank Scenic Road, then turn right at the stop sign onto Navesink Avenue. Continue for 0.3 mile to the Buttermilk Valley parking area for Hartshorne Woods Park, on the left side of the road. (Do not turn right at the intersection of Memorial Drive and Navesink Avenue in Atlantic Highlands.)

THE TRAIL

From the parking area, proceed ahead to a kiosk with a large trail map (free park brochures with maps are usually available

---

Pinxterbloom Azalea   CLAUS HOLZAPFEL

section, where greenbrier—a vine-like plant with a green, smooth, and thorny stem—is abundant. You'll also pass a few huge hickory and tulip trees. Smaller sassafras trees are scattered about, and in the understory are jack-in-the-pulpits.

Soon, a view of water appears ahead, particularly when the leaves are off the trees. This is the Navesink River. The trail now curves sharply to the right and begins to climb. You'll notice chunks of conglomerate rock (sand fused with pebbles) along the trail here. This resistant rock has acted as a protective cap over softer sediments, creating highlands among sea-level plains. Another change you may note is in the vegetation itself. There is little mountain laurel or holly along this section of the trail, and oaks are now the predominant tree.

After the trail levels off, you'll reach a junction with a side trail to the Claypit Creek Overlook, the highest point on the hike (elevation 248 feet). Turn left onto this trail and head through dense mountain laurel thickets to the viewpoint over the Navesink River. Unfortunately, the vegetation has largely grown in, and even in leaf-off season, you get only a limited view of the river through the trees. This area makes a good rest stop. Return to the junction when you are ready to continue the hike.

Turn left at the junction and head downhill, first along a stone-bordered switchback and then through mountain laurel thickets. Some of the descent is over soft dirt that in places may be torn up from mountain bike usage. If you are lucky, you may spot a deer or two. Two side trails lead off to the left, but follow the main Laurel Ridge Trail ahead until you reach the kiosk adjacent to the parking area where the hike began.

here), and turn left onto the Laurel Ridge Trail, marked with a blue circle to indicate it is of moderate difficulty. You'll be following this trail in a clockwise direction for the entire hike. The trail heads gradually uphill on a wide, sandy road that begins a gradual climb. Beyond the crest of the hill, the road descends to a four-way junction, marked by signposts. The Grand Tour Trail begins on the left, and the Cuesta Ridge Trail proceeds straight ahead, but you should turn right to continue on the Laurel Ridge Trail.

In about five minutes, you'll come to another junction. The other end of the Grand Tour Trail is on the left, but you continue ahead on the Laurel Ridge Trail. Follow the path along the side of a slope through thickets of mountain laurel. It is for this plant, abundant throughout the hike, that the trail is named. The trail meanders up and down as it swings around the slope, passing a few holly trees, also green throughout the year. After a while, you enter a denser stand of holly and continue through a thickly vegetated

41

Allaire State Park

Total distance: 3.7 miles
Hiking time: 2.5 hours
Vertical rise: 120 feet
Rating: Easy
Maps: USGS Farmingdale, Asbury Park; DEP Allaire State Park map
Trailhead GPS Coordinates: N 40° 09' 26.5" W 74° 07' 16"

Allaire State Park (4265 Atlantic Avenue, Farmingdale, NJ 07727; 732-938-2371; www .njparksandforests.org) was a gift in 1941 to the people of New Jersey from the widow of Arthur Brisbane, a prominent newspaper man. The original 1,000-plus acres has now expanded to more than 3,200 and includes a narrow-gauge railroad, a car camping area, and a historical village dating from the boom days of the bog iron industry in the 1830s. The park, located in one of the northern-most sections of the Pinelands, straddles the Manasquan River, which is popular with canoeists. Interstate 195, which bisects the park, pollutes the park with sound, depriving it of the isolation it once had. On the other hand, the Interstate highway also makes the park more accessible to the public.

Within Allaire's boundaries are a large number of sand and gravel roads and an abandoned railroad bed that are used for hiking, biking, and horseback riding. Because the park is essentially quartered by the river and the freeway, a complete tour is not possible, and we have chosen a route that takes you through some wooded areas as well as the park's main attraction, historic Allaire Village.

HOW TO GET THERE

Take the Garden State Parkway to Exit 98. Beyond the toll booths, bear left at the fork, following signs to Route 34 South. After merging onto Route 34, make the first right onto Allenwood Road, and proceed for 0.7 mile to a stop sign at a T-intersection. Turn right onto Atlantic Avenue (County Route

524), and continue for 1.0 mile to a large gravel parking area on the left, just past the entrance to the Spring Meadow Golf Course. (Alternatively, you can take I-195 to Exit 31B and head east on Atlantic Avenue to the parking area, 0.6 mile beyond (east of) the main entrance to Allaire State Park.) By parking here, you avoid both the fees and the crowds of people who visit the park only to see the historic village. Most of the hike is on sandy trails. Sneakers as well as boots are fine here. A trail map is available at the park office.

THE TRAIL

From the parking area, cross the road, turn left, and head west along the grassy shoulder. You'll pass a private residence (#4210), with a split-rail fence and a row of evergreens along the road. In about 750 feet, just beyond the end of the evergreens, you'll see two gates—first, a metal gate, then a wooden gate with a State Park Service NO PARKING sign. Go through the opening to the right of the wooden gate, and continue along a lane that runs between two properties, with old metal fences on either side. The lane may be somewhat overgrown with grass, but it is the correct route to follow. The park map shows this route as the Orange Trail, but there are no orange markers for the first part of the hike. The lane is shadowed by tall sumac trees and vines, with a few patches of holly along the way. As you move away from the highway and the sound of traffic, the sounds of birds, plentiful in this area, may be heard.

After about 10 minutes, the lane widens into a sand-and-gravel road (typical of the Pinelands), and the walking becomes more pleasant. You'll notice several orange-blazed brown wands on the left, as well as orange paint blazes on trees to the right, indicating that you are following the Orange Trail.

Carpenter shop at Allaire Village

DAN BALOGH

Coastal Plain

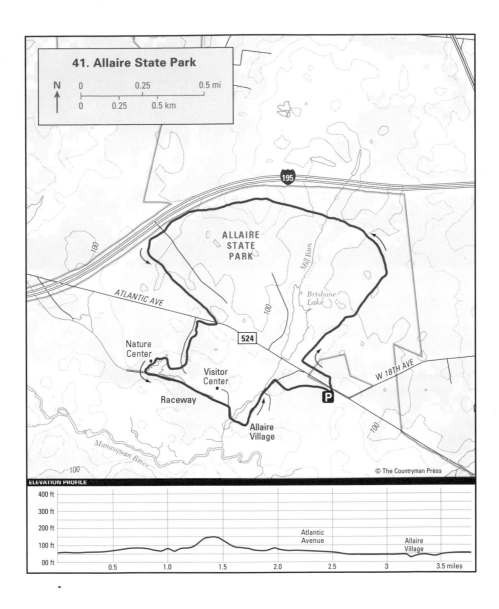

Lowbush blueberry and mountain laurel form the ground cover, and oak and sassafras are the dominant trees (along with stands of holly).

Soon, the trail bears left and begins a gradual ascent. You'll be gaining only about 50 feet in elevation, but this is the most significant climb of the entire hike. As it swings left, the trail begins to parallel I-195 (always busy with cars heading to and from the Jersey Shore), which it follows for about half a mile. At the top of the climb, about 1.3 miles from the start, you'll pass through an abandoned gravel quarry, with a blue water tower visible on the left, through the trees. You'll know when you reach this spot because the

---

Along the Raceway

oak/sassafras forest is suddenly replaced by a stand of pitch pines.

From the quarry site, the trail begins to descend, now closely paralleling I-195, which can be seen through the trees on the right. The noise of the traffic on I-195 spoils the peacefulness of the area, but soon the sand-and-gravel road curves to the left, away from the busy Interstate highway, and the sounds of birds once again become more prominent. The road now begins to parallel the right-of-way of the abandoned Freehold and Jamesburg Agricultural Railroad (visible below on the right). This railroad was built in 1853 to transport produce from Monmouth County farms to city markets, and it was acquired by the Pennsylvania Railroad in 1879. For many years, it served as a main route for passenger traffic from Philadelphia to the Jersey Shore. In 1939, the Royal Train carrying King George VI of England passed over this line. From 1949 until passenger service was discontinued in 1962, the daily passenger train consisted of a gas-electric self-propelled railroad car, popularly known as the "Doodlebug."

Continue along the sand-and-gravel road until you come to Atlantic Avenue, 2.3 miles from the start. (You've followed a semicircular route to reach this point.) Bear slightly left, cross the road at the crosswalk, and turn right onto a wide paved path with purple blazes. (To your left, you'll see the tracks of the Pine Creek Railroad, a short, narrow-gauge-loop tourist railroad established in Allaire in 1963.) Follow the paved path as it curves left, away from the highway, and enters the woods, paralleling the park entrance road on the right.

After passing a small toll booth, you'll see a sign on the right for NATURE CENTER PARKING. Turn right, leaving the paved path, cross the park entrance road, and continue through the parking lot. At the end of the parking lot, bear right and follow a concrete path that crosses a wooden footbridge over a stream and continues through the woods to the Nature Center. If the center is open, you'll want to stop and visit the interesting exhibits. Continue past the Nature Center, following an unmarked path that leads to another footbridge over a stream. Cross

Coastal Plain

the bridge and immediately turn left onto a gravel road known as the Raceway. On the park map, this is shown as the Green Trail, and you'll see some green blazes on trees along the way.

Proceed ahead on the Raceway, passing an attractive pond on the right, and continue along the route of a former canal. Soon, you'll pass a large picnic area on the right. You're now traversing a developed section of the park, and you should expect to see many people here, especially on summer weekends. After passing a large parking lot on the left, you'll enter the historic Allaire Village. Back in the 18th century, this village site was known as Monmouth Furnace and later as the Howell Works, after Benjamin Howell, the first iron maker here. In 1822, the property was acquired by James P. Allaire of New York, who was already established as a brass worker. At the Howell Works, Allaire put together a community of more than 400 people to turn bog iron into pots, kettles, cauldrons, stovepipe, and other common items. The self-contained community included a wide variety of craftspeople to both run the industry and serve the population.

Bog iron, found in the Pinelands, is smelted from iron oxides leached from the sand and deposited in accumulations of decaying swamp vegetation. Interestingly, bog iron is a renewable resource as long as the vegetation decay cycle is not interfered with. The operation at Allaire's village prospered in the 1830s, but the discovery of higher-grade iron ore in Pennsylvania, the development of improved smelting technology, and a national depression made the operation less profitable, and it was closed in 1846. Although the village no longer functioned as an active industrial community, the Allaire family continued to live there until James Allaire's son Hal died in 1901.

In 1907, the property was acquired by the journalist Arthur Brisbane, and it remained in his family until, in 1941, it was deeded to the state by his widow. In 1957, a group of concerned citizens, including several descendants of James Allaire, formed Allaire Village, Inc., a nonprofit organization, and restoration of the historic buildings began. Today, most of the historic buildings have been restored, and the village is reminiscent of its heyday in the middle of the 19th century.

The visitor center, a long brick building built in 1820, is on your left and offers a number of interesting displays about the park and the village. A map and guide to the village can be obtained here. After viewing the exhibits, continue straight ahead to the end of the visitor center, make a right, and follow the main road as it heads downhill, turns left to cross a stream, and proceeds through the Historic Village at Allaire. The historic brick buildings you'll pass include a foreman's cottage, blacksmith shop, bakery, general store and carpenter shop—all built in the village's heyday, between 1827 and 1836. Many of the buildings are open during summer months from Wednesday to Sunday and feature historical demonstrations. Refreshments are offered for sale in the bakery, and the general store is now a well-stocked gift shop. You'll want to spend some time visiting these historic buildings and exploring the surrounding area.

After taking in the sights of the historic village, continue along the road as it heads north, leaving the village area. A short distance beyond, you'll come to a locked gate. Here, you should turn right onto a paved path (marked with orange and purple blazes) which follows the route of the abandoned Freehold and Jamesburg Agricultural Railroad. Continue to follow the paved path as it bears left, leaving the railbed, and soon reaches the parking area where the hike began.

42

Cattus Island

Total distance: 3.2 miles
Hiking time: 2 hours
Vertical rise: Minimal
Rating: Easy
Maps: USGS Toms River/Seaside Park; Cattus Island Ocean County Park trail map
Trailhead GPS Coordinates: N 39° 58' 55" W 74° 07' 45"

Cattus Island County Park (1170 Cattus Island Boulevard, Toms River, NJ 08753; 732-270-6960; www.co.ocean.nj.us/ocparks) preserves a small portion of the salt marshes and pine forests on Barnegat Bay. Located in the midst of New Jersey's most popular summer vacation area, which has been extensively developed, Cattus Island offers the hiker a variety of natural environments to explore, including pinelands, open marshes, holly forests, and bay beaches. The excellent views over vast marshes, across inlets, and out over the bay, plus the variety of wildlife found in the park, are further reasons to walk the trails in this 500-acre Ocean County park.

Cattus Island was first settled by the Page family, who moved here in 1763. Timothy Page, born on the island that year, served in the local militia during the American Revolution. Most probably he was a privateer, essentially a pirate licensed by the Continental Congress. During the war, British ships were lured into Barnegat Bay through Cranberry Inlet only to be attacked and have their cargoes sold for profit. Cranberry Inlet, an opening to the Atlantic near present-day Ortley Beach, existed between 1750 and 1812. It was opened and closed by strong storms.

After the death of Timothy Page, the family house burned down, and the property was sold to Lewis Applegate. He moved there in 1842 and developed the southeastern section of the island, now named for him. He built a sawmill and a port for lumber boats. The island was sold again in 1867 and was slated to be developed as a resort, but the 1873 depression canceled the project.

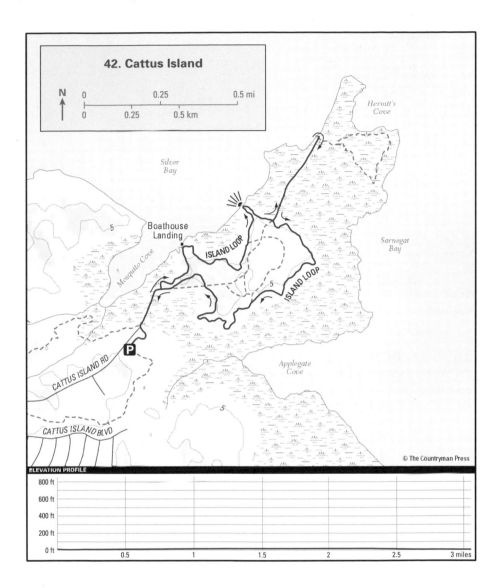

In 1895, the island was purchased by John V. A. Cattus, an importer and Olympic-class athlete. He used the island and its buildings for weekend vacations, not as a full-time residence. Cattus loved boating, owned many boats, and built a hunting lodge on the island. After he died, the land was sold in 1964 by his sons to developers. New state laws passed in the early 1970s that limited development in wetlands and along the coast discouraged the developers, and they sold the land to Ocean County in 1973. The property was acquired with county tax dollars and state Green Acres funds. In 1976, the park opened to the public, and in the following year trail development began.

Raised wood-chip path along the Island Loop

DANIEL CHAZIN

HOW TO GET THERE

From Exit 82 on the Garden State Parkway (Toms River/NJ 37), take NJ 37 east 4.4 miles to Fisher Boulevard. Proceed north on Fisher Boulevard for 2.0 miles, and turn right onto Cattus Island Boulevard (just after Bellcrest Plaza). The park entrance road is 0.1 mile ahead on the left. Another 0.5 mile will bring you to the large parking area.

THE TRAIL

To begin the hike, follow the asphalt path to the Cooper Environmental Center. The environmental center building was heavily damaged by Hurricane Sandy in October 2012 and, as of this writing (December 2013), it is closed to the public. When you reach the building, turn left and walk around the porch, descend a ramp, pass a kiosk, and turn right onto a sand road. This road, more like a causeway, penetrates the salt marsh that surrounds the slightly higher and drier land ahead. The body of water to the left is Mosquito Cove. The sand road leads straight ahead into the woods and eventually out to the tip of the island, which extends well into Barnegat Bay. Our hike utilizes this sand road and footpaths on either side of it.

Just after leaving the marsh, turn left onto a blue-blazed footpath, called the Island Loop. This path winds through a pine forest, makes a small loop out to the shoreline, then swings out again to the grassy shore of Mosquito Cove at the old Boathouse Landing.

Leave the landing, and continue following the blue blazes through a forest of oak, pines, and enormous thickets of greenbrier. You'll pass the gnarled trunk of a dead cedar tree and the fallen trunks of many pine trees toppled by Hurricane Sandy, and you'll traverse a holly forest, green in all seasons. Notice that the red berries do not grow on all the holly trees—only the female trees bear fruit. These bright red berries are found on the tree year-round, and the bird population is well supplied with food.

A short distance beyond, the white/blue-blazed Cedar Line Short Cut Trail begins on the right, but you should continue ahead, following the blue blazes through dense phragmites on a raised wood-chip path and wooden boardwalk. Soon, the trail comes out on the shore of Silver Bay, with broad views across the bay. Several cedar trees shade this pleasant spot, and a bench is provided if you wish to take a break.

Continue on the blue-blazed trail until you reach the sand road, then turn left onto the road and follow it across a causeway, bordered by salt marsh on both sides. Towering over the marsh to the left is an osprey nesting site. Other water birds, such as the great egret, may be feeding in this area. In about a quarter of a mile, the road ends at the narrow sandy beach that forms the northern tip of Cattus Island. You may wish to walk along this narrow strip of sand to the most northerly point of the island. After this short exploration, return to the sand road and retrace your steps across the causeway.

At the end of the causeway across the salt marsh, turn left onto the blue-blazed Island Loop, which follows a raised wood-chip path through a wet area, with a boardwalk on one section. After passing through an open area, with several large pines felled by Hurricane Sandy, you'll reach an observation blind over a salt marsh, with an osprey nesting platform visible in the distance. The trail now goes through an area dominated by highbush blueberry and passes the end of the white /blue-blazed Cedar Line Short Cut Trail, on the right. To the right, you'll notice a large clearing, with several benches. This is the site where the island's residents once lived.

Continue ahead on the blue-blazed trail, which cuts through a dense stand of phragmites, reenters the woods on a sandy footpath, and passes several stands of holly. You'll pass another observation blind, traverse a dense growth of phragmites on a boardwalk, and reach the sand road. Cross the road and follow the blue-blazed trail for a short distance until you reach the sand road once more. Turn right onto the road, and follow it back to the Cooper Environmental Center. Then take the wide path back to the parking area.

Salt marshes

43

Island Beach State Park

Total distance: 3.7 miles

Hiking time: 2.5 hours

Vertical rise: Minimal

Rating: Easy

Maps: USGS Barnegat Light; DEP Island Beach State Park map

Trailhead GPS Coordinates: N 39° 47' 6.5" W 74° 05' 41.5"

Along the 127-mile boundary between New Jersey and the Atlantic Ocean are a number of long, thin barrier islands. Separated from the mainland by large bays, these islands are part of a chain that runs from New England to the Gulf Coast of Mexico. The constant movement of sand pushed by the ocean waves, called littoral drift, both maintains and changes these relatively fragile land forms. Severe storms often open or close inlets, wash out beaches, and even extend barrier islands, creating new land. With the exception of Island Beach State Park (P.O. Box 37, Seaside Park, NJ 08752; 732-793-0506; www.njparksandforests.org) most of these islands have been developed with row after row of summer beach homes, board-walks, and restaurants. If it were not for this park, many New Jerseyans would have no idea of what the shoreline in its natural state would look like.

Island Beach State Park occupies the southern end of a long spit that is joined to the mainland near Point Pleasant. This sec-tion of the spit was an island at one time; an inlet connecting the ocean and Barnegat Bay was once located near present-day Ortley Beach. This inlet, known as Cranberry Inlet, was created overnight by a storm in 1750 and was just as quickly destroyed by a storm in 1812. More recently, in 1935, a storm opened up an inlet just south of the present park entrance. Local rum runners wanted it to remain open, but the owners of the tract at the time had it closed.

Originally, Island Beach was owned by Lord Stirling, owner of vast acreages in New

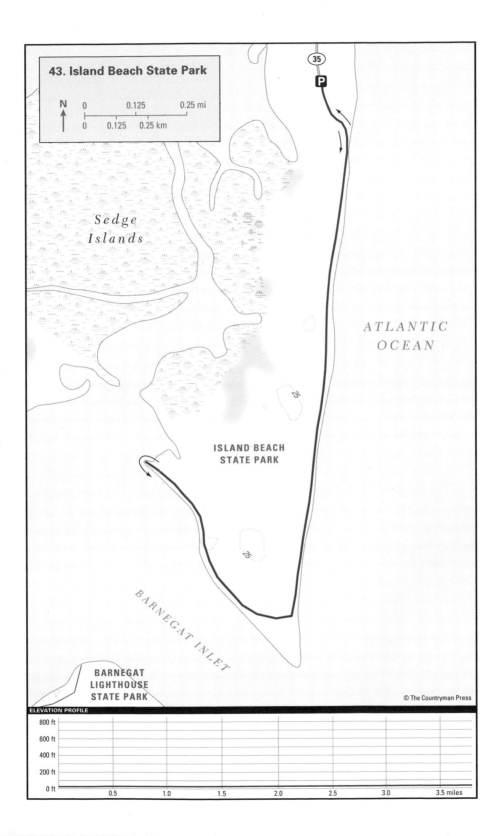

43. Island Beach State Park

N

| 0 | 0.125 | | 0.25 mi |
| 0 | 0.125 | 0.25 km | |

35

P

Sedge Islands

ATLANTIC OCEAN

25

ISLAND BEACH STATE PARK

25

BARNEGAT INLET

BARNEGAT LIGHTHOUSE STATE PARK

© The Countryman Press

ELEVATION PROFILE

| 800 ft |
| 600 ft |
| 400 ft |
| 200 ft |
| 0 ft |

0.5   1.0   1.5   2.0   2.5   3.0   3.5 miles

Jersey during the 17th century. During this period, the island was called Lord Stirling's Isle. Not much happened here during the next 100 years. These beaches were remote from industrial areas and were occupied only by squatters who lived in part from materials that washed ashore. In 1926, Henry Phipps purchased the island with a shore resort in mind. He was able to build three large homes before his project was halted by the stock market crash and Depression. During World War II, Island Beach was used by the army for rocket experiments and, as such, was restricted to the public. The squatters and leaseholders who lived on the island were forced to leave, though they were allowed to return after the war. In 1953, after much talk about preserving the area, the state purchased the land from the Phipps estate and opened the park in 1959. The island residents who held leases were allowed to live there for the rest of their lives.

The 3,003 acres of the park are divided into three sections, the northernmost and southernmost being natural areas, the central section public beaches and concessions. Located 1.2 miles south of the entrance are the park office and a nature center. A short, circular, self-guiding nature trail, which begins at the Aeolium (the nature center) is a good introduction to the park's vegetation. Farther ahead on the left is one of the original homes Phipps built; it's now used as a summer residence for New Jersey's governor. Beyond this house are the two large beach areas with their huge parking lots.

HOW TO GET THERE

From Exit 82 on the Garden State Parkway, take NJ 37 east through Toms River and over the Barnegat Bay Bridge. The entrance to the park is 2.5 miles south of the bridge at the southern end of NJ 35. There are many signs directing you to the park along the way. You will find that a fee is charged at the entrance gate. In 2013, this was $6 on weekdays and $10 on weekends from Memorial Day through Labor Day; $5 daily the rest of the year (with nonresidents of New Jersey being charged a higher fee). Although a large number of parking spaces are spread along the 8-mile road in the park, they often fill up quickly during peak season, and late arrivals are turned away at the gate. In fact, use of the area is so high that computer signs on the Garden State Parkway advise motorists of the park's opening or closing. The best time to explore Island Beach State Park on foot is definitely during the off-season, especially during the week.

To begin the hike, drive the full 8 miles south from the park entrance to parking area A-23, the last one on the paved road. This area is very popular and may be filled on sunny days, even during the off-season. If so, park at area A-22 or A-21 and walk the extra distance along the road. The area between A-19 and A-20 is a bird observation area.

THE TRAIL

From parking area A-23, walk through the gate toward the shoreline. You will be walking in a southerly direction toward the Barnegat Inlet and Lighthouse. You can walk either on the beach buggy tracks or along the water's edge, both far easier to walk on than the soft sand. The compacted sand along the water is probably the most interesting choice because it offers a fascinating variety of ocean debris that is constantly being reorganized by the tides and waves. Here are shells, dead fish, crabs, and driftwood. You will also encounter seagulls and fishermen with their beach buggies and campers. You will never be bored walking along what you may at first think to be a monotonous stretch of beach.

After about 1.75 miles, you will reach the

Coastal Plain

Footprints along the beach   DAN BALOGH

southern tip of Island Beach. This is Barnegat Inlet, where the Atlantic Ocean meets Barnegat Bay. Barnegat Lighthouse, built in 1858, stands across the inlet at the northern tip of Long Beach Island. In Barnegat Inlet, the ocean currents are steadily moving sand southward toward Long Beach Island. The accumulation of sand from this drift is awesome when you consider that the end of the road, more than a mile back, was once much closer to the end of the island. The Army Corps of Engineers struggles to keep this inlet, which is constantly filling with sand, open to navigation. It was hoped that the inlet would be stabilized by the two jetties, but even these structures don't prevent the sand from filling the inlet. During low tide, a sandbar or breaking waves are often visible between the two.

Walk west along the jetty toward Barnegat Bay. To your right is a protected bird nesting area and, beyond that, the dunes. The stability of the entire state park depends on these dunes, which are in turn stabilized by dune grass and other plants such as seaside goldenrod and Hudsonia or beach heather. These plants are very tolerant of the salty sea spray, which kills other species. Continue walking westward until you are nearly opposite the lighthouse. Comparing the present topography with that of the geological survey map reveals the incredible changes constantly taking place here. To your right are the Sedge Islands, a large area of salt marsh inhabited by countless birds and visited by many kayakers. Also to the right are the higher backdunes, separating the foredunes and the bay, which support a thick barrier of holly, bayberry, and other shrubs that cannot tolerate salt spray. You can also see a residence from here, one of several at the southern end of the park.

A small promontory made of jetty stone juts into the inlet, most often a private spot for lunch or simply for viewing the bay, ocean, and inlet all at once. To the south, the lighthouse and a steady parade of fishing and pleasure boats are a sharp contrast to the wild, virtually inaccessible Sedge Islands to the northwest.

When you are ready to continue, retrace your steps to the parking area. The first large gap in the dune fence that parallels the shore is your access to parking area A-23.

Island Beach State Park

44

Wells Mills County Park

Total distance: 4.5 miles

Hiking Time: 3 hours

Vertical rise: 500 feet

Rating: Easy to moderate

Maps: USGS Brookville; Ocean County Parks & Recreation Wells Mills trail map

Trailhead GPS Coordinates:
N 39° 47' 45" W 74° 16' 38"

Wells Mills County Park (P.O. Box 905, Wells Mills Road, Waretown, NJ 08758; 609-971-3085; www.co.ocean.nj.us/ocparks/) is located at the site of the former town of Wells Mills. Here, sometime in the late 1700s, James Wells established a sawmill. He created the lake, which supplied water power for the mill, by damming Oyster Creek. Others settled in the area, and over the years the ownership of the mill was passed along, with each owner benefiting from the local abundance of Atlantic white, or "swamp," cedar. This wood is not only strong but also extremely rot resistant and was used to build ships. Shingles and house-building lumber were other products of the mill.

During the 1870s, Christopher Estlow and his sons operated two mills in the area, which explains why the name of the hamlet, and now the park, is plural. In addition to the sawmill business, Estlow's grandson Tilden mined clay, which was sent to Trenton to be made into pottery. In 1936, the property was sold to Charles M. Conrad and his brother Grove. A year later, they began constructing the cabin that stands today on the shore of the lake at the boat dock. In 1979, the Conrad family found a buyer for all of their 200 acres in the New Jersey Conservation Foundation, a private organization that moves quickly to purchase land that might otherwise be developed. Later, it sells the land to public agencies, in this case Ocean County. Additional acquisitions by the county have increased the size of the park to 910 acres.

The staff of the Ocean County Park System has created an excellent trail system.

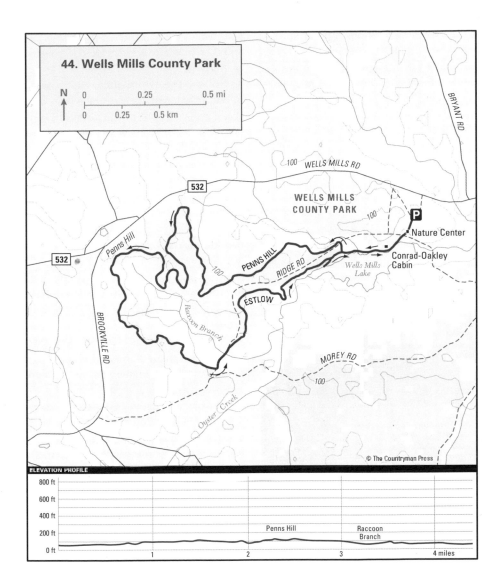

44. Wells Mills County Park

ELEVATION PROFILE

Several blazed hiking trails traverse the park, the longest being the 8.4-mile Penns Hill Trail (also known as the Macri Trail). The first section of this trail will be used in this hike. Except for one designated bicycle trail, which follows a sand road, all of the trails in the park are for hiking only. One of the surprises you will find here is the frequent ups and downs. Most of the New Jersey pinelands are flat. Here, and also just to the north in the Forked River Mountains (privately owned), the flatness is broken by small hills.

HOW TO GET THERE

Wells Mills County Park is on the eastern edge of the Pinelands, not far from the Garden State Parkway. Take the Parkway to Exit

69, turn left at the bottom of the ramp onto County Route 532 West, and proceed for 2.2 miles to the park entrance, on the left. Follow the entrance drive past the maintenance garage to the large parking lot.

THE TRAIL

Walk toward the restrooms and fountain, then follow the paved path to the nature center. Be sure to sign in at the kiosk just past the restrooms, and stop in at the nature center to see the displays illustrating the natural and human history of Wells Mills.

When you are ready to start hiking, descend the steps in front of the nature center and face the lake. You should see a tree with three white paint blazes to your right. This marks the start of the Penns Hill Trail, which

Along the Penns Hill Trail   DANIEL CHAZIN

first follows the shoreline of Wells Mills Lake and then traverses a remote and hilly section of the park.

Follow the white trail, which winds through the forest, parallel to the lake. Soon, you'll pass in front of the Conrad-Oakley Cabin, built in 1937. Just beyond, a dock extends into the lake. You can walk out on the dock to get a good view of the lake. Beyond the cabin, the trail goes through a stand of holly and then traverses a deep woods of tall Atlantic white cedar trees, with an understory of highbush blueberry and mountain laurel. You'll cross several streams on wooden bridges, including a picturesque one-log bridge. After bearing right, away from the lake, the trail crosses Ridge Road, a yellow-blazed sand road open to mountain bikes.

From here, the trail winds through a forest of pitch pines and scrub oak, with an understory of mountain and sheep laurel, crossing several fire ditches along the way. The trail snakes its way deeper and deeper into the pineland forest, crossing over wet areas on puncheons. About 20 minutes from the road, the trail reaches the top of a small rise called Raccoon Ridge. This is the 1-mile point. From here the trail alternately rises and descends, a highly unusual pattern for the Pinelands.

About a mile and a half into the hike, you will approach County Route 532 and hear the sounds of traffic. But the trail soon loops away from the road and heads south. As the trail curves to the west, the understory of highbush blueberry and mountain laurel thickens, and in places the vegetation arches over the trail.

After a short but rather steep climb, the trail attains a small ridge. This is Penns Hill, which is about 125 feet above sea level and about 70 feet higher than Wells Mills Lake. Although this relief seems inconsequential

Picturesque one-log bridge along the Penns Hill Trail   DANIEL CHAZIN

when compared with the mountains of northern New Jersey, it is unusual in the Pinelands.

Over the next mile, the trail climbs the 130-foot-high Laurel Hill, descends, and continues along what is called Laurel Ridge. Like Penns Hill, neither of these high points is much more than 50 feet above the surrounding woods, but the many ups and downs you encounter on this hike add up to a total elevation gain of over 500 feet. Along the way you'll walk through a small clearing, descend a few wooden stairways, and cross several wooden bridges and boardwalks over wet areas.

Eventually, you'll cross a wooden barrier and emerge onto Ridge Road. Leave the white-blazed trail and turn left onto this sand road, marked with both yellow bike trail blazes and the green blazes of the Estlow Trail. Soon, you'll enter a cedar swamp. The narrow, perfectly vertical cedars and the dark waters of the brook are a sharp contrast with the pine forest you have traversed for the last few miles. After crossing Raccoon Branch on a wooden bridge, turn right onto a footpath, following the green blazes of the Estlow Trail. For the next mile or so, this trail parallels Ridge Road. As you approach Wells Mills Lake, a short black-dot-on-yellow side trail on the right leads down to an observation blind on the lake.

A short distance beyond, you'll reach a junction with the white-blazed Penns Hill Trail. Turn right and follow the white blazes back through the cedar swamp and past the cabin, and continue to the visitor center, where the hike began.

45

Bass River State Forest

Total distance: 4.2 miles

Hiking time: 2 hours

Vertical rise: Minimal

Rating: Easy

Maps: USGS New Gretna; DEP Bass River State Forest Hiking Trails (sketch map)

Trailhead GPS Coordinates: N 39° 37' 21" W 74° 26' 25"

Bass River State Forest (762 Stage Road, Tuckerton, NJ 08087; 609-296-1114; www .njparksandforests.org) is New Jersey's first state forest. Land acquisition began with 597 acres in 1905, and today it includes 29,147 acres. The Garden State Parkway passes through the eastern parts of the forest, making it very accessible by automobile. The 50-mile Batona Trail (see also Hikes 46 and 47 in this volume) terminates in the western portion of the forest. The focus of recreational activities in Bass River State Forest is Lake Absegami, which offers swimming and boating and is surrounded by 176 car campsites, six group campsites, and a number of cabins, shelters, and lean-tos. Entrance to this section of the forest is via Stage Road, and a fee is charged during the summer season. (The hike below utilizes a free parking area.) Trails in Bass River State Forest are marked with flexible plastic posts containing the trail blaze color and international symbols indicating usage. These posts are found only at junctions.

A memorial to the Civilian Conservation Corps (CCC) is found in Bass River State Forest. The CCC was a New Deal program designed to get the many unemployed men, who were victims of the Depression, working on civic projects. During the 1930s, some 3 million men served in the CCC, and they worked on many park and forest projects that still stand today throughout the United States. Bass River State Forest had its own camp, one of the earliest in the nation. The men who served at this camp, S-55, planted 4,500 acres of timber and were noted for

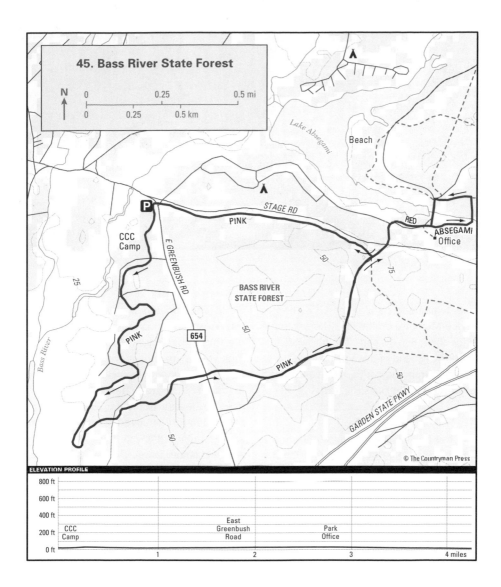

45. Bass River State Forest

ELEVATION PROFILE

their valor in fighting fires in the Pinelands, including an especially tragic one on May 30, 1936. The CCC also dammed two streams in the forest and created Lake Absegami. The camp was later used by the military during World War II. Very little remains of this camp today, but you will have the opportunity to hike through its remnants on the hike described below. A kiosk at the parking area contains photographs of some of the corps back in the 1930s, making the memorial more personal.

HOW TO GET THERE

If coming from the north on the Garden State Parkway, take Exit 52 and turn right onto East Greenbush Road (County Route 654), following signs to Bass River State Forest.

Boardwalk across the white cedar bog

Drive 1 mile and park at the CCC Forest Service Memorial on the left. There is parking for about 8 to 10 cars. The trailhead is at the northwest end of the small parking area. (If coming from the south, take Exit 50 and follow the signs to Bass River State Forest.)

THE TRAIL

From the parking area, head south on the Pink Trail (not to be confused with the Batona Trail)—you'll soon see a trail marker with a pink blaze. For the next hundred yards or so the trail passes alongside the remains, mostly floor and foundations, of the former CCC camp that existed in this location. The first one you pass is labeled Site A, the partial foundation of the kitchen/mess hall for the corps. The trail then swings to the left and passes several other foundations. Site B is unknown, but Site C is distinguished by a wide stairway and is thought to be either a medical building, officers' quarters, or an administration office. Just ahead is Site D, a large slab of concrete with small holes for drainage, which was apparently the bathhouse. Site E was the trash pit, and Site F was where the five wooden barracks of the

camp were located. As you walk along the trail, notice that portions of the trail retain the former pavement. At the clearing, the Pink Trail bears right, leaving the camp area.

You now enter a typical Jersey Pinelands forest. The coarser-barked pitch pines (three needles per clump) rise above a low understory of several common shrubs, among them highbush blueberry, leatherleaf, and sheep laurel. The trail next meets a wide sand lane, the route of a buried AT&T cable, onto which the trail turns left. After just a few minutes of walking, the Pink Trail turns right, leaving the AT&T line, and enters the woods on a four-wheel drive lane. Notice how different the forest in this section is from that in the vicinity of the CCC camp. Here are white pines, distinguished by clumps of five needles and finer bark ridges. Pay attention to the route here—in the midst of the white pines, the Pink Trail turns left onto another lane and then heads in an easterly direction. You may notice that white oaks are more prominent in this section of the forest. Follow the lane out to paved East Greenbush Road.

Cross the road and follow the Pink Trail

as it continues to head east in a pitch pine forest. A lane comes in from the right, and then the trail veers to the left onto a sand road. In places the sand is soft and limits traction. This is one of the characteristics of pineland hiking—a beach in the woods! Soon you will arrive at a junction with the AT&T line again, which is also a junction with the Green Trail. Turn left and follow the Pink Trail in a northerly direction straight across the AT&T line. Parts of this trail are on soft sand, other parts are more solid. After several minutes of walking you will come to a junction (the trail on your left will be your return route) and then reach Stage Road. Slightly to the right and ahead of you is the official entrance to Bass River State Forest. This is roughly the halfway point of the hike.

Cross Stage Road (be careful people drive fast on this country road) and continue on the Pink Trail. Follow the trail across the power line right-of-way until you come to the Red Trail. Turn right onto the Red Trail, crossing the paved south-shore campground road. The park office, where you can pick up maps and other information, will be on your right. Just past the office, you will come to the paved north-shore campground road. Continue across the road onto a silver-blazed trail with a surface of crushed cinders. This is the 0.4-mile Absegami Trail, which penetrates the Absegami Natural Area.

Proceed east on this easy-to-follow trail through mountain laurel and other common pineland plants and around a white cedar bog. Signs along the way explain the preservative properties of a bog. The anoxic conditions in a bog preserve pollen and other botanical remains, as well as ash from fires or even distant volcanic eruptions. A core taken from the bog (3 inches equals about 100 years) contains botanical markers and ash particles dating back as far as 12,000 years, the end of the previous Ice Age. The

Lake Absegami   DANIELA WAGSTAFF

bog itself, dark even on a bright day, is entered on a boardwalk. Here are densely packed Atlantic white cedars rising from a carpet of sphagnum mosses on the moist ground. Leave the bog, turn left at a junction, and continue to follow the silver blazes back out to the paved road. Make a left here and, immediately, another left onto the south-shore campground road.

Walk back in a southerly direction toward the park office. Pass over the Falkinburg Branch drainage that feeds the cedar bog, with a wonderful view of the southern end of Lake Absegami. After crossing the drainage, follow the Red Trail on your right. When you come to the paved south-shore campground road, you will find good water at a pump at the sanitary dump station to your left. After crossing the road, continue on the Red Trail for a short distance, then turn left onto the Pink Trail, heading in a southerly direction.

After crossing Stage Road (be careful), turn right onto a branch of the Pink Trail that heads in a westerly direction, closely paralleling Stage Road. This trail is not heavily used, but it is quite passable. Along the way, the trail becomes lined with ferns. After crossing East Greenbush Road, follow the Pink Trail as it turns left. Continue for about 300 feet to the sign for the CCC Memorial, then turn left to reach the parking lot where the hike began.

46

Brendan T. Byrne (Lebanon) State Forest

Total distance: 8.1 miles

Hiking time: 5 hours

Vertical rise: Minimal

Rating: Moderately strenuous

Maps: USGS Browns Mills; DEP Lebanon State Forest; DEP Batona Trail maps

Trailhead GPS Coordinates: N 39° 53' 42" W 74° 34' 32"

With over 37,000 acres, Brendan T. Byrne State Forest is the state's second largest forest. The original name, Lebanon State Forest, was after the Lebanon Glass Works, manufacturers of window glass and bottles, located here during the middle of the 19th century. The availability of sand and wood for charcoal supported the glassmaking industry from 1851 until about 1867, when the wood supply became exhausted. About 150 men worked here, and a small town of 60 homes, a few shops, and a post office was established but later abandoned. In 1908, the state began to acquire land in the area. Also part of Brendan T. Byrne State Forest is deserted Whitesbog Village, the birthplace of the cultivated blueberry and at one time the state's largest cranberry farm. The historic village is now being restored, and the not-entirely-abandoned cranberry bogs are appealing to hikers. Cranberries are still harvested in some sections of Brendan T. Byrne State Forest by farmers who lease the land from the state. The reservoirs are used to flood the bogs in the early fall for harvesting. Machines are run through the bogs to shake the berries off the vines. The berries, which float, are scooped up and loaded, via conveyor belts, onto trucks that take them to processing plants.

The forest was renamed in 2002 to honor former New Jersey Governor Brendan T. Byrne, who worked to designate the New Jersey Pine Barrens as a National Reserve. During his two terms as Governor of the State of New Jersey (1974 through 1982), Byrne was a leader in the difficult and

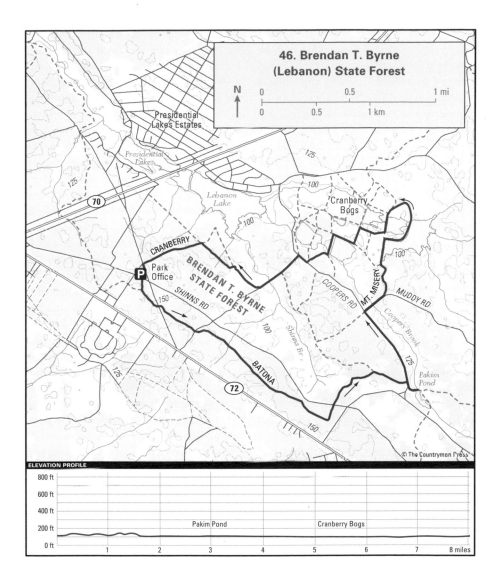

Presidential
Lakes Estates

Presidential
Lakes

125

70

Lebanon
Lake

CRANBERRY

Park
Office

BRENDAN T. BYRNE
STATE FOREST

SHINNS RD

150

125

72

BATONA

Shinns Br

125

Cranberry
Bogs

100

COOPERS RD

MT. MISERY

MUDDY RD

Coopers Brook

Pakim
Pond

150

© The Countryman Press

ELEVATION PROFILE

			Pakim Pond		Cranberry Bogs		
800 ft							
600 ft							
400 ft							
200 ft							
0 ft							
	1	2	3	4	5	6	7	8 miles

controversial effort to protect the New Jersey Pinelands. "Pinelands" is the politically correct name, though locals and scientists still respect the historical name "Pine Barrens." With so many interests, public and private, involved in the large Pinelands region, the type of protection eventually settled on involved a combination of local, state, and federal agencies that would manage the Pinelands through land acquisition and land-use controls. This unique arrangement required that the Pinelands be called a National Reserve, the country's first. Without such protective measures, the Pinelands would surely have been developed commercially and for housing by now. The Pinelands National Reserve is said to be the largest assemblage of open space in the northeastern United States and has achieved recognition as a Biosphere Reserve by the United States Man and the Biosphere Program and also by the United Nations Educational, Scientific and Cultural Organization (UNESCO).

Utilizing a section of the Batona Trail and the gravel and sand roads that crisscross the Pinelands, the hike described below takes in much of what Brendan T. Byrne State Forest (P.O. Box 215, Route 72, New Lisbon, NJ 08064; 609-726-1191; www .njparksandforests.org) has to offer. A section of the 735-acre Cedar Swamp Natural Area will be traversed twice, and you will visit Pakim Pond, a good spot for lunch. The trail then uses sand roads to explore the shores of reservoirs and cranberry bogs. In this latter section, your navigational skills may be challenged. Though long in mileage, this hike is not especially strenuous because the land is so flat; however, hot weather and biting deer flies could make it seem difficult, and, like most long hikes in the Pinelands, it should probably be hiked in cooler weather. Hikers are advised to stay on the trail and out of the brush, because ticks and chiggers have become common in recent years. It is best to wear long, light-colored pants tucked into socks, along with tick repellent.

HOW TO GET THERE

The main entrance to Brendan T. Byrne State Forest is on NJ 72, 1 mile east of the traffic circle where it intersects NJ 70. The entrance is on the north side of the road and is well marked with a large sign. Proceed 0.3 mile on this entrance road and bear right at the first intersection. The park office is just ahead on the left. Park here.

THE TRAIL

From the parking area, follow the blue-blazed trail that leads south toward the Batona Trail. After a short walk, you will reach the Batona Trail, marked with pink paint blazes. Bear left here, heading southeast and parallel to, though some distance from, NJ 72. You'll be walking through a mixed pine and oak forest on a well-used footpath. The walking is pleasant, and the trail surface, mostly sand, is soft and comfortable. After a short distance, the trail crosses a sand road and reenters the woods, continuing in the same direction. Here, stands of scrub oak, sassafras, pink and white mountain laurel, and blueberry bushes close in on the trail. Tall ferns line the trail in darker places. Farther along, the Batona Trail crosses another sand road, this one wider, and reenters the woods on a narrow sand road. Gradually, the trail climbs to its highest elevation, about 150 feet above sea level. The land is dry here, and blackjack oak, scrub oak, and pitch pine predominate.

About 2 miles into the hike, the trail turns left and crosses paved Shinns Road. Continue following the pink blazes of the Batona Trail, and enter a swampy area, crossed on puncheons and boardwalks. You are now in the Cedar Swamp Natural Area, a dense jungle of Atlantic white cedars surrounded by the pitch pine forest. The cedar wood, which is soft but durable, is used in boatbuilding, for some kinds of furniture, and for shingles and stakes. The management of this tree is an important project in the forest. Below the tall cedars, the vegetation is dense and the lighting is dark. Plant life includes rare orchids, curly grass ferns, pitcher plants, and sundews. After leaving the Cedar Swamp Natural Area, you'll come to a junction with a gravel road. Here, a red-blazed trail begins on the left, but you should bear right and follow the pink blazes through an area where cedars have been harvested. After you pass a few sand roads leading off to the right, the road swings left and meets a wider gravel road, Coopers Road. Turn right and follow the pink blazes into the Pakim Pond area.

Pakim Pond

Pakim Pond takes its name from the Native American word for cranberry. Its water is the reddish brown, acidic water typical of the Pinelands. Known as cedar water, it picks up its color and acidity as it moves very slowly through thick cedar swamps. Next to the pond is a swamp, a former cranberry bog. When the bog was actively cultivated, Pakim Pond was used as a reservoir to store water for the fall flooding of the bog. There are restrooms and picnic tables at Pakim Pond, but swimming is not allowed.

A short nature trail, which explores both the pond and the swamp, begins just off the Batona Trail at the southern end of the dam. A guidebook, which explains the points of interest indicated by numbered posts, is available at the park office. Carnivorous plants can be found here, including the pitcher plant and at least two types of sundew. The pitcher plant has funnel-like leaves that are filled with water. Insects are attracted to the leaves by their odor and color and, should they fall in, are drowned and digested by the plant. The sundew is very small and grows in clumps in very wet but sunny areas. Its leaves, round or stemlike, have numerous sticky hairs that trap insects and then digest them. These plants can be found along the northeastern shore of the pond just off the Batona Trail.

After either exploring or resting at Pakim Pond, leave the way you came in and return to the gravel road. Do not turn left on the

Batona Trail at the junction, though; stay on Coopers Road. From now on you will be following sand and gravel roads and will need to pay attention to the text and map.

Coopers Road, like most of the gravel and sand roads in the Pinelands, is straight, flat, and lined with pines. It can be very hot and buggy during the summer. After about 15 minutes (0.7 mile), you'll come to a junction. Turn right here, onto a smaller gravel road known as Muddy Road, marked with the white blazes of the Mt. Misery Trail. (Bicycles are permitted on this trail.) Along the side of the road are rhododendron, pepperbush, spicebush, and various species of blueberry. You will pass through a cedar swamp with towering Atlantic white cedars, densely packed, looking down on you from both sides of the road. In 0.2 mile, where the road curves to the right, follow the white blazes that lead left onto a sand road. This road has some soft "sugar-sand" sections, and the going may be slow in places.

Farther along, you'll pass an open area that is, in fact, a former cranberry bog in various stages of regrowth. Follow the white blazes and the road as it swings around the bog and heads north (ignore the road going off to the left); then head west again until the road ends at a T-intersection. Bear right here and head north toward the reservoir, which, like Pakim Pond, was used to flood

Mt. Misery Trail through cranberry bogs

Coastal Plain

cranberry fields. The scenery as you walk along the dam is beautiful, with the backdrop of pines and the green shades of water lilies and other aquatic vegetation. Wildflowers, not found in the shady woods, thrive in this sunny and well-watered environment. When you come to the corner of the reservoir, bear right, leaving the white markers. Now follow the reservoir's perimeter. The walkway heads east, then swings to the north, eventually leaving the reservoir with its dark cedar water, standing dead trees, and elusive pickerel. The sand road now winds through a quiet and remote pine woods, with a forest carpeting of pine needles.

When you come to a junction with another sand road, keep left. Stay on this sand road (which is the white trail again) heading south for about 750 feet, then make a right turn onto a sand road heading west. (From this junction, the edge of the first reservoir is visible.) An overgrown bog will be on your right and an open swamp, possibly with some waterfowl activity, on your left. From this point you will be working your way back to Coopers Road through a maze of old cranberry bogs, reservoirs, and sand roads. Don't be surprised if some large military aircraft fly by as well—these bogs are not far from Fort Dix and McGuire Air Force Base.

Take the second left turn at a T-intersection, and head south out to another reservoir. At this junction, another T-intersection, bear right, heading west along the shore of the reservoir. Next, bear left at the end of the reservoir, and head south along the dam. At the next T-junction, turn right onto a sand road that first swings to the left and then comes to a fork. Take the left fork, and walk through an area where sand has been excavated, staying on the main path which swings left and soon arrives at Coopers Road. Turn right onto Coopers Road, then turn left onto another gravel road only 200 yards ahead. There may be some yellow markers on this lane.

After a few minutes of walking on this lane, you'll pass a junction on the left with the red-blazed Cranberry Trail. (From this point on you can follow red markers back to your car.) Once again, you will cross a cedar swamp, now on a path separated from the road by a railing. Here the cedars are particularly tall and completely shade the road. Just after you leave the swamp, follow the red markers to the right onto a sand road that heads west. After about 250 yards on soft sand, the markers lead to a small sand road on the left. Take this road south for about 200 feet, then bear right and west again on a very straight sand road, still following red markers. This road is shady, surrounded by pine forest with an understory of blueberries. Pass over a small mossy bog and then, after another 10 minutes or so, reach an intersection with a somewhat larger sand road. Bear left here, heading south with the red markers. Another 10 or 15 minutes of walking will bring you to a paved road. Follow the trail across the paved road and back to the park office and your car.

47

Carranza Memorial to Apple Pie Hill

Total distance: 8.2 miles (or 5.2 miles with car shuttle)

Hiking time: 5 hours

Vertical rise: 166 feet

Rating: Moderately strenuous

Maps: USGS Chatsworth, Indian Mills; DEP Batona Trail; DEP Wharton State Forest maps

Trailhead GPS Coordinates: N 39° 46' 37" W 74° 37' 55"

Walking uphill in the Pinelands is unusual. The entire region is just above sea level, and the very few "hills" are usually only 25 or 30 feet above everything else. There are a few exceptions, however, and this hike leads to the highest elevation in the Pines, a dizzying 205 feet above sea level and about 125 feet above the land around it. This is Apple Pie Hill, on which a fire tower is located. En route, the hike will take you over another hill, 139 feet above sea level, as a warm-up for the big climb. Another feature of the hike is a camping option. One of Wharton State Forest's primitive camping areas is located at the start of the hike and makes a great base camp. Camping permits are issued at the Atsion and Batsto forest service offices.

The Carranza Memorial, where this hike begins, commemorates the tragic crash and death of Mexican pilot Emilio Carranza. Carranza, only 23 at the time of his death, had been a Mexican hero for five years, his fame resting on both his aviation and his military accomplishments. On June 11, 1928, he took off from Mexico in a Ryan monoplane, the same as Lindbergh's, and attempted a nonstop flight to Washington. He was grounded by fog in North Carolina but was still received with speeches and parades in both Washington and New York. Carranza was on the return leg of this goodwill flight when he flew into a thunderstorm over this remote section of the Pinelands and crashed. The local American Legion holds an annual observance of this event on the first Saturday after the Fourth of July. Each year on this day, wreaths are placed around

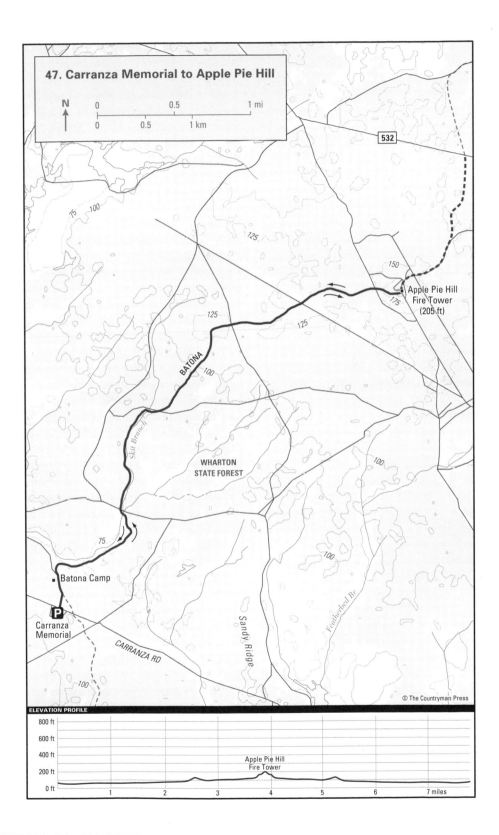

47. Carranza Memorial to Apple Pie Hill

N

| 0 | | 0.5 | | 1 mi |
| 0 | 0.5 | | 1 km | |

532

75 100

125

150

Apple Pie Hill
Fire Tower
(205 ft)

175

125

125

BATONA

100

125

Skit Branch

WHARTON
STATE FOREST

100

75

100

Batona Camp

100

Sandy Ridge

Featherbed Br

P
Carranza
Memorial

CARRANZA RD

100

© The Countryman Press

ELEVATION PROFILE

| 800 ft |
| 600 ft |
| 400 ft |
| 200 ft |
| 0 ft |

Apple Pie Hill
Fire Tower

| 1 | 2 | 3 | 4 | 5 | 6 | 7 miles |

the memorial—a stone marker made in Mexico that portrays a diving Aztec eagle.

HOW TO GET THERE
To reach the parking area at the memorial in Wharton State Forest, turn left (east) off US 206 just south of its junction with NJ 70. The sign here directs you to the town of Tabernacle and the Carranza Memorial. You'll reach the little town of Tabernacle and cross County Route 532 in 2.3 miles. Continue straight ahead through farms and a residential area into Wharton State Forest (Atsion Office, 744 Route US 206, Shamong, NJ 08088; 609-268-0444; njparksandforests. org). Seven miles from Tabernacle you will find the Carranza Memorial, which has ample parking, on the right. If you wish to do the hike as a one-way trip of 5.2 miles, leave a second car on County Route 532 where the Batona Trail crosses it, about 7 miles east of Tabernacle and 3 miles west of Chatsworth.

THE TRAIL
Cross the paved road and head north into the Batona Camp. A sign indicates the location of the campsite, which is not far from the main road. In about 500 feet, you'll reach the pink-blazed Batona Trail, which connects with the camp access road from the right. From here to Apple Pie Hill and back you'll be following these pink markers. The 50-mile Batona Trail, begun in 1961 by the BAck TO NAture Hiking Club, is a foot trail only. Mountain bikes or motorized vehicles are not permitted. A map of the entire trail is available from the New Jersey Department of Environmental Protection, as well as at the Atsion and Batsto state forest offices.

Batona Camp is one of several primitive camping areas located in Wharton State Forest. The site is accessible by car and offers numerous spaces to pitch a tent, also providing a water pump and several pit toilets. If you wish to camp here, you'll need a permit, available from the Atsion Ranger Headquarters farther south on US 206 or from the office in Batsto. In 2013, the camping fee was $3 per night per person for New Jersey residents, and $5 per night for nonresidents. Pets are not permitted in the campsite for overnight camping.

When you reach the end of the camping area, the Batona Trail bears right past a toilet and enters the woods on a footpath. Immediately, the typical flora of the Pinelands surrounds you. Highbush blueberries, which are found along the trail over much of this hike, make their first appearance. Blackjack oak and, of course, pitch pine surround you. Within a few hundred feet, the trail emerges onto a wide sand road, which it follows for a short distance. For the next half mile, the trail parallels this road, playing tag by using it for short stretches then cutting back into the woods on a footpath.

After a section that skirts the edge of a cedar swamp, the Batona Trail emerges onto the road for a final time to use its bridge. The brook you are crossing is the Skit Branch of the Batsto River. Like all Pinelands water, it is tea colored from the cedar wood that grows in it. The bridge offers a good view of the swampy brook and its plant life. If you look closely at the clumps of grasses growing in and around the water, you'll see hundreds of tiny sundew plants. If you look even closer, you may find a few miniature pitcher plants as well. These plants survive in this nutrient-poor environment by digesting insects that get trapped in their sticky leaves or no-exit entrances.

After crossing the bridge, the trail turns right and reenters the woods on a footpath, this time for good. For the next half mile, Skit Branch and its white cedar swamp will be on the right. The many dead cedars, still standing tall in the water, were killed by fire.

Along the Batona Trail

Unlike pitch pines and shortleaf pines, Atlantic white cedars do not regenerate after a burn; only the water protects them from fire. In this section, the trail crosses a wet area on loose logs. Be careful, or you may sink into deep black mud. The next crossing is of the stream itself, again on logs and, once more, potentially perilous for your shoes.

The Batona Trail now leaves the wet area surrounding Skit Branch and heads into drier and higher territory. About 2 miles from the start of the hike, the first climb begins. The ascent is noticeable by the change from soft white sand underfoot to a harder gravel path. After a "climb" of about 40 feet, you'll reach the table-like summit of this unnamed hill and, before you know it, begin heading downhill. Pay close attention ahead as the trail veers left off the path, crosses a sand road, and then reenters the woods.

One of the creatures of the Pinelands you may encounter on this hike, particularly in the drier areas, is the aptly named fence swift lizard. You may see a blur and hear the rustle of leaves, yet not get a look at this speedster unless you catch him sunning on a piece of dead wood. This rather attractive lizard has a gray-brown body and some very jagged scales along his head and back. The males have a dark marking under their lower jaws.

After crossing three more sand roads, the Batona Trail begins another climb, this one more serious. Views out to the southern horizon appear between the trees. The trail winds along the hill until the summit and its fire tower appear. This rise is Apple Pie Hill, and at 205 feet it's the highest summit in the Pinelands.

Although the hill, which is accessible by car or truck, is the scene of many a wild party, the view from its tower is spectacular. To the south, a wilderness of green pines

Apple Pie Hill Fire Tower

extends as far as the eye can see. To the west in the distance is the slight rise of Mount Holly. To the north are pines and, far in the distance, a water tower and a few other protrusions of civilization. To the east is a cranberry field—and more pines. To the southeast, a sand road runs from the hill in a perfectly straight line. For the most part, the view is one of vastness and wilderness that gives you an idea of the magnitude of the Pinelands.

Fire towers, which are frequently manned, play an important role in controlling the frequent fires (about 400 a year) in the Pinelands. The soil in the Pinelands drains the water so well that the oil- and resin-rich pine needles and dead branches are nearly always dry as tinder. There are no earthworms or bacteria to digest the dead materials on the forest floor, so the tinder accumulates year after year until it burns. The shortleaf pine and the pitch pine, the most common pines here, are two of only three pines in the United States that can sprout from buds lying deep within their trunks or large limbs, thereby assuring their quick recovery following a fire. The persistence of fires in the Pinelands, many of them started by arsonists, has ensured the dominance of these two pines in the forest. Ecologists believe that without regular fires, oaks would probably make up the bulk of a climax forest.

Because it is somewhat abused, Apple Pie Hill may not be the best place for a rest or lunch. We suggest that you find a resting place nearer to the first hill you climbed, which shows little sign of use other than from hikers. If you parked at the Carranza Memorial, this will be on your way back. If you left a car on County Route 532, it is 1.1 miles ahead on the Batona Trail. This trail section has been rerouted to traverse the Franklin Parker Preserve of the New Jersey Conservation Foundation.

48

Mullica River Wilderness

*Total distance: 7.5 miles round trip
(8.5 miles from visitor center)*

Hiking time: 5 hours

Vertical rise: Minimal

Rating: Moderately strenuous

*Maps: USGS Atsion; DEP Wharton
State Forest map*

*Trailhead GPS Coordinates:
N 39° 38' 42" W 74° 38' 46"*

Backpacking in the Pinelands is a unique experience for those more familiar with mountainous areas. The pines are not so dense or tall that they shut out a good view of a starlit sky. In fact, the effect is sometimes more like camping in a desert than in a forest. The pine needle cover on the sandy ground also makes for a comfortable bed. From Batsto, in the heart of the Pinelands, a 4-mile walk leads to the Mullica River Camp in Wharton State Forest (31 Batsto Road, Hammonton, NJ 08037; 609-561-0024; www.njparksand forests.org), a good choice for such an experience. You'll be camping alongside the Mullica River at a designated primitive campground. It has a water pump and pit toilet, is expansive enough for private folks, and is monitored by the forest rangers. You'll have to get a permit from the office in Batsto to camp here, however. In 2013, the camping fee was $3 per night per person for New Jersey residents and $5 per night for nonresidents.

Batsto was the site of an iron forge that produced kettles, stoves, cannon, pipes, and other iron products during the latter part of the 18th and the early 19th centuries. Like Allaire Village in the northern extremes of the Pinelands, the iron was made from bog iron—accumulations of iron oxides leached from the sand by groundwater and deposited at or near the soil surface. During the Revolutionary War, Batsto was a major source of military iron, and its workers were exempt from military service. At its peak, the village that developed around the furnace had a population of nearly a thousand. When the

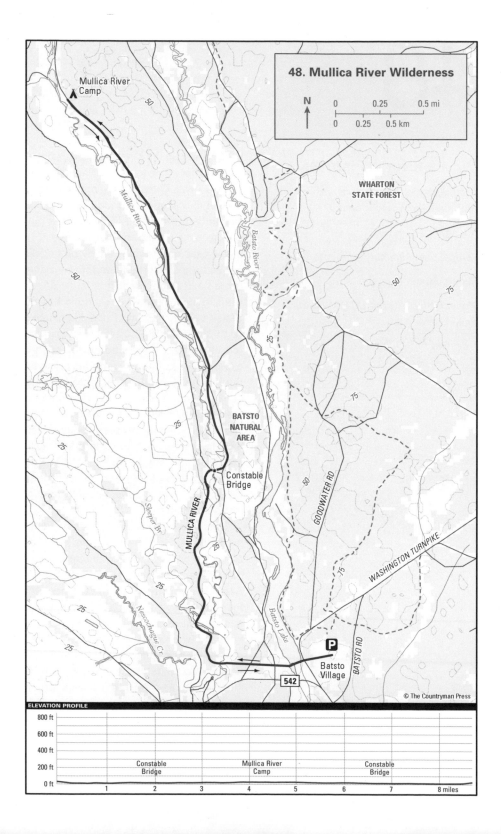

48. Mullica River Wilderness

N

| 0 | 0.25 | 0.5 mi |
| 0 | 0.25 | 0.5 km |

Mullica River Camp

WHARTON STATE FOREST

Mullica River

Batsto River

BATSTO NATURAL AREA

Constable Bridge

MULLICA RIVER

GOODWATER RD

Sleeper Br.

Nescochague Cr.

Batsto Lake

WASHINGTON TURNPIKE

P

Batsto Village

BATSTO RD

542

© The Countryman Press

ELEVATION PROFILE

800 ft								
600 ft								
400 ft								
200 ft		Constable Bridge		Mullica River Camp		Constable Bridge		
0 ft								
	1	2	3	4	5	6	7	8 miles

iron industry declined, a glassmaking factory was built, and the town produced window panes and other flat glass products for a few years. In 1876, after a major fire in the village, Joseph Wharton bought the property as part of his plan to acquire major tracts of land in the Pinelands and sell its water to the city of Philadelphia. The state of New Jersey responded by passing a law prohibiting the export of water, effectively halting this project. Eventually the Wharton holdings were acquired by the state, forming the present-day Wharton State Forest. Information about the interesting history of Batsto and the Pinelands can be found at the visitor /interpretive center.

The route of this hike is the route of the Mullica River. Hikers will immediately notice its color. "Cedar water" is the usual name for it. The water of the Pinelands is dark, the color of tea, and comes in part from the tannins from decaying vegetation washed out of swamps and in part from the iron-colored sandy mud. Because the water in the Pinelands tends to stay fresher longer, sea captains used to sail up the rivers that drain the Pinelands and take on barrels of what they called "sweet water." The water table in the Pinelands is shallow, but the reserve of water is vast. As an aquifer, there is no equal to the Pinelands in the northeastern United States. Because the water lies so close to the surface, and the sand, which takes in the rain that falls on it, is not a good filter, the Pinelands aquifer is extremely vulnerable to pollution. For this reason, development—which constantly threatens this area—has been kept at bay.

HOW TO GET THERE

Batsto, a part of Wharton State Forest, is on County Route 542 and is easy to find—signs directing you to it (it is a major historical site) are strategically placed within a radius of 20 miles. From the Garden State Parkway, take

Batsto Lake

Mullica River

DANIELA WAGSTAFF

Exit 52 and follow the signs. If you plan to backpack and spend the night at the Mullica River Camp, it is advisable to leave your car overnight at the parking area behind the state forest office in Batsto.

THE TRAIL

The entire hike is within the Batsto Natural Area on sand roads and paths. Although you will be following the well-marked, yellow-blazed Mullica River Trail, pay close attention at junctions as many paths and lanes intersect the main route. Markers are found on flexible plastic posts, and also as paint marks on trees. Sections of the sand roads utilized by the trail are very soft, with poor traction.

If you are backpacking, or wish to also explore Batsto Village and have parked at the main Batsto parking area, walk west on the main walkway through Batsto Village, across the dam on Batsto Lake, and go straight ahead until you arrive at a sand road. You will find a trailhead with yellow and orange markers here. If you are day-hiking and have parked among the trees adjacent to the west end of Batsto Village, just off County Route 542, follow the lane that heads due north to find the yellow and orange trail on your left in about 100 feet. Turn left here and follow the path into a dark woods that leads out to the Mullica River. The trail next crosses the river on a magnificent wooden bridge built in 1999. Continue following the markers though the forest—posts bearing botanical identification information will be found along the way. At a junction, the trail will turn right on a sand and pine needle walkway. Just ahead at a fork, the trail turns left. At the next major junction, the yellow-blazed Mullica River Trail turns right, leaving the orange-blazed Tom's Pond Trail. From here on you will be following only yellow markers. The trail now crosses a tributary of the Mullica River on a wooden bridge. The next section of trail is particularly beautiful, with a swamp, a river, white and yellow sand, stunted pitch pines, and a lot of open sky. The route next utilizes a soft white sand road on which tracks—evidence of usage by vehicles, hikers, and deer—can be found. The soft sand will slow down your progress and give you a taste of some of what is to come. A more compact section is just ahead.

About a mile into the hike you will arrive at a bend in the Mullica River that is noted as a scenic overlook on the forest map. A few rails stabilize the trail, keeping hikers away from the steep drop down to the river. There are inviting beachlike qualities to this river bend in the deep forest. The Mullica, along with the Batsto, Wading, Great Egg Harbor, and Rancocas, is one of the major rivers draining the vast water reserves lying just below the sands and forests of the Pinelands. Though the river widens considerably farther downstream, the Mullica here in the forest is typical of other rivers in the Pinelands. The river is not wide, but it can be deep enough in some places to be over your head. There are no rapids, but the current is strong. The fact that it remains at a constant water level throughout the year and during droughts indicates the extent of the aquifer underlying the Pinelands.

Continue hiking north on the yellow trail. In the summer the insects may be aggressive. Wildlife, including deer and flying squirrels, may be encountered. You may spot the red wasp, which looks like a giant ant, alongside the trail. Soon you will arrive at the Constable Bridge. If you're hiking on a busy summer weekend, expect regular deliveries of canoes to this popular boat-launching point. Next, cross over the Mullica River and continue following the yellow markers in a northerly direction, now on the east side of the river. After another mile you will reach the entrance to the Mullica River Wilderness Area, a section of the forest where no vehicles (except the ranger's) are allowed. A sign here marks the boundary. About a mile from the beginning of the wilderness area is the Mullica River Camp, a good place to have lunch—or spend the night. There's a pump for clean water here, and there are plenty of campsites within the limits, posted and marked by a ditch. Along the banks of the Mullica are several beachlike areas.

After a lunch, rest, or possibly an overnight, leave the campsite area and walk south, following yellow markers and retracing your steps past the entrance to the wilderness area, over the Constable Bridge, and back to Batsto Village.

49

Parvin State Park

Total distance: 4.6 miles
Hiking time: 3 hours
Vertical rise: Minimal
Rating: Easy to moderate
Maps: USGS Elmer; DEP Parvin State Park map
Trailhead GPS Coordinates: N 39° 30' 38" W 75° 07' 53"

In 1930, the New Jersey legislature began the acquisition of Parvin State Park with an appropriation of just less than $74,000. Nine years later, following 19 separate transactions, Parvin entered the state park system. During the Depression, a Civilian Conservation Corps (CCC) camp was established in the park. The men hacked out trails through the dense forest, using the wood to build bridges across the swamps. They cleared the main beach and picnic area and constructed the cabins—each with its own boat landing—along the shore of Thundergust Lake.

A German prisoner-of-war camp was located in a section of the park in 1942. When the European hostilities ended, the camp was converted to intern Japanese-Americans transported from the West Coast. The year 1952 saw the last nontraditional use of Parvin. Six years earlier, Soviet dictator Joseph Stalin had the Kalmyck people and some other Tartar groups transported to Siberia in retaliation for their revolt against the Communist government. Only about a quarter of the 400,000 people involved survived the ordeal, some of whom escaped to the United States. They came to Parvin in three groups, but stayed only a few months. Some are now settled in the Philadelphia area and in Howell Township in New Jersey.

This hike starts on the Parvin Lake Trail and uses the Long Trail for the rest of its route. Many of the trails in the park, even those in the natural area, are open to bike use, and some are also available for equestrians.

HOW TO GET THERE

Parvin State Park is located in southern Salem County along the Cumberland County border. The park entrance is on County Route 540, just over 1 mile east of Centerton, or 6 miles west of Vineland. The surrounding area has many road signs to point you in the right direction. The office (701 Almond Road, Pittsgrove, NJ 08318; 856-358-8616; www.njparksandforests.org) is located in one end of the park bathhouse, with a large parking lot across County Route 540. Stop in the office to obtain a trail map. The trails are named on the park map, and there are some trailhead signs indicating permitted uses.

THE TRAIL

Your hike starts just outside the park office. Facing Parvin Lake and the bathhouse, walk to the right (west) along a brown dirt path and then beside a green chain-link fence. The trail is over flat terrain, and the walking is easy. It proceeds between the highway and the lake, passing a children's area and some picnic tables. Holly trees and mountain laurel abound.

After crossing a small brook on a tiny stone bridge, continue straight as the route swings closer to both the road and a few houses seen through the woods. Large pitch pines with their distinctive, thick, shingle bark are much in evidence. Ground pine moss abounds on the forest floor.

You may notice a short side trail leading left down to the edge of Muddy Run. Continue straight ahead, also avoiding the trail to the right. A short distance beyond, there is another path to the water's edge. Muddy Run is a typical slow-moving stream of South Jersey. A tributary of the Maurice River, its water eventually empties into Delaware Bay. In the 1880s, small ponds were formed by

damming to provide power for gristmills and sawmills. One of these was owned by a family named Parvin.

Proceed ahead, crossing a series of small plank bridges to reach a paved road at a pavilion. This road forms the main boundary between the developed area and the designated natural area of Parvin State Park—the latter to be retained in a "forever wild" condition. A short walk to the left (suggested) along this road leads to both Muddy Run and an interesting bridge likely designed to discourage illegal motorbikes. Back on the main trail, continue straight ahead as the path gets a little sandier. In a few minutes you will reach an area known as Second Landing. Uphill to the right is a picnic area with a rain shelter and rest rooms. The shore of Muddy Run is just to the left. You will probably find that the footpath is very wet in spots—a minor price to pay for the peace, solitude, and natural dignity here.

The League for Conservation Legislation, the New Jersey Chapter of the Sierra Club, and Assemblyman (later Governor) Thomas Kean deserve credit for the 1976 passage of the Natural Areas System Act. This landmark legislation, which followed in the footsteps of the Forest Preserve article of the New York State Constitution, allows the designation of areas to be left forever in their natural state. Except for trails, they remain fundamentally undeveloped, and the trees remain uncut.

Continuing ahead, avoid the nature trail fork to the right and proceed over two small wooden bridges, following the footpath onto land slightly raised from the surrounding marsh. This part of the trail has many small plank bridges. Like most other trails in Parvin, this trail was built during the 1930s by the CCC. Considering that many years have elapsed since then, it is easy to admire their fine, long-lasting workmanship.

The route through the natural area is

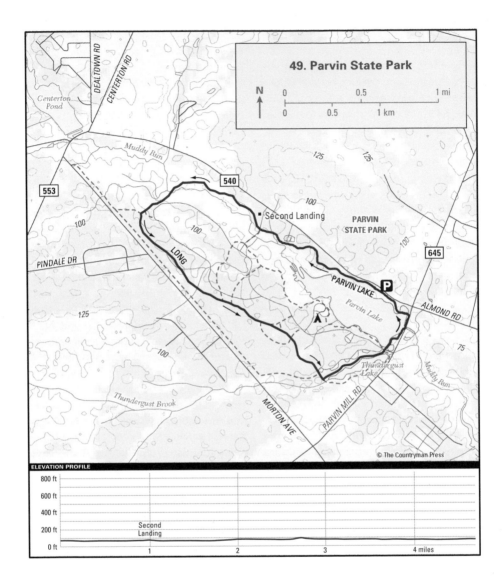

49. Parvin State Park

obvious. In one wet, open area, the trail bends somewhat to the right, but otherwise it is mostly straight with gentle curves. The wooden posts seen occasionally along the route are long-neglected mile markers, which may even date back to CCC days.

You'll cross three or four small feeder inlets as the trail bends slowly left toward Muddy Run. Be sure to take time to observe the forest around you. Left alone by humanity, it has developed a distinctly wild feel. Birds seem to like the area—you will hear many, but see few. In about 20 minutes, you will reach a substantial bridge over the Muddy Run. Shortly after crossing it, and just as the main trail takes a distinct turn to the left, watch for and take the fainter path on the right. Just ahead, you'll see a plastic post

Muddy Run

with a red blaze, indicating that you are following the red-blazed Long Trail. If you miss this turn, you'll soon climb gently to a paved park road. Just retrace your steps, find the correct path, and resume the hike.

The trail continues ahead, crossing many two- and three-plank bridges. It soon comes to and parallels a small inlet creek flowing through the dense brush and forest, then crosses an unmarked trail. The trees begin to open up a little, and the trail resumes the wide, groomed look it had at the beginning of the hike. Through the trees to the right are glimpses of some houses as the trail nears the southern border of the park.

The plant community now resumes the character it had early in the hike. The large pitch pines attest to the years the area has been undisturbed by logging. Young white pine trees add to the gentle feel, with their long, light green needles. Holly trees canopy the trail at one point. The holly is an evergreen tree that, like mountain laurel, keeps its leaves throughout the year. The trees can be either male or female, and both sexes are needed before berries develop.

When the trail comes to a T-intersection, turn right, crossing over a sand road after a minute or so. Continuing ahead, you will pass some indistinct trails, one on the right and one just beyond it on the left. Soon, you'll reach another intersection, with a red-blazed brown metal post on the right (and both red and yellow blazes on the left). Continue ahead, and in a short distance you'll reach yet another unmarked intersection. Here you should turn right (even though the more obvious trail continues straight ahead). Should you miss this turn, you'll soon reach a paved road and will need to retrace your steps.

Thundergust Lake

DANIELA WAGSTAFF

You're now following a trail that is raised from the surrounding forest floor. After crossing a yellow-blazed trail, the footpath gets a little narrower. In less than five minutes, the Long Trail ends and the Black Oak Trail starts to the right. Continue straight ahead, with the paved park road on the left. Soon, you'll approach the cabins in the Thundergust Lake area and reach a wooden footbridge over Thundergust Brook, a pleasurable place to pause as the hike draws to a close. Eighteen rental cabins, each sleeping four or six people, are available from April through October. Each is well equipped with a refrigerator, stove, toilet, shower, and electric lights.

This route does not cross the bridge, though. Turn left onto the trail that follows the shore of Thundergust Lake, passing the cabins and sandy boat-launch beach. Stay between the lake and the service road, passing a wooden fishing platform and small brick structure. As the trail approaches the main highway, you'll notice a dam with a wrought iron railing on your right and the campground entrance road with the park entrance booth on your left. Turn left toward the booth, then turn left onto the paved park entrance road heading toward a 20 MPH sign, and turn right just after the sign. Proceed toward Parvin Lake, then turn left onto the path along the lake, soon crossing a footbridge over a small section of the lake. The park office and bathhouse, where your hike began, are now visible.

From here, no formal directions are required. Just continue through the more developed part of the park, always remaining close to the shoreline. The outlet dam of Parvin Lake is especially interesting, with its Art Deco lines and unusual curved spillway. Two bridges, one concrete and the other wooden, cross what appear to be streams, but they actually take you on and off Flag Island.

You will be back to your car before long.

Coastal Plain

50

Belleplain State Forest, East Creek Trail

Total distance: 7 miles

Hiking time: 4.5 hours

Vertical rise: Minimal

Rating: Moderate

Maps: USGS Woodbine, Heislerville; DEP Belleplain State Forest map

Trailhead GPS Coordinates: N 39° 13' 27" W 74° 53' 11.5"

Located at the southern tip of the Pinelands, Belleplain State Forest (P.O. Box 450, Woodbine, NJ 08270; 609-861-2404; www.njparksandforests.org) is a popular camping spot containing a few hundred family camping sites, 14 all-season cabins, five yurts, two group campsites, which can each accommodate 75 people, a group cabin for up to 30 people, hot showers, and flush toilets. Belleplain has, in fact, more campsites than any other state forest in New Jersey. Central to the camping areas in this 21,250-acre forest—90 percent of which is part of the Pinelands National Reserve—is Lake Nummy, a transformed cranberry bog with white sand beaches. It was named in honor of King Nummy, chief of the Kechemeche tribe and the last to rule in the Cape May area. For hikers, Belleplain offers many short trails in the camping area, along with the East Creek Trail, a white-blazed footpath that will be used in this hike. Most trails in the forest are multiuse; there are even motorized trails.

Please note that from mid-January into June of each year, a section of the East Creek Trail may be closed for nesting eagles. Call ahead to check if the trail is open.

The East Creek Trail is a 7-mile white-blazed loop trail, which you will hike clockwise. It encircles the area drained by Savages Run between Lake Nummy and East Creek Pond. The trail generally traverses dry oak-and-pine forests but frequently descends into deep, dark cedar brooks and swamps, more characteristic of the Pinelands to the north. Unlike the Pinelands, shore vegetation—particularly greenbriers and holly trees—is found throughout the forest, revealing the transitional nature of the region.

Be warned that some footbridges and planks may be slippery, and a few areas have become very overgrown and may also be under water. Expect to get your shoes wet and muddy.

HOW TO GET THERE

Take the Garden State Parkway to Exit 17 (Woodbine/Sea Isle City). Follow signs for Woodbine and soon turn right (north) onto US 9. Continue for 0.6 mile and turn left onto County Route 550 (Woodbine–Ocean View Road). After 6.3 miles, you reach the town of Woodbine, where County Route 550 makes a left turn near Spirit Chevrolet, then a right turn at a blinking light. This is still County Route 550—stay on it. It's another 1.4 miles to the state forest. Turn left at the entrance near the park office, pass the entry station (a fee is collected seasonally), and drive 0.5 mile to an intersection. A right turn here will lead in another 0.5 mile to Lake Nummy on the right and the nature center on the left. Park at the nature center. If you are hiking during the peak summer season, you may need to continue to the beach, where there is also a large parking area and a refreshment stand.

THE TRAIL

With your back to the lake and facing the nature center, the East Creek Trail starts

Along the East Creek Trail

DANIELA WAGSTAFF

Coastal Plain

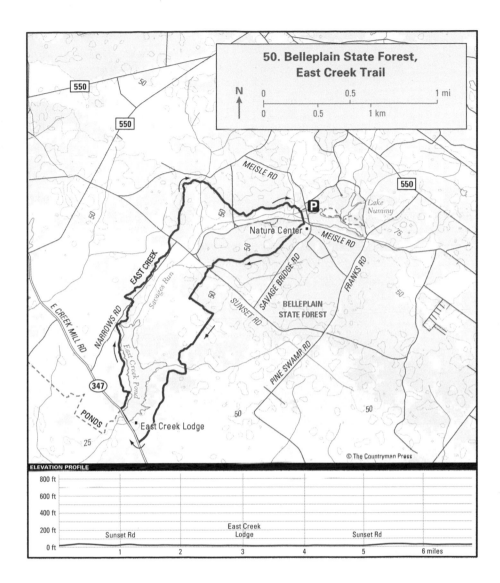

50. Belleplain State Forest, East Creek Trail

ELEVATION PROFILE

© The Countryman Press

about 300 feet to the right, near a sign for the campers-only trash recycling center. A sign indicating the hiking trail is just beyond.

Still following the white blazes, begin hiking southward. The trail, a moss-covered footpath, first penetrates an open forest of young oaks, then a pitch pine forest reminiscent of the Pinelands. Where the trail parallels a fire ditch, the first of many along the

trail, be alert for a sudden right turn where the ditch swings left. Clumps of mountain laurel, small pine trees and, in places, bracken ferns form the ground cover seen here and all along the trail. About a mile into the hike, the trail crosses a creek in the dark shadows of tall cedars. Here are the first of many holly groves and tangles of greenbrier that threaten to overwhelm the trail. After

East Creek Pond

crossing the small brook, reach and cross paved Sunset Road.

The trail now follows the perimeter of an abandoned field filled with wildflowers in season. The transition from field to forest is evident here, and wildlife, including deer and game birds, is abundant. After reentering the woods, the trail joins an old sand road, following it through a pine forest for only 100 yards or so before turning sharply left. Here is an old boardwalk, the first of many that will—hopefully—aid you through the wet sections ahead. The narrow trail now penetrates an older, deeper, and darker forest; some of the pines are very large. In the wetter areas, huge holly trees are found.

Beyond this low and wet area, the trail crosses another stream on planks at the edge of a dense stand of cedars. Then it recrosses where the same stream is wider, the cedars denser. The trees seem to be standing on their roots to keep out of the wet, green earth. If the going gets wet, look to both sides of the trail for hiker-made bypass routes.

The next section of trail is very green, dominated by pine, holly, and laurel. After traversing more sections of boardwalk, the trail winds through an open section of trees killed by the gypsy moth caterpillars. Follow an old woods road through a forest of young pines before you reach an open area. Walk straight ahead, following markers, toward the building at the southern end of East Creek Pond. This is the rebuilt East Creek Lodge, available through the state forest for group use. The front of the lodge has a dock and many picnic tables; if it's not already in use, this makes a good spot for a snack or lunch. This location is the halfway point of the hike—about 3 miles from the start.

Nowadays, the view over East Creek Pond is a calm one—blue water lined with tall, green pines. If anything, the pond is underused, yet it is regarded as an excellent pickerel lake and does attract some anglers. A hundred years ago, however, this area was the scene of much activity; both a lumber mill and gristmill were located here.

When ready to continue, walk to the other side of the lake along the busy paved road, following white markers. The parking area here was built to accommodate users of the multiuse Ponds Trail to Pickle Factory Pond, dedicated on National Trails Day in June 1995. Still following the white markers, reenter the woods, heading north. The trail parallels the lake for a distance before it arrives at the shoreline near an inlet. Here is a wilderness vista of the lake. With the possible exception of anglers in boats, the entire panorama is of water and forest. From this point the trail turns left, skirts a wet section, then heads toward higher ground.

You now traverse a forest of young pines on both cut trail and woods road. As the trail nears the northern end of East Creek Pond, it meanders through a dense cedar forest and, farther on, crosses a swamp on puncheons. At the swampy northern end of the lake, the trail makes a sharp left and meets, in 100 feet, a woods road. You will use this road for only a short distance, then bear left at the fork (a right would lead to a last look at the pond) and almost immediately turn left

again, off the road and cutting back into the woods on a footpath. After a short walk, arrive at gravel Tom Field Road, which is open to vehicles.

Because the next section of the hiking trail ahead was and may still be badly maintained and hard to follow, we can no longer recommend you use it. Instead, stay on Tom Field Road when the marked trail bears left from it. Follow the road north for 0.75 mile to its junction with the paved Sunset Road, turn left, travel a short distance, and again pick up the marked foot trail on the far side of Sunset Road.

North of Sunset Road, the trail traverses some higher and more open land, making for easier hiking. After about a quarter mile, the trail, now heading northeast, descends and crosses Tom Field Road, then a smaller sand road. From here the trail once again enters a cedar swamp, crossing a brook on a wooden bridge and a wet area on a boardwalk. After a grassy road, the trail proceeds through a mature white pine forest, where some large holly trees may be seen as well. Ahead, it makes a final road crossing and heads toward Lake Nummy. This last section begins on fairly high ground but descends toward a large cedar stand. In the heart of this river of cedars lies Savages Run, the stream that drains Lake Nummy and feeds East Creek Pond. After keeping its distance from the cedars, the trail finally enters what may be the darkest and wettest of all the cedar brooks on the trail so far. Be careful here, for the trail can be slippery and very muddy in places. After emerging from the cedars, the trail bears left, then right on a utility line cut; in a short distance it meets the paved road that crosses Lake Nummy's dam. If you parked at the main parking area, bear left and then right on paved roads. If you parked at the nature center, turn right, then left.

Resources

Bennett, D. W. *New Jersey Coastwalks.* Sandy Hook Highlands, NJ: American Littoral Society, 1981.

Boysen, Robert. *Kittatinny Trails.* Mahwah, NJ: New York–New Jersey Trail Conference, 2004.

Brooks, Christopher & Catherine. *60 Hikes within 60 Miles: New York City: with Northern New Jersey, Southwestern Connecticut, and Western Long Island.* Birmingham, AL: Menasha Ridge Press, 2004.

Buff, Sheila. *Nature Walks in and Around New York City: Discover Great Parks and Preserves Throughout the Tri-State Metropolitan Area, 1st edition.* Boston: Appalachian Mountain Club Books, 1996.

Card, Skip. *Take a Hike: New York City: 80 Hikes within 2 Hours of Manhattan, 2nd edition.* Berkeley, CA: Avalon Travel, 2012.

Case, Daniel. *AMC's Best Day Hikes near New York City: Four-Season Guide to 50 of the Best Trails in New York, Connecticut, and New Jersey.* Boston: Appalachian Mountain Club Books, 2010.

Chazin, Daniel. *Hike of the Week: A Year of Hikes in the New York Metro Area.* Mahwah, NJ: New York–New Jersey Trail Conference, 2013.

Chazin, Daniel. *New Jersey Walk Book: A Companion to the New York Walk Book, 2nd edition.* Mahwah, NJ: New York–New Jersey Trail Conference, 2004.

Dann, Kevin. *Twenty-Five Walks in New Jersey.* Piscataway, NJ: Rutgers University Press, 1982.

DeCoste, Paul E. and Ronald J. Dupont, Jr. *Hiking New Jersey: A Guide to 50 of the Garden State's Greatest Hiking Adventures.* Guilford, CT: Falcon Guides, 2009.

Della Penna, Craig. *24 Great Rail-Trails of New Jersey.* North Amherst, MA: New England Cartographics, 1999.

Harrison, Marina, with Lucy D. Rosenfeld. *A Walker's Guidebook: Serendipitous Outings near New York City: Including a Section for Birders.* Michael Kesend Publishing, Ltd., 1996.

Kjellstrom, Bjorn. *Be Expert with Map and Compass.* Hoboken, NJ: John Wiley & Sons, 1994.

Kobbe, Gustav. *The New Jersey Coast and Pines.* Baltimore: Gateway Press, 1982.

Lenik, Edward J. *Iron Mine Trails,* revised edition. Mahwah, NJ: New York–New Jersey Trail Conference, 1999.

Mack, Arthur C. *The Palisades of the Hudson.* Edgewater, NJ: The Palisade Press, 1909.

McClelland, Robert J. *The Delaware Canal.* Piscataway, NJ: Rutgers University Press, 1967.

McPhee, John. *The Pine Barrens.* New York: Farrar, Straus and Giroux, 1968.

New York–New Jersey Trail Conference. *Appalachian Trail Guide to New York–New Jersey* (with 4 maps), 17th edition. Harpers Ferry, WV: Appalachian Trail Conservancy, 2011.

Perls, Jeffrey. *Paths along the Hudson: A Guide to Walking and Biking along the River.* Piscataway, NJ: Rutgers University Press, 1999.

Petty, George. *Hiking the Jersey Highlands: Wilderness in Your Back Yard.* Mahwah, NJ: New York–New Jersey Trail Conference, 2007.

Ransom, James M. *Vanishing Ironworks of the Ramapos.* Rutgers University Press. 1966.

Rosenfield, Lucy D. and Marina Harrison. *A Guide to Green New Jersey: Nature Walks in the Garden State.* Piscataway, NJ: Rutgers University Press, 2003.

Scherer, Glenn. *Nature Walks in New Jersey: A Guide to the Best Trails from the Highlands to Cape May,* 2nd edition. Boston: Appalachian Mountain Club Books, 2003.

Waterman, Laura and Guy. *Forest and Crag: A History of Hiking, Trail Blazing, and Adventure in the Northeast Mountains.* Boston: Appalachian Mountain Club Books, 1989.

_____. *Backwoods Ethics: Environmental Issues for Hikers and Campers,* 2nd edition. Woodstock, VT: The Countryman Press, 1993.

_____. *Wilderness Ethics: Preserving the Spirit of Wilderness, 2nd edition.* Woodstock, VT: The Countryman Press, 1993.

Zatz, Arline. *Best Hikes with Children in New Jersey,* 2nd edition. Mountaineers Books, 2005.

HIKING MAPS

(Published by the New York–New Jersey Trail Conference)

Hudson Palisades Trails 5-map set. 2012

Jersey Highlands Trails 2-map set. 2011.

Kittatinny Trails 4-map set. 2012.

North Jersey Trails 2-map set. 2014.

USEFUL ROAD MAPS

AAA New Jersey. Latest edition.

Rand McNally/New York City, Metro Area Counties, Long Island. Latest edition.